# A DAILY DEVOTIONAL
## OF THE WORD, REFLECTION AND PRAYERS OF PRAISE

By: Herbert Crawford

Author of 366 Prayers For All Seasons

# Contents

INTRODUCTION ................................................................................................. 5

DEDICATION .................................................................................................... 7

JANUARY ........................................................................................................ 9

FEBRUARY ..................................................................................................... 40

MARCH .......................................................................................................... 68

APRIL ............................................................................................................. 99

MAY ............................................................................................................. 129

JUNE ............................................................................................................ 160

JULY ............................................................................................................. 190

AUGUST ....................................................................................................... 221

SEPTEMBER ................................................................................................. 252

OCTOBER .................................................................................................... 282

NOVEMBER ................................................................................................. 313

DECEMBER .................................................................................................. 343

# Introduction

This Daily Devotional is my first attempt at doing a full devotional based upon requests I have had from many persons who have purchased copies of 366 Prayers For All Seasons. The intent of this devotional is to focus on God's Word and how it speaks to us individually through reflection on the Word and prayer. All the scripture passages used encourage us to give thanks and praise to God and that is exactly what is expected from us as Christians.

May this devotional be an inspiration to all those who will read it and that many lives will be blessed as a result. To God be the glory great and mighty things He has done.

Dear Readers,

Welcome to my collection of Prayers of Praise and Reflection, a daily devotional born out of an overwhelming response from loved ones and the wider public. I invite you to join me in expressing gratitude to God for His countless blessings, abundant provisions, and unwavering protection that He lavished upon us.

From Genesis to Revelation, the Bible resounds with praises, acknowledging the goodness of our Creator. Inspired by the profound impact of the COVID-19 pandemic, I felt compelled to shed light on the Lord's past and present interventions during troubling and challenging times. As a result, I have carefully curated Bible verses of praise and adoration to serve as the foundation for these devotionals.

Regardless of the situations or circumstances we find ourselves in, the holy pages of God's book offer words of comfort and solace. Prayer is an integral part of our Christian journey, a means through which we connect with God's grace and favor. Therefore, I encourage you to embrace these daily prayers, allowing them to guide you in seeking the joy of the Lord as you meditate and internalize His precious Word.

May these Prayers of Praise and Reflection become a faithful companion on your spiritual path, providing daily inspiration, renewed hope, and a deepened relationship with our Heavenly Father.

Blessings,
Herbert

# **Dedication**

To my dear wife Marisa,

This book is a testament to the unwavering dedication and support you have shown me throughout this incredible journey. Your tireless commitment to my dreams and aspirations has been the guiding light that illuminated my path, and for that, I am eternally grateful. Your keen insights and meticulous attention to detail have undoubtedly shaped this book into something far greater than I could have ever imagined.

As we embark on this new chapter together, I offer my sincerest gratitude to you, my love. Your love, encouragement, and belief in me have been my constant source of inspiration. May the Lord's blessings be upon you, safeguarding and guiding you, just as you have done for me.

With all my love,

Herbert

## January

# Giving Thanks Forever

## Day 1

*"O give thanks unto the Lord, for he is good; His love endures forever."*

*Psalm 107: 1-2*

Have you ever really thought about the goodness of God and all that He has done for us? The song Count Your Blessings reminds us how important it is for us to count our blessings and to appreciate all the provisions God has made for us despite our unworthiness. Too often we forget that all that we have is all because of Him and His great love for us. Every day we need to give him our thanks and gratitude and acknowledge that He is indeed a good God and His inexpressible love for us endures forever.

*O God of love, we thank You for Your goodness and mercy which are new every morning. Father, may we ever sing songs of praises and thanksgiving to Your most holy and righteous name for journeying with us through another year and to this the beginning of a new year. Lord we are so thankful to You for accepting us as we are and for Your continued care and protection.*

*Loving and gracious Father God, as we set our eyes on You at the outset of this new year, we ask You Father to help us to come to You with an attitude of gratitude. You have done so much for us during the past year and for all that You have done, we just want to give You thanks and to let You know how much we really appreciate You. Father, it is in your name we pray. Amen.*

# January

# Walking In His Image

## Day 2

*"Rejoice in the Lord you who are righteous and praise His holy name."*

Psalm 97: 12

God our Father requires us to give to Him all the praise, glory and honor which are due to His holy name. Because He is holy, He wants us to be holy too. It is our duty as God's chosen people to strive to be holy even as He is holy. Holiness means to be 'set apart" and so as Christians we are to set ourselves apart from the world. God wants us to live a life of discipline, focus and attention to matters of righteous living.

*We thank You Lord God that You are indeed a righteous God and You require us Your children to praise Your name always. Help us Father to remain faithful in ever thanking You everyday of our lives. We thank You Lord for our redemption through the blood of Your Son, Jesus Christ which was shed on Calvary's Cross, for the sin of lost humanity.*

*Father God, we acknowledge that we have not always spent enough time with You. We have been guilty of devoting so much of our time to doing things to get praise from others instead of really spending quality time with You. Forgive us Lord and enable us to make a change this New Year in rejoicing more in You and in praising Your name because You are truly deserving of it. This we pray Lord in your name. Amen.*

# January

# Our Rock And Deliverer

## Day 3

*"The Lord is my strength and song, and He has become my God, and I will praise Him; my father's God and I will extol Him."*

*Exodus 15: 2*

Our whole duty to God is to give Him thanks constantly for He is worthy to be praised. There is absolutely no other god besides Him who is worthy to receive our praise and adoration. Let us not forget that every day it is God who gives us the strength to do the many things we have to do and therefore it is our duty to show our appreciation by thanking Him as often as we can.

*Almighty and all-powerful God, we thank You for being our strength and song. We thank You for being our Father and the one in whom we can trust. Lord You are just an awesome God and we thank You for all Your blessings on us. We thank You Father that when we are feeling weak You make us strong and that we can always depend on You to supply our every need.*

*In every situation Father, You have proven time and time again Your goodness and faithfulness towards us. Thank You Lord that You are our God and we are Your people. We have no choice Father but to keep on thanking You for being the loving and compassionate God You are and we just want to sing praises of thanksgiving to You. It is in your name we pray Lord. Amen.*

# January

# A Class By Himself

## Day 4

*"Who is like You among the gods, O Lord? Who is like You, majestic in holiness, awesome in praises, working wonders?"*

Exodus 15:11

Our God is truly a wonder working God. His ways are mysterious and there is no one else like Him. When we consider what the Lord has done for us and the many times He has delivered us out of harm and danger, we can only agree with the songwriter in saying how great Thou art, how great Thou art. There's certainly no one else like God to be compared to in the whole wide world. Our God is an awesome God indeed and He keeps on mystifying our minds with His wonders.

You are indeed worthy our God to receive all our praise, all our respect, all our gratitude, all of who and what we are. We thank You for being an awesome, holy and righteous God who is constantly working on our behalf and keeping us safe and well protected from the storms of life.

Holy Father, we know that there is none like You for You are God and God alone. Thank You Lord for spanning time and eternity and for being in control of our very existence. We praise You and glorify Your name and we thank You for remaining constant in all that You do for us on a daily basis.

Father, it is in your name we pray. Amen.

## January

# Before Your Very Eyes

### Day 5

*" He is your praise and He is your God, who has done these great and awesome things for you which your eyes have seen."*

*Deuteronomy 10:21.*

God never fails to challenge and to boggle our minds with His unbelievable and marvelous work. He is just such an awesome and powerful God who is to be praised, adored and glorified in all our ways. When last have you really spent some time with the Lord thanking Him for His goodness and for all His continuous blessings He has poured down upon you? Why not take the opportunity today to just praise the Lord in ways you have never done before and see the difference it will make in your life.

*Lord we want to thank You for the ways in which You perform Your mighty work. It is so amazing to see how You make the impossible to our eyes, possible. We really thank You for all the wonderful things You have done for us and for investing so much in us to ensure that all our needs are met.*

*Heavenly Father, we can never understand or comprehend the great love You have for us Your wayward children. When we wandered far away from You, You sent Your Son Jesus to become the Way, the Truth and the Life so that we could find our way back to You. We thank You for never leaving or forsaking us.*

*It is in Jesus' name we pray. Amen.*

# January

# Hear Ye God's People

## Day 6

*"Hear this, you kings! Listen, you rulers! I will sing to the LORD, I will sing; I will sing praise to the LORD, the God of Israel."*

Judges 5:3

It is a good thing for us to sing praises to God for all the blessings He has bestowed upon us. God being a just God does not withhold His blessings from anyone. He sends His rain on both the just and the unjust and He truly has no favorites. This is why it is so important that we spend time to sing our praises to Him and to give to Him what He deserves. Never take God for granted because the time will come when our blessings could be taken away from us as it has happened to so many others.

*Thou art worthy O Lord to receive glory and praise and honor because You are deserving of all the accolades we can give to You. Thank You precious God for taking care of us even when we do not deserve it. We need to sing Your praises daily Father because You have been so good.*

*Thank You Dear Father for the many ways in which You have demonstrated Your might and power over and over again and how You have delivered Your people in mysterious ways. We give You our praise and gratitude for Your constant care and protection especially during times of hardships and challenges.*

*All these and other mercies we pray in your name. Amen.*

# January

## Prayer Saves

### Day 7

*"I call upon the LORD, who is worthy to be praised, and I am saved from my enemies."*

2 Samuel 22:4

It is God and God alone who can save us from all adversity. When things seem at times hopeless, He breaks forth and delivers us from all dangers. Many times in our lives we have had to face up to adversity of one kind or another and only through the mercies of God why we were able to overcome. God has a way of dealing with our problems in ways that we will never understand. Trusting Him is our only option since He alone knows what trials and tribulations we will encounter in this life.

*Dear Lord, thank You that You are our Rock, our Fortress and our Deliverer. Help us to take refuge in You O God for we know we will be safe. When we are worried and distressed Lord, help us to cling to You because You are our hiding place. Thank You Lord for giving to us Your Son, Jesus who remains closer to us than a brother and who is beside us at all times.*

*Today Father we call upon Your name because our hope is in You and You are the Light of our lives. We thank You for building a hedge around us to protect us from our enemies. Help us Father to surrender our lives to You so that we can always feel secured in Your everlasting arms. Hear our prayer Lord and let our cry come unto You. Amen.*

# January

# How Much Is Enough

## Day 8

*"Therefore I will give thanks to You, O LORD, among the nations, and I will sing praises to Your name."*
2 Samuel 22:50

How can we ever stop praising the name of the Lord? This must be part of our daily routine. He is deserving of it all. When we consider how sinful and unrighteous we have been and for God to love us the way He does, it is our duty to not only sing praises to Him but also to surrender our very lives to Him in humility. With God in our lives, we have nothing to fear but fear itself. He has promised never to leave us or to forsake us, and so every day we need to express our gratitude to Him in ways that we have never done before.

Father in Heaven, we give to You today all our thanks, all our praise and all of us. Lord, we thank You for showing unfailing kindness to us over and over again. We know Lord that we cannot repay You for all the wonderful blessings You have bestowed upon us so we just want to thank You for all Your blessings and to let You know that we appreciate everything You are doing for us.

Loving Father there have been times when we doubted whether or not You cared for us or loved us because You took so long in responding to our cries. Forgive us Lord for our foolish thinking and we want to thank You for proving to us that You truly love and care for us by providing us with all that we need and more. It is in your name we pray Lord. Amen.

## January

# Celebrate God's Amazing Wonders

*Day 9*

*"Sing to Him, sing praises to Him; speak of all His wonders."*

1 Chronicles 16:9

Again and again we are encouraged to give God our praise and gratitude for the ways in which He has demonstrated His goodness and awesome wonders to us. Certainly there is no other god like Jehovah and we need to just magnify and lift up His holy name. Let us make this year one of praise and thanksgiving to our God by exalting His name and making Him the central figure in our lives.

*Loving Lord we just glory in Your holy name today and rejoice for all the wonders You have performed from the time of creation until this new day. We thank You for creating the heaven and the earth and for displaying Your great workmanship. Father, nothing that man does can be compared to Your beauty and majesty and we adore You for this.*

*Heavenly Father when we consider the moon and the stars You have made and all of creation, we can't help but to lift up Your name on high. Father You are all that we need and desire and with You in our lives, we are happy and glad to have such a wonderful, amazing and compassionate Father like You. We subscribe to You all praise and glory. Amen.*

## January

# The Greatness Of God

### Day 10

*"For great is the LORD, and greatly to be praised; He also is to be feared above all gods."*
1 Chronicles 16:25

There is certainly no other god to serve but the one, true and living Father God who is the Creator of this great universe. He is the only one to be feared, adored and worshipped. Our Father God is indeed a great God and as His people we should always remember to salute Him and to yield our lives to Him. He alone can make the single most difference in our lives now and in the future.

O God of grace, power and might, we know that You are a great God whose name is to be praised and feared above any other gods. Everything else that we might worship is false because You made the heavens and the earth and You created all things living and inanimate. Let us rejoice today in singing Your praises and giving You thanks.

Lord we thank You that to fear You is the beginning of wisdom which You give to all those who ask of You liberally. In this world Father where so many fail to fear You, may You in Your wisdom touch their lives so that they will come to You to praise and honor Your name. It is in Your name we pray. Amen.

## January

# Worship God With Our All

## Day 11

*"Ascribe to the LORD the glory due His name; bring an offering, and come before Him; Worship the LORD in the splendor of His holiness."*

1 Chronicles 16:29

The least we can do as Christians is to offer ourselves to the Lord as a holy and living sacrifice to Him. We do so when we fall down and worship Him with our praise and songs of thanksgiving. The right thing we need to do as followers of God is to remain faithful and submissive to Him and this we do by heaping all the accolades of praise, thanksgiving and honor to His holy name. Our worship of Him is one way of showing our loyalty to Him.

O Triune God, today we ascribe greatness to You because You are our Rock and all Your ways are just and Your work perfect. Thank You Lord God that You are a God of righteousness and justice and all that You do is good and upright. Help us this day to truly worship You in the beauty of splendor and holiness.

Lord we thank You for Your mercy which is new every day and which reminds us that we are forever Yours. Dear Father, help us to rejoice and be glad in Your presence even as we bow down before You and worship You in the beauty of holiness. Thank You for Your constant love and provision and for always supplying our every need. It is in Your name we pray. Amen.

## January

# God's Name Be Lifted Up

### Day 12

*"O give thanks to the LORD, for He is good; for His loving-kindness is everlasting. Then say, "Save us, O God of our salvation, and gather us and deliver us from the nations, to give thanks to Your holy name, and glory in Your praise." Blessed be the LORD, the God of Israel, from everlasting even to everlasting. Then all the people said, "Amen," and praised the LORD."*

1 Chronicles 16:34-36

The whole duty of man is to recognize our Creator God by giving Him thanks and blessing His name for His unfailing love for humanity. God has proven His love for us again and again and yet so often we fail to recognize His faithfulness and kindness towards us. We should at all times devote some of our time in thanking and praising the Lord on a daily basis because we have such a wonderful Father who never fails in supplying our needs.

*Wonderful and Awesome God, we thank You that Your loving-kindness is better than life. May our lips praise and bless You Lord and may we lift up our hands and hearts to praise Your name. Help us Father to continue thanking You forever and ever because Your love for us is just so special and we bless Your name for that.*

*We thank You Lord for enabling us to be able to praise You and to acknowledge Your loving-kindness and affection You bestow upon all those who love and serve You. We owe You Father a great debt of gratitude and praise for continually providing our needs. Blessed be Your name O Father from everlasting to everlasting. This we pray in Your name. Amen.*

# January

# Without God We Are Nothing

## Day 13

*"Now therefore, our God, we thank You, and praise Your glorious name."*

1 Chronicles 29:13

God's name is to be praised and lifted up as often as we humanly can do so. There is no time limit placed on us in giving thanks to Almighty God and neither has He placed a limit on what He can do for us. What a blessing and a privilege it is to know the extent to which God cares for us. He is always rendering service to us as often as we call on Him. How about stopping for a moment right now and just send up a word of praise and thanks to our God.

*Praise and honor, dominion and power are due to You O Lord our Father. Our tongues cannot find words adequately enough to express to You all of our gratitude to You for all that You have done for us throughout our lives. We are really very thankful to You Lord for every blessing we have received from Your hands.*

*Thank You Father that at the name of Jesus every knee shall bow and every tongue shall confess You as Lord. Help us Dear Lord to truly focus on You in everything that we do and may we sincerely render our praise and thanksgiving to Your most glorious and precious name. For all that You do for us Father we give You thanks and this we pray in Jesus' name. Amen.*

# January
# The Glory Of The Lord
## Day 14

*"The trumpeters and singers joined together in unison as with one voice to give praise and thanks to the Lord. Accompanied by trumpets, cymbals and other instruments, they raised their voices in praise to the LORD saying, "He indeed is good for His love endures forever.," Then the temple of the LORD, was filled with a cloud, and the priests could not stand to perform their service because of the cloud, for the glory of the LORD filled the temple of God."*

2 Chronicles 5:13-14

How powerful and magnificent the glory of the Lord truly is. When we stand in the presence of this Holy God we must expect nothing less than the spectacular. We are encouraged to make a joyful noise to the Lord and to come into His presence with praise and thanksgiving. Anything we do should bring praise and glory to the name of God. Our songs of praise and thanksgiving can take many forms. The Lord is happy with the different ways in which we show our love and appreciation to Him. Why not sing a love song to God today and just worship Him.

*Lord from the rising of the sun to the setting of it, let our hearts, our voices, our tongues, our total being sing praises to Your holy, unmatchable, unchanging and unstoppable name. Help us to come into Your presence Lord with awe, silence and reverence and fall prostrate before You and just worship You Lord God Almighty.*

*We are thankful to You Lord that You alone exemplifies goodness and Your name is unparalleled. All of creation Father is in awe of Your magnificent splendor and amazing power and we fall down before You in humility and obedience to lift up Your most holy and righteous name. We thank You for satisfying the longings of our hearts and for showering Your love upon us. All these mercies we pray in Your name. Amen.*

## January

# Just Simply Amazing

*Day 15*

*"All the sons of Israel, seeing the fire come down and the glory of the LORD upon the house, bowed down on the pavement with their faces to the ground, and they worshiped and gave praise to the LORD, saying, " Truly He is good, truly His loving-kindness is everlasting."*

2 Chronicles 7:3

Let us acknowledge God's glory and holiness even as we try to worship Him. We truly cannot face a righteous God until we have surrendered our own unrighteousness to Him. As human beings who have fallen short, we stand in awe of the One who has created us for His purpose. When we experience the glory of the Lord as the sons of Israel did, we need to bow down and give praise and adoration to our Father God who is our King of Kings and Lord of Lords. What a privilege we have to know that we have such a good, loving and kind Heavenly Father.

*Holy and majestic, awesome God of power and might, our hearts will always praise You and Your name will always be lifted up and honored. We bow before You O God to love and adore Your matchless name. Thank You that You are our Father and You beckon us to come into Your presence and gaze into Your glory. We thank You today Lord for new life in Jesus Christ Your Son.*

*Living and loving Lord, we thank You that You are the all-powerful, all transforming and all-consuming God who orders everything in our lives. Thank You Father that when we come into Your holy presence, we are to come with a sense of reverence and awe as we fall down and worship You. Father it is in Your name we pray. Amen.*

# January

# God Is The Reason For Our Praise

## Day 16

*"With praise and thanksgiving they sang to the Lord: He is good, His love to Israel endures forever." And all the people shouted with a great shout of praise to the Lord because the foundation of the house of the LORD was laid."*

Ezra 3:11

God's goodness, greatness and love need to be repeated over and over again. The more we focus on what he has done for us is the less we have to think about what He has not done or should have done. The more praise and adoration we attribute to our loving Father, is the more we show our love and appreciation for His kindness, protection and goodness towards us. Let us like the children of Israel express our thanksgiving and praise to God because His love for us endures forever.

*Precious Lord, today we want to praise You in Your sanctuary, we want to praise You in Your mighty heavens, we want to praise You and thank You for Your greatness and power and might. We want to praise You Lord for all musical instruments that help to make melodious sounds in singing songs and hymns to You. Father we want to thank You for the gift of music and for all those who dedicate their time to playing.*

*Lord we come to You with our praise and thanksgiving because You have been so good and faithful to us. You, Heavenly Father, always go above and beyond to supply our every need and Your loving hands are never short in doling out Your blessings upon us. Father we are so happy that we can come to You with our songs of rejoicing and praise. We thank You in Jesus' name for all Your blessings on us. Amen.*

## January

# Stand Up And Praise The Lord

## Day 17

*"And the Levites—Jeshua, Kadmiel, Bani, Hashabneiah, Sherebiah, Hodiah, Shebaniah and Pethahiah—said: "Stand up and praise the Lord your God, who is from everlasting to everlasting. "Blessed be your glorious name, and may it be exalted above all blessing and praise."*

Ezra 9:5

We are to bless the Lord's name daily with songs and praises and lift Him up high above the heavens. He is worthy of our praise indeed and nothing should prevent us from giving Him all the praise and glory that is due to Him. When we think about the goodness of God to us His unworthy children, we should not hesitate to find the time to thank the Lord because without His love for us what would we do. Sometimes we are stretched for time but do not forget that He has blessed all of us with the same twenty four hours and we need to make the effort to give back to Him just a little of what He has given to us in praise and adoration.

*Lord of lords and King of kings, to You we give our thanks and gratitude for guiding, protecting, caring and providing us with all we need or desire. Your name is from everlasting to everlasting Lord, and we will praise You continually with our entire being.*

*We thank You and praise You for the gift of lips and voices with which we can utter sweet songs of melody to Your adoring and adorable name. Lord we pray that You will help us never to allow anything or anyone to prevent us from sincerely offering our thanks because we cannot praise and thank You enough. This we pray in Your name. Amen.*

# January

# Never Afraid Of God

## Day 18

*"Serve the Lord with fear and celebrate his rule with trembling."*

Psalm 2:11

We do not fear God in the same way we fear man. Fear of God is to show honor, love and respect because He is God and it is He who created us, therefore it behooves us to be submissive to Him in all things. The psalmist tells us that the fear of the Lord is the beginning of wisdom and so all those who fear God, He will bless them with His wisdom. The fear of God is different from the fear of man because God will not cause us any hurt or harm as man can do. Instead God will stand by us in every situation and will never become upset or mad with us.

Lord we come into Your holy presence today with gladness in our hearts. We come with a love song to sing to You O God knowing that it is You who made us Lord in Your own image and we just need to celebrate You as our Lord and King. Help us to serve You Lord with fear and trembling because You are Almighty God.

Loving Father we thank You that when we fear You it is the beginning of being wise. You enable us Lord to make the right decisions and to remain in You. Thank You Father that You will not allow anyone to pluck us from You but that we will remain secured and well protected in Your tender and loving arms. We thank You today Lord for Your act of creation and for creating us in Your own image. This we pray in Your name. Amen.

**January**

# Grateful And Thankful Hearts

*Day 19*

*"I will give thanks to the* Lord *because of his righteousness; I will sing the praises of the name of the* Lord *Most High."*

Psalm 7:17

Our living, righteous and loving God is deserving of all our sincere gratitude and praises so let us always seek to sing praises and spiritual songs to His most precious and holy name. We do so because He is Lord and it is He who has made us and not we ourselves and we must learn to honor our Maker and Creator. Too often we give honor to others for their earthly work and neglect to give God what is due to His name.

*Dear God, thank You for Your presence with us each and every day. Remind us to take the time every day to listen to Your still small voice and hear Your direction and reassurance. Help us Father, to feed upon Your strength to cope with the unforeseen things that come suddenly upon us.*

*Thank You Lord that You are a righteous and perfect God and who is deserving of all our adoration. No appreciation or accolade is too much for us to offer up to You Father because You are indeed a special Father who always make Yourself available to us. Help us we pray Father to give You thanks for all the bountiful blessings You shower down on us each day. It is in Your name we pray. Amen.*

# January

# Our God Most High

## Day 20

*"I will be glad and rejoice in you; I will sing the praises of your name, O Most High."*

Psalm 9:2

As children of God, we must become excited in singing, rejoicing and just praising the Almighty for all His goodness towards us His most undeserving children. To rejoice in God we need to do so with our souls, bodies and minds focusing our thoughts solely and completely on Him. We must at all times align our lives with what He has called us to become and never forget to magnify and glorify His name.

We do not presume mighty and everlasting Father that we have what it takes to truly come into Your holy presence. We have sinned Father God and we need Your forgiveness. Prepare our hearts O God so that we can sing praises to Your priceless name and rejoice in knowing that we are children of the King most high.

Almighty Father, every day You call us to be faithful to You by putting You first and foremost in our lives. We cannot praise and magnify Your name Father as we ought to until we have a personal relationship with You. We invite You Holy Father into our lives and into the deep recesses of our hearts so that we can just offer up our thanksgiving to You without being afraid. Father, this we pray in Your name. Amen.

## January

# Our Sovereign Lord

### Day 21

*"Sing the praises of the Lord, enthroned in Zion; proclaim among the nations what he has done."*
Psalm 9:11

As followers of our Lord, the only voice God has in proclaiming His praises is the voice of those whom He has called. This is a mandate we have and should not fail in carrying it out to the world. We all are guilty of singing the praises of our favorite movie, sportsperson, leader or friend, but yet we spend so little time in proclaiming the name of the Lord. He is worthy of far more than we attribute to Him, which is not good enough.

O Great Architect, who has designed our lives to be able to withstand natural as well as other disasters, we pray Lord that You will teach us how to build our lives on the unshakable foundation of Your Son Jesus Christ as revealed through Your word. Grant us Lord the zeal and the desire to be worthy to share this good news with the world in praise of You.

We thank You Father that our praise of You is not limited in any way, shape or form. All that You desire of us Father is to come to You with humble and contrite hearts and to pour out before Your throne of grace our profound gratitude and praise for Your plenteous blessings on us even when we do not merit such blessings. May we always seek Father to adore and lift up Your name in all places. Here us we pray Lord. Amen.

# January

# God Hears Us When We Call

## Day 22

*"I called to the Lord, who is worthy of praise, and I have been saved from my enemies."*

Psalm 18:3

When we sing praises to God, He will protect us and guide us from the evil one. We should not be slack in praising Him continuously because He never fails to supply our needs. When we are afraid and uncertain about life' challenges, the only one on whom we can call and be sure that He will be there for us is our Father God. Let us never take Him for granted but rather give to Him our loyalty and undivided attention.

We praise You heavenly Father from whom all our blessings flow. We praise You in the morning, we praise You in the evening and we praise You all the time. Your praise O Lord is continually on our lips and we will not fail to praise You day and night. We thank You Father for saving us from our enemies when we sing praises to You.

On this bright and beautiful day Lord that You have made, we rejoice and are happy in it because once again we can see Your beauty and splendor all around us. We thank You Father for giving to us the knowledge, wisdom and understanding to read Your word and to put it into practice. When we praise and magnify Your name we are doing what You want us to do in obedience to Your word. Hear our prayer Lord, and let our cry come unto You. Amen.

**January**

# In Moments Like These

### Day 23

*"Therefore I will praise you, Lord, among the nations; I will sing the praises of your name."*

Psalm 18:49

Those who sing praises to God will be blessed at all times. He is to be thanked and appreciated for all that He does for us. It is important that as believers we endeavor to make it our duty to be sincere and consistent in the way we honor God. We should not honor Him halfheartedly but we should do so with vigor and vitality and with our total being. Nothing is more satisfying to God than when we find time to have fellowship and communion with Him in a quiet place.

*Come dear Lord God into the darkness of our lives and illuminate the darkest part of our souls with Your gifts of truth, light, gladness, strength and Your love above all else. Enlighten our lives O God and may we serve to reflect the brightness and beauty of who You are to others. May our lips sing Your praises endlessly day in and day out for as long as we live.*

*Merciful Father, sometimes we allow other gods to consume our time so much that we begin to lose our way with You. Forgive us loving Father for not staying focused on the things that matter most which includes giving You our undivided loyalty. We thank You Father for making it possible for us to be able to worship and praise You without being fearful of anyone preventing us from doing so. This we pray in Your name. Amen.*

## January

# Always Exalting God's Name

### Day 24

*"Be thou exalted, Lord, in Your own strength: so will we sing and praise Your might."*

*Psalm 21:13*

God's name is to be exalted and given pre-eminence above every other name. Our thanks and praise for Him must constantly flow from our hearts. In order for us to exalt the Lord we must study His word and adhere to His teachings and know what He desires us to do. God does not expect us to do the impossible because that is His task. All that He expects from us is to do what is possible and leave the rest to Him.

*Most gracious and loving Lord, we need You every second, every minute, every day, every hour, every week, every month and every year of our lives. We just cannot exist without You Lord. You give us strength when we are weak, You lift us up when we fall and You give us Your grace to carry us through our trials*

*O Lord God, lover of our souls, let us to Your bosom cling while we praise and glorify Your name. We adore You Father for who You are and we acknowledge Your might and power which no one can dispute because You have proven time and time again how great You are. The world stands in awe Lord of You because of the awesome and mysterious ways in which You accomplish Your promises. We thank You Father, in Jesus' name. Amen*

## January

# God's Name Is Awesome

### Day 25

*"I will declare your name to my people; in the assembly I will praise you. You who fear the Lord, praise him! All you descendants of Jacob, honor him! Revere him, all you descendants of Israel!"*

Psalm 22:22-23

Whose name is worthy to be revered, reverenced and exalted? No other name but the name of our Lord God who lives in the highest heaven. We stand in awe of His holiness and should bow before Him and give Him all the thanks and praise due to His name. Our duty as God's followers is to proclaim and declare His name to every nation, tongue and tribe. Remember until all peoples hear the name of God and know about Him, we will have to wait for a longer time for the return of His Son, Jesus. Let us get busy in going out into the highways and byways telling others about the God whom we serve.

*Heavenly Father, help us to understand how we can praise and thank You more and more. We try our best Lord but sometimes it seems that our best is not good enough. Still we keep on trying Lord and we need to hear from You. Let us not be found wanting in short-changing You Lord in our worship of You.*

*Loving Lord it is our desire to declare Your name to the world through Your holy word. We realize Father that we are Your voice on earth and if Your word is to be heard by all, we have to be the ones to proclaim it to those near and far. We thank You Father for the many opportunities You have given to us in spreading the good news of Jesus Christ to the world. May You inspire us to keep on spreading the good news of salvation in the name of the Father, in the name of the Son and in the name of the Holy Spirit. Amen.*

# January

# Vows Fulfilled

## Day 26

*"From you comes the theme of my praise in the great assembly; before those who fear you I will fulfill my vows. The poor will eat and be satisfied; those who seek the LORD will praise him- may your hearts live forever!"*
Psalm 22:25-26

Forever and forever God's name will be praised, adored and glorified by all those who call Him their Lord and their God. It is our duty as Christians and believers to lift up the name of the Lord in praise and thanksgiving as long as we have the breath of life in our bodies. We would not be fulfilling our vows if we do not use every opportunity we have to testify about the goodness of the Lord and what He has done for us. It is truly amazing how God has blessed us and provided all our needs and that is why we need to constantly give Him thanks and praises.

Great Jehovah God, it is in You that we live, move and have our very being and we want to thank You for this. We come to You today Lord with fear and trembling because we have sinned in thought, word and deed and we want to thank You for the provision You have made for the remission of our sins. For us to truly and sincerely praise You O Lord, we ask that You will forgive us of our sins and cleanse us from all unrighteousness.

We come to You earnestly in penitence and humility Lord conscious of all our shortcomings and pride which have often times prevented us from sincerely serving You as we ought to. Help us Father to be steadfast in our faith and remain loyal to You no matter what trials or temptations we may be going through. Our praise and worship of You Father will continually be on our lips and in our hearts. This we pray Father, in Your name. Amen..

## January

# Remembering God's Goodness

## Day 27

*"All the ends of the earth will remember and turn to the* Lord, *and all the families of the nations will bow down before him."*

*Psalm 22:27*

Every day we are called to bow down before our God and Maker and lift up our praise and thanksgiving to Him for He is good and His mercies endure forever and ever. In the same way we are committed to our jobs or our families, we need to be even more committed to God in executing what He has laid on our hearts to do for Him. We often make excuses that we do not have enough time to pray or to read our Bibles but yet we can find the time to do anything else that we want to do. This is not right in the sight of God and we need to reconsider our priorities.

*Living, Loving Lord, we pray that today You will be our vision, our best thought, our delight, our dignity, our inheritance now and always. We pray Father God that You will be our wisdom, our true Word, our battle-field, our soul's shelter and our high tower. May You be first and foremost in our hearts Lord and may we bow down and praise and worship You Lord of our lives.*

*Lord teach us to offer to You our hearts of thanksgiving and praise in all our daily experiences of life. Help us Father to be joyful at all times and to pray and give You thanks continually in all our circumstances. Do not let the devil have a foothold on our lives but rather help us to defeat him through our sacrifice of praise to You. This we ask in Your name and for Your sake. Amen.*

# January

# God's Splendor And Holiness

## Day 28

*"Ascribe to the LORD the glory due his name; worship the LORD in the splendor of his holiness."*

Psalm 29:2

We should ascribe greatness to our God because He is our rock, His work is perfect and all His ways are just. Let us all bow down and worship Him in the beauty and splendor of His holiness. What a joy we feel, when we just focus on God and God alone in the quiet moments that we spend with Him. It is so fulfilling when we speak to God and He listens to us just like a father listens to his earthly children. The challenge for us is that in this fast paced world and the many voices beckoning for our attention and time, we tend to miss out on the times God tries to get our attention. Let us try to give Him a bit more of our time that He has given to us so generously.

*Father God, we pray that You will enable us to bow down and worship You today in spirit and in truth. We acknowledge Lord that You are our rock and shield and a very present help in time of trouble. We thank You Father that You are a God of faithfulness and without injustice and that You are good and upright in all that You do and deserving of all our praise.*

*We thank You Father for this wonderful and amazing blessing of today and for the hope You have given to us which gives us strength to press on in this life. We thank You Lord for Your grace, which renews and restores our lives and we praise You for everything You have done for us to make a difference in our lives. Lord, forgive us for not always being consistent in our worship of You, and we ask You to challenge us to do better than we have been doing. This we ask in Your name. Amen.*

# January

# Never Fail To Praise God

## Day 29

*"Sing the praises of the Lord, you His faithful people; praise His holy name."*

*Psalm 30:4*

How do we sing the praises of God if we do not know Him? Our praise to God must come from a humble and contrite heart. Our desire at all times must be one of praise and thanksgiving to God even when we think or feel there is nothing to praise or to thank Him for in those moments of adversity and trials. However, we need to remember the promise of God who says He will never leave us nor forsake us and He faithfully keeps His promise..

*Lord, help us to sing praises to You as long as we live and have our being. Our mediation of You Father will be sweet and we will be glad to rejoice in You O Lord our God. Father, we ask that You will teach us how to bless and to praise Your name while we patiently wait upon You. You are our only hope when we feel weak and weary because then You give us the strength and courage to keep going on.*

*Thank You Father that You are a faithful and compassionate God and one who is always guiding and protecting Your children. We confess Lord that we have not always shown our gratitude to You in the halfhearted way in which we try to elevate Your name. Forgive us Lord, for not living up to Your expectations from us for whom You have done so much. This we pray in Your name. Amen.*

## January

# Bruised But Not Broken

### Day 30

*"You turned my wailing into dancing; you removed my sackcloth and clothed me with joy, that my heart may sing your praises and not be silent. LORD my God, I will praise you forever."*

Psalm 30:11-12

In the midst of crisis and impending danger, God delivers us from our terrorizing experiences and places us where we find safety. How wonderful it is for brethren to sing praises to the Lord at all times and not only when we face insurmountable challenges. Consider this if God would only do things for us when we call upon Him, how would we feel? He is always thinking about us and knows our needs and supplies them whether or not we ask. We too need to come to God every day full of praise and thanksgiving.

*O God our Father, night and day we cry unto You to deliver us from all our troubles and You heard and answered our cries. You Lord removed our sackcloth and clothed us with Your joy so our hearts can sing praises to You forever and ever. You are our God and early in the morning will we seek You.*

*Have mercy on us Father and blot out all our transgressions as we seek to serve You. Lord help us to draw nearer to You this week and be more devoted to living faithfully for You instead of ourselves, Help us to start each day with thanksgiving in our hearts, giving praise to you, O Almighty God because You are deserving of all our praise. It is in Your name we pray. Amen.*

# January

# Giving To God Our Best

## Day 31

*"Sing joyfully to the Lord, you righteous; it is fitting for the upright to praise him. Praise the Lord with the harp; make music to him on the ten-stringed lyre. Sing to him a new song; play skillfully, and shout for joy."*
Psalm 33:1-3

Every day we should come to the Lord singing a new song of praise to Him for all the wonderful and marvelous wonders He has performed again and again. Our God is a great and good God who is fitting for us who call Him Lord to praise Him in every way we can. The Lord is worthy of our undivided loyalty and as His followers we should never fail to do so. Let us rise up and do our part in showing our honor and praise to our Almighty God.

*O Lord our God, when we in awesome wonder, consider all the works Your mighty hands have made. When we see the stars and we hear the mighty thunder, Your power throughout the universe displayed. Lord we can't help but just to let our souls sing to You to say how great You are indeed. We thank You for all the splendor and majesty of the universe and we just praise and lift up Your name Most High.*

*Give us Lord we pray the tenacity to call You Abba Father, knowing very well how undeserving we are to come into Your holy presence because of our sins. We thank You for giving us a second chance to be called Your children by confessing our sins and accepting You as our Lord. Fill us Father with Your Holy Spirit, the Comforter who affords us the privilege to sing songs of praises to You. This we pray in Your name. Amen.*

# February

## Rejoicing In Affliction

### Day 1

*"I will extol the Lord at all times; his praise will always be on my lips. I will glory in the Lord; let the afflicted hear and rejoice. Glorify the Lord with me; let us exalt his name together."*

Psalm 34:1-3

Let us all exalt the name of the Lord as often as we can with a song on our lips and praise flowing from our hearts. We are encouraged by God's word to extol His name at all times and our praise of Him to always be on our lips. It is not ok for us just to pay lip service to the Lord, but everything that comes out of our mouth must be from the heart. God knows when we are genuine in our worship and praise of Him so it behooves us to be sincere and faithful in honoring Him.

*Heavenly Father, give us hearts to praise You O God. Give us hearts that are from sin set free, hearts that always feel Your blood so freely shed for us. Lord give us hearts resigned, submissive, meek, humble, lowly and contrite which neither life nor death can separate from You who dwells within us. Lord give us hearts today to sing to You melody of praise and thanksgiving.*

*Gracious God, You desire from us hearts that are pure and free from hypocrisy and pride. Help us Father to glorify and magnify Your name in all that we do and say so that others can see Your beauty being reflected in us and be drawn closer to You. Lord, You are our all in all and we owe You our wholehearted allegiance and this we pray in Your most precious and holy name. Amen.*

## February

# Everyday A Promise

### Day 2

*"I will give you thanks in the great assembly; among the throngs I will praise you."*

Psalm 35:18

God is everywhere and so He is deserving of all our praise wherever we may go or worship Him. The Bible is our source and inspiration on how to shower our praises and accolades on our God who constantly reminds us of His love for us even when we disobey Him. Each day as we think about God, let us remember that it is He who has made us and not we ourselves and that we owe our very life to Him. Praising God should be a part of our daily routine.

*Father God we stand in awe because of You and all praise and honor, dominion and power are due to Your most holy and precious name. Holy Father to whom all praise should be given, we stand in awe of You God because You are beautiful beyond description, too marvelous for words, too wonderful for comprehension and there is nothing ever seen or heard to grasp Your infinite wisdom.*

*Lord we thank You for Your absolute beauty and the splendor of Your creation. When we look around us and see all that You have made, we just marvel at Your handiwork and offer a prayer of praise and thanksgiving to You. It is beyond our human comprehension Father to grasp the length, breadth, depth and height of Your power and might. Thank You for just being such an awesome, loving and wonderful God and to You we offer up ourselves even as we are. Hear our prayer Father, and let our cry come unto You. Amen.*

## February

# Little But Tallawah

### Day 3

*"My tongue will proclaim your righteousness, your praises all day long."*

Psalm 35:28

We should offer our entire body to God as a sacrifice of praise to Him. Let us praise Him with our whole being because He is the vine and we are the branches and we are all intertwined with Him. None of us can survive without God no matter how hard we may try because those who think they can have only discovered how poor their lives have been without Him. The Bible tells us in Psalm 34:8 to taste and see how good the Lord is and those who have done so can truly testify to that goodness. The Lord has given to all of us a special organ that is our tongue to be used to glorify Him. It is little but can be used to turn the world upside down for Him. Let's all use it wisely to bring glory and honor to God's name.

Father God, we thank You for allowing us to celebrate even when life is uncertain. We thank You Lord that through the uncertainties of life, we can still praise You and glorify Your name. We realize Lord that when we trust in Your salvation, we do not have to depend on circumstances for joy. As we follow in Your footsteps Father and receive the blessings of Your righteousness, our hearts and souls are filled with joy.

Lord we thank You for giving us peace and joy even in the midst of trials and tribulations. Thank You Father for the way in which You respond to our cries for help and for seeing us through difficult and challenging times. We know Father that even in the midst of our pain and agony we can still praise and worship You because You are always by our sides to comfort us. All this we pray in Your name. Amen.

## February

# Daily Renewals

## Day 4

*"He put a new song in my mouth, a hymn of praise to our God. Many will see and fear the Lord and put their trust in him."*

Psalm 40:3

Every day gives us a new opportunity to praise and thank the Lord for some special blessings He has bestowed upon us. Sometimes our focus is only on the big and spectacular but the little things are also very important. For example the air we breathe is so very important because it sustains life and without it we literally die, yet we take it for granted and it is something for which we must give thanks. Today consider all the little things in life that we really cannot do without and make it a part of our routine to give thanks for each.

Ah Lord God our Father, You have made the heaven and the earth by Your great power. There is nothing too difficult that You cannot do. Thank You Lord for the many new blessings You pour down upon us daily including all the things we so often take for granted. Keep us always open to You Lord so that we can live with the confidence that You will never abandon us.

Dear Father, we praise and thank You for working within us and enabling us to proclaim You as Lord and work with You in telling others about Your love and forgiveness. Give us we pray Father the energy and strength we need for this task and fill us with Your presence and peace. This we pray in Your name and for Your sake. Amen.

## February

# No Matter What God Be Praised

### Day 5

*"Why my soul, are you downcast? Why so disturbed within me? Put your hope in God, for I will yet praise him, my Savior and my God."*

Psalm 42:5

There are many things in life that can knock us down leaving us disturbed and downcast. God is able to deliver us from such situations once we put our trust and hope in Him. Many people have been through really difficult and challenging times but they have not allowed their circumstances to prevent them from pressing on. We too as God's followers must not allow anything from preventing us to remain faithful to our God because He is always in control of our lives and will see us through even to the end.

Lord, living in today's world places a great strain on us as we worry as to what tomorrow will bring. We need to heed Your word Lord that there is no need for us to worry, because You take care of the sparrows so how much more will You take care of us. Help us Father to rejoice in You and give You praise and put our hope in You. With You Father in the driving seat, our future is secured.

Father we thank You that the lines of Your grace have no limits because they extend to all people in the world. Thank You Father that Your forgiveness and salvation have been offered to all people. As we consider the boundary line of our lives Father, we thank You for the rich inheritance with which You have blessed us and the assurance that You have given to us not to worry or become concerned about tomorrow. This we pray in the name of Jesus. Amen.

## February

# Downcast But Hopeful

## Day 6

*"Why, my soul, are you downcast? Why so disturbed within me? Put your hope in God, for I will yet praise him, my Savior and my God."*
Psalm 42:11

Some things are worth repeating over and over again until the message is heard. Thank God for His word that keeps on reminding us to praise Him. As we reflect on these words from Psalm 42:11, let us look back on Psalm 42:5 and pause and wonder why the psalmist repeats this verse again. Notice that we are encouraged to put our hope in God even when we are under the weather and to praise Him because He is in control of every area of our lives and He will always see us through the hard and difficult times.

*Father, forgive us for the times when we have been too afraid and ashamed to call upon Your name for help. Yet we know that we have no one else to help us but You. Remove from our hearts all doubts and fear of You and help us to learn to trust You always. We put our hope and trust in You alone Father and we praise Your name forever and ever.*

*Gracious Father, let Your ears always be attentive to our prayers of praise and adoration. We pray loving Father that You will touch the hearts of those who do not adore You and help them to love You with all their hearts, souls and strength. Please remind us Lord of the many things You do for us daily and help us to spend more time in praise and adoration of You. This we ask in Your name. Amen.*

# February

# Never Stop Praising Our Creator

## Day 7

*"Sing praises to God, sing praises; sing praises to our King, sing praises."*

Psalm 47:6

The more praises we sing to our God, the closer we feel to Him and the more we keep the devil out of our lives. God wants us to give Him our total undivided attention in response to His love and protection for us. All of us as His followers must make it our duty to ascribe all praise and thanksgiving to our Maker who has shown us over and over again how much He cares for us His erring children. There can be no substitute for God in our lives and this we need to recognize and acknowledge.

We praise and thank You Lord God for coming into every area of our lives. May the power of the Holy Spirit fall on us and ignite our hearts to sing praises to You Lord Most High. Lord we pray that Your Holy Spirit will breathe on us, inspire us and dwell in us. Heavenly Father we pray that You will help us to realize that Your grace, mercy and forgiveness are always available if we would only ask of You.

Forgiving and Righteous Lord, forgive us for our sins of pride, rebellion, disobedience, selfishness, hatred and bitterness which so often prevent us from sincerely worshipping You as we ought to. Forgive us Father for halfhearted worship and for disrespecting Your name and treating You with irreverence. Give us the zeal and desire Lord to truly worship You in Spirit and in truth. This we pray in the precious name of Your Son, Jesus our Lord. Amen..

# February

## Mountain Of Praise To God

### Day 8

*"Great is the* Lord, *and most worthy of praise, in the city of our God, his holy mountain."*

Psalm 48:1

Our God is a great God and greatly to be praised by His people. We should never hold back or be reluctant to praise the name of our God who has done so much for us. When we consider where we are coming from and where the Lord has brought us, it is enough for us to fall prostrate before Him and honor Him from the depth of our hearts. Only God could do all that He has done for us in such amazing and mysterious ways. We should all give Him a mountain of praise that He so well deserves.

*Lord You are great and mighty and Your name is worthy of our praise day and night. Father we just want to lift Your name on high. We want to thank You for the works You have done in our lives and Lord we trust in Your unfailing love for us, for You alone are God eternal and indeed worthy of our praise.*

*Lord God, the Almighty Father, You reign supreme in heaven and on the earth. You are our great Father and the works that You do are just marvelous. You alone are holy Lord and all nations will one day come and worship before You because Your righteous deeds have been revealed to all people. Help us Father to continually praise Your name even until the end of the earth. It is in Your name we pray Lord. Amen.*

# February

# God of Heaven and Earth

## Day 9

*"Like your name, O God, your praise reaches to the ends of the earth; your right hand is filled with righteousness."*

Psalm 48:10

Once we give thanks and praise to the Almighty, we will never go away empty-handed because His blessings are ever new. When we think about all the things that are happening around us and competing for our time, we become very challenged to remain focused on the things that are most important to us. That is why we have to become well-grounded in our faith and hold on to what we believe. God is in control of our lives and we need to surrender our all to Him, giving Him all the praise and glory.

New every morning Lord is Your love for us even as we awake and rise from our slumber. We thank You Lord for guiding and protecting us through another night and for restoring us to life, and power and thought. We thank You for Your mercies Lord which are new every day and for Your constant love and protection for us,

Help us Father that as we go through another day, we will learn to sing Your praises and be obedient to Your word. Father, we cannot do without You because You are our very dependable God on whom we can call upon at any time. We thank You for Your righteousness and for the way You execute Your love and mercy for all peoples on earth. You are indeed worthy of our honor and adoration. This we pray in the name of the Father, in the name of the Son and in the name of the Holy Spirit. Amen.

# February

# Open Lips, Open Hearts

## Day 10

*"Open my lips, Lord, and my mouth will declare your praise."*

*Psalm 51:15*

Our praise of God can be in silence or we can shout our praises from the mountaintop. God has not placed any restriction or preference on how we must praise Him. As long as we sing praises to Him that is what matters most. The most significant thing we need to remember is that God is always available to us no matter where we may be or what we might be going through. He just wants us to remain faithful and true to Him and He will honor His promises to us.

*Lord we pray today that You will open our lips so that we can bear good tidings of Your mercy everywhere we go. We pray Father that You will open our hearts and let us prepare love to share with others. Open our minds Lord that we may read more of Your word so that we can impart Your truth to those who do not know You.*

*Thank You Father that Your word is a lamp to our feet and a light to our path and we shall never walk in darkness as long as You are with us. Every day Father we will seek to declare Your praise to those with whom we come in contact and especially those who do not have a personal relationship with You. Thank You for making a difference in the lives of all those who have accepted You as Lord. Father we give to You all the praise and glory in Jesus' name. Amen.*

# February

# We Are Not Afraid

## Day 11

*"In God, whose word I praise; in God I trust and am not afraid. What can mere mortals do to me?"*
Psalm 56:4

Those of us who put our faith and trust in God do not have to be afraid because no one can pluck us from His hand. God's hold on us is secured and His protection is firm and we are all well anchored in Him. No matter what storms we might be going through, God's anchor will always hold and we certainly do not have to be afraid because He is in charge of our destiny. Each day we should put Him before everything else and continue to give Him praise.

Lord we are not dismayed and we are not afraid to praise You and to put our trust in You. When others try to beat and tear us down we know Lord You will lift us up and set us on solid ground. Father we thank You for being the Alpha and Omega, the first and the last of our lives. Lord we know that as long as we place our trust and faith in You, no one can touch us because we are safe with You.

We thank You today for all that You have been doing for us and as long as we put our faith and trust in You, we will be saved from all that is evil. We ask You Father to look down on us with mercy, love and compassion and keep on drawing us closer and closer to You and enable us to remain faithful to You even as we lift up our voices to You in gratitude and praise. These mercies we ask in Your name Father. Amen.

## February

# A Fixed Heart

### Day 12

*"My heart is fixed, O God, my heart is fixed: I will sing and give praise."*

*Psalm 57:7*

When we serve God, there can't be any unwavering of our faith. Our mind, heart and soul must be fixed on Him day in and day out. Every day we need to make an endeavored effort to stay focused amidst all the distractions we encounter daily. It is good for us to resign ourselves to a quiet place where we can truly concentrate and meditate on the word of God. When we do so, we will experience the big difference it makes in our relationship with God.

*Lord we know that our faith cannot be in things or even other people but it must be vested in You and You alone. Everything and everyone else will fail us when we put our trust and hope in anything that is not eternal. Help us dear Lord to put our trust in You so that You will not only take care of us in this life but in the life to come. Lord we thank You today for all that You do for us on a daily basis and we just want to give to You all the praise and glory due to Your name.*

*We thank You Father for transforming us by the renewing of our minds in Your holy word so that we can be living proof of that good and acceptable and perfect will of Yours. Lord, we thank You and praise You that through You we are destined to win and not to lose because You have made us to be more than conquerors in this world of ours. For all Your mercies and blessings Lord, we give You thanks in the name of Jesus. Amen.*

# February

# Only One God

## Day 13

*"I will praise you, Lord, among the nations; I will sing of you among the peoples."*

Psalm 57:9

God is everywhere and because He is everywhere, we need to proclaim the good news of salvation so that all nations and all the peoples of the world will know about Him. Jesus in the Great Commission in Matthew 28, exhorts Christians to take the good news of salvation to every corner of the globe so that all peoples everywhere would bow down and worship the God of all creation. We must not fail in carrying out this mandate the Lord has given to us.

Lord help us today to praise You, seek You and serve You forever. We seek Your forgiveness Father and pray that You will cleanse us from all our sinful ways. May we learn Lord to praise You wherever we go and to tell others of Your mercy, love and grace which are available to all who would seek You. Grant us we pray Father Your wisdom so that we will be able to prepare ourselves for the task You have called us to do.

Teach us Heavenly Father through Your word to be obedient, true and faithful to You in everything that You have placed on our shoulders to do for You. Give us the ability to be able to impart Your word to others in such a way that they will readily and willingly accept You as Lord and bring glory and honor to Your name. Father, help us that this day we will exhibit true love to all those with whom we may come in contact because You are a loving God and it is Your will for us to love others even as we love ourselves. This we ask in Your name. Amen.

## February

# Vows For Life

### Day 14

*"Then I will ever sing in praise of your name and fulfill my vows day after day."*

*Psalm 61:8*

A vow is a promise we take such as a marriage vow and we are held responsible and accountable in keeping to that promise. So it is when we make a vow to God to praise Him we must honor that promise as He does His. Unfortunately, due to the many demands on our time, we so often forget to do the things we promise God that we will do. Paul alludes to the fact that the things he should be doing, he finds himself doing the opposite and we too have fallen into the same trap. Let us call upon the name of the Lord daily for Him to help us to remain focused on Him and His word.

*Father this is our solemn vow to You that we will honor, respect, praise and love You with all of who we are for the rest of our lives. We know Lord that we will fail You along the way and when we do we ask You to forgive us and cleanse us and continue to use us Lord for Your glory. Lord we are weak but You are strong so help us to lean on Your everlasting arm.*

*Father God, we thank You today for the dark periods of our lives that we may experience and for the way in which You will see us through. You Father have declared in Your word that nothing can separate us from Your love and that gives us reasons to rejoice and be glad in You. We thank You Father for enabling us to express our joy no matter what the circumstances of life might be and for Your promise ever to be with us always. This we pray in Your name. Amen.*

# February

# God's Love Is Better Than Anything

## Day 15

*"Because your love is better than life, my lips will glorify you."*

Psalm 63:3

God's love for us is better than life itself because He never stops loving us despite our shortcomings. Consider what He did for us when there was hopelessness in the world and mankind was lost in sin. He took it upon Himself and sent His only Son, Jesus Christ to pay the ultimate price for our sin. We have ten thousand reasons why we should at all times praise and glorify the name of the Lord without hesitation. Think of the amount of time we spend on watching our favorite movie or game and yet compared that to how little time we spend with the Lord. Are you satisfied with the amount of time you spend in prayer or reading God's word? If not why not begin today.

*Your loving-kindness Lord is better than life; therefore our lips will praise You and we will lift up our hands in Your name to glorify and to magnify You O Lord our God. Father in Heaven, You have acted with power in the past so help us to trust You with our future. We know Father that we can always depend on You to see us through any and all situations.*

*Oh loving and living Father God, we stand in awe of You because of Your resplendent beauty and awesomeness. Thank You Father that You are the immovable, immutable and unchanging God who sits on Your throne in the highest heaven and yet You remain ever so close to us. We thank You indeed Lord for Your inexpressible love which is better than life itself. Lord, as we lift up our praises to You, we do so in the precious name of Your Son, Jesus. Amen.*

# February

# Singing Lips of Praise

## Day 16

*"I will be fully satisfied as with the richest of foods; with singing lips my mouth will praise you."*
Psalm 63:5

God gives to us the best of whatever He has in His storehouse and our duty is to keep on thanking and praising Him for His loving-kindness and tender mercies. Have you ever taken time out to reflect on God's goodness towards us? He has never ever failed in giving to us the best even when we do not deserve it. Think of how we treat our God who is so generous, kind and loving with our stinginess in the giving of our time, talents and treasures. Remember that all we possess comes from God and we really do not own anything in this life as everything belongs to Him. May we make an effort to honor Him daily with an attitude of gratitude.

*Lord how many blessings have You heaped on us in our life time and yet we find it so difficult at times to acknowledge your generosity towards us. Not only do You provide us with our daily food and other material things, but our spirits feel Your goodness and our souls flourish like a well-watered garden carefully tended by You our Father. Lord how can we thank You enough for all Your blessings You give to us so freely and unconditionally? We offer our lives to You Lord in obedience to Your word.*

*Heavenly Father, we thank You that Your name is awesome and that You are the King of Kings and Lord of Lords. We thank You that You are our omnipresent, omniscient and omnipotent Father God who is the Supreme Leader of all the heaven and the earth and there is just no one else like You. We thank You Father for loving to hear us sing and pray to You and to make music with our voices that reverberate throughout all the earth. We ask You Lord to hear our prayer and let our cry come unto You. Amen.*

# February

# Full Of Praise For God

## Day 17

*"Shout for joy to God, all the earth! Sing the glory of his name; make his praise glorious."*

Psalm 66:1-2

We must speak glorious things about our God who deserves all our time in praise and gratitude for His wonder, working power and might. In the same way we put our energy in cheering for our favorite sports person without feeling constrained to do so, it's the same way we need to put in that energy when we are praising the Lord. God is not afraid of how loud we shout out to Him. He enjoys hearing our melodious voices and so at no time should we be afraid to express our love and gratitude to Him the best way we can.

Glorious things of You our God are spoken by all those who acclaim You as their Lord and King. Lord, help us never deride or belittle Your name or do anything to bring Your name into disrepute. Let us give thanks to You always with a grateful and thankful heart and help us to learn how to praise You without fail.

Merciful and forgiving Father, how we thank You so much for choosing us to bring glory, praise and honor to Your name. Every day we pray Father, that You will give us the strength to shout for joy to You because of the great and wonderful things You have done for us Your erring children. We are so underserving of Your love and yet You keep on loving us just the same. May we always express our love and gratitude to You in the name of Jesus. Amen.

## February

# Countless Praises To God

### Day 18

*"All the earth bows down to you; they sing praise to you, they sing the praises of your name."*

Psalm 66: 4

God's people must bow down and worship Him in spirit and in truth even as we lift up His mighty name in songs and hymns of praise. In these difficult and trying times of uncertainty, there is much for us to be thankful for. We could be in a worst situation had it not been for the mercy and grace of God which He has seen fit to bestow on us. Consider life without a God who cares and protects us from all of the trials and tribulations that are so pervasive in our world today. He certainly is worthy of our praise and gratitude all the time.

O Lord Jesus we will bow down and worship You today as our King of kings and Lord of lords. We will adore and magnify Your name without ceasing. You are worthy Oh God to be exalted and lifted up on high because of Your greatness, Your amazing power and might and Your absolute beauty. Lord we come to You today before the throne of grace, to bow down in worship and to sing Your praises ceaselessly.

O God our Tower of Strength, we thank You for doing so much for us and for reassuring us that You will never leave us nor forsake us. We exalt and magnify Your name Father because there is no one else like You. Because of the freedom You have given us to worship You Father, we know that You will accept the various ways in which we express our love and adoration for You. It is a good thing Father that You have given us the freedom to truly and sincerely worship You in Spirit and in truth. This we pray in Your name. Amen.

# February

# An Attitude of Praise To God

## Day 19

*"Bless our God, O peoples, give Him grateful thanks and make the voice of His praise be heard."*
Psalm 66:8

Let us bless the name of the Lord by lifting up our voices to Him in praise and thanksgiving. As we read the word of God daily, we can draw our comfort from the fact that God truly loves us and wants us to love Him too. By loving God first we will be able to love others and to be exemplars to those with whom we come in contact. The Bible tells us that by our fruits people will know whose we are and so we should always make the effort to celebrate the God whom we serve in praise and adoration.

*Lord, help us today to bless Your most holy and precious name with songs and hymns of praise and adoration. Our souls bless Your name our Lord God because of Your holiness and righteousness. You have done great and mighty things for us Father and so all that we have within us, we just want to pour it out to You Lord to honor and magnify Your precious name.*

*Almighty God, we come before You with grateful hearts, praising You with all our being. We thank You Father that every good and perfect gift comes from You- the One who never changes. We recognize those good things both large and small with which You have blessed us and we thank You sincerely Lord for Your generous blessings that You have bestowed upon us Your wayward children. Lord, it is in Your name we pray. Amen.*

# February

# Our Merciful and Gracious God
## Day 20

*"God be merciful and gracious to us and bless us and cause His face to shine upon us and among us! That Your way may be known upon earth, Your saving power (Your deliverances and Your salvation) among all nations. Let the peoples praise You [turn away from their idols] and give thanks to You, O God; let all the peoples praise and give thanks to You." (AB)*

*Psalm 67:1-3*

The God whom we serve is a merciful and gracious God, who is slow in getting angry and plenteous in mercy. The more we focus on God's mercy and grace, the more we should be compelled to turn away from our wicked and evil ways and turn to Him in total obedience. Remember that God does not really need us but we desperately need Him and so our loyalty should be to Him and no other. As we live each day, let us do so with the knowledge that it could be our last day so we need to be connected to God at all times through our praise and adoration for Him.

*Lord we pray that You will be merciful and gracious to us today. We ask Father God that You will bless us and cause Your face to shine upon us and deliver us from all that is evil. Help us Lord not to fall into temptation and when we do, prepare a way for us to escape from the evil one. Let us praise You and give You thanks loving Father so that others in return will also give You thanks and praise.*

*Father the world we live in and all that You have created belongs to You. We thank You for giving us the opportunity to live on this earth and to be able to enjoy all that You have made available to us. Forgive us Father for the times when we have abused that which You have created and to turn a blind eye to the mess we have made. Forgive us Lord because we have sinned and fallen short and we are not worthy to call You Abba Father. Forgive us we pray Father and cause Your face to shine upon us in the name of Jesus we pray. Amen.*

## February

# Gladsome Praise To Our Father

### Day 21

*"Sing to God, sing praises to His name, cast up a highway for Him Who rides through the deserts—His name is the Lord—be in high spirits and glory before Him!" (AB).*
Psalm 68:4

When we praise God we should do so joyfully and with a willing and gladsome heart. He is no ordinary God so we should become excited in our praise for Him. Let us remember that our worship of God wherever or however we gather is through Jesus Christ, His Son. Our personal relationship with God in our worship of Him is to love Him with all our hearts, souls, and with all our minds with the help of the Holy Spirit.

Lord our souls find rest in You alone and our salvation comes from You. You alone Lord are our rock and our fortress and we shall never be shaken. We put our trust in You O Lord because You are our refuge and strength. We will continually praise You our Father and we will always seek to do Your will.

Speak to our hearts Father even as we listen to Your still small voice. May we respond to Your call to tell others about You as we have never done before. We know Father it is our duty to sing praises to Your name in the company of others especially those who do not have a personal relationship with You. Lord may we use every opportunity we have to witness to those with whom we come in contact with songs of praise and adoration. This we pray Father, in Your name and to Your glory. Amen.

# February

# All Sing Praises To God

## Day 22

*"Sing to God You kingdoms of the earth, sing praises to the Lord." Who must sing praises to our God?*
Psalm 68:32

All the peoples, nations and kingdoms of the world are to sing praises to God our Creator and Maker of the earth. Our worship and devotion to God is demonstrated by our submission to His Lordship over and through our lives to become the persons of faith He desires us to become. The faith we received when we accepted Jesus into our hearts and into our lives is critical for our learning to more fully trust, honor and obey God in every circumstances of life,

*Lord God of might and power, Creator and Sustainer of all life, help us this day to become encouragers and enablers to all those who do not know You. We know Father that it is Your will that all the peoples of the world should sing praises to Your holy name and to thank You without ceasing. Help us Lord to spread the good news of salvation not only through the lives we live but also through personal witnessing to all those with whom we come in contact daily.*

*Loving Lord, we pray that every day You will help us to make a concerted effort to come to Your throne of grace where we find forgiveness for our souls and the strength to carry on. We praise You Father for the ways in which You have enabled us to sour like eagles and to be counted even by our enemies. Give us we pray Father the patience to remain steadfast in Your love. This we pray in Your name sake. Amen.*

# February

# Magnifying God's Name

## Day 23

*"I will praise the name of God with song and magnify Him."*

Psalm 69:30

It is a good and wonderful thing for us as God's people to magnify and sing praises to Him not only because it is the right thing to do but because He is worthy of our praise. Everything we do, say or think is so very important because through these sin can enter into our lives and cause us to be separated from God. The Christian walk is not always easy but with God in our lives and with His leading, we can certainly praise and magnify His name.

Heavenly Father thank You for this beautiful day we are able to enjoy with family and friends. Thank You for the beauty of Your creation and we thank You that we are a part of Your family- the family of God. It is our duty Lord to praise and to magnify Your name in everything we do and we thank You for the freedom we have in doing so.

Today Father as we lift up our voices to You in praise and adoration, help us to do so with humble and contrite hearts. Lord we thank You that You are always looking out for us and for providing us with our daily needs. There is no one else besides You on whom we can call Father for help especially when we need it most and so we want to thank You for making Yourself available to us always. It is in Your name we pray. Amen.

## February

# Everything Give Praise to God

*Day 24*

*"Let heaven and earth praise Him, the seas and everything that moves in them." (AB)*
*Psalm 69:34*

Our God made the heaven and the earth and set the mighty seas and oceans in motion. He has given us responsibility to care for all that He has created and He wants us to be careful in doing so. Unfortunately, today we are paying the price for not taking care of God's creation, as we should. The world is warming up more than ever and the environmental changes taking place are huge and concerning. As Christians we need to play our small role in protecting and preserving our environment wherever we live.

O Creator of heaven and earth and all living and non-living things, we thank You Lord for the uniqueness of Your creation and the way in which everything works together so perfectly well. Father we pray that all of creation will truly recognize You as their God and Creator and will give You all the praise, thanks and glory which You are so well deserving of.

Lord we know that we have not always been good stewards in taking care of our environment and for this we seek Your forgiveness. We ask Father to help us to do all we can to take care of all that You have entrusted to us and to realize that You are depending on us to protect that which You have created. We thank You Father for the beauty of the earth and for everything with which You have blessed us. This we pray in the name of the Father, Son and Holy Spirit. Amen.

## February

# Our Sovereign Lord

### Day 25

*"For You have been my hope Sovereign Lord, my confidence since my youth. From birth I have relied on You; You brought me forth from my mother's womb. I will ever praise You."*

Psalm 71:5-6

Almighty God has been good to us ever since our existence. All that we are and will become it is because of His love and goodness towards us. This gives us more reason why we should praise and show our gratitude to Him continually. When we think of how God created us in His very own image and filled is with His breath of life, we should consider how special and fortunate we are for Him to have done this for us. His goodness is certainly from everlasting to everlasting and our praise of Him should continually be in our mouths.

Loving God, we thank You for being our Hope in ages past, our Confidant, our Creator, our Sustainer and our Deliverer from the beginning of the world. Father, You have given to us life and You have kept us safe from our childhood. You gave us wonderful parents to care for us and You never took Your eyes off us. We thank You dear God for everything You have given to us and for all the blessings we have received from You Lord.

Heavenly Father we are thankful to You for having provided Your Word which is life to us. The orderliness of nature tells us of Your existence Father and we thank You that every day we can enjoy the beauty and splendor of this world You have so uniquely created. Thank You loving Father for having taken a personal interest in us and we thank You that Your Word gives us a glimpse of Whom You are. We thank You for blessing us in the name of Jesus. Amen.

# February

# Our Daily Praising of God

## Day 26

*"My mouth is filled with Your praise and with Your glory all the day."*

Psalm 71:8

God's word declares that out of the mouths of babies and suckling praises are uttered, even so much more important it is for us as matured Christians for our mouths to be filled with praise and thanksgiving for the King of kings and Lord of lords. We should never be at a loss for words when it comes to expressing our appreciation to our God and Creator because He has done so much for us. In the same way we can shower kind expressions of love on our earthy fathers so it should be for us too to do the same for our Wonderful God who has made all things good.

*Oh Lord and our God, teach us how important it is for us to come to You singing praises and lifting our voice to You in thanksgiving. Let our mouths praise You O God night and day without ceasing. You are worthy our Father of all our adoration for You, because You are our God, our High Priest, our Provider and our Bright and Morning Star.*

*Father God, we thank You that little with contentment is great gain and that we must always be appreciative of what we have. Lord, help us that rather than being discontent and looking for a better situation, we pray that You would help us to focus more on You and what You have given to us. This we pray in Jesus' name. Amen.*

# February

# More Praise For God

## Day 27

*"But as for me I will hope continually, and will yet praise You more and more."*

*Psalm 71:14*

No matter what life may dish out to us, let us always put our faith and hope in God and keep on trusting Him more and more. God has promised not to give us more than we can endure and we should give Him thanks for this reassurance. When things are not going well and when our spirits are down, let us remember that the Lord is our only hope and we are to look to Him from whence comes our help. Instead of giving Him less praise when times are rough and tough, let us increase our praise and gratitude to Him for the good times as well as the bad times for He never fails.

*Precious and awesome Father, help us we pray never to lose our hope in You even when the going gets rough and the rough gets going. Lord, You have proven Your love and care for us over and over again and we have no reason for not continuing to trust You. Father we realize that the more and more we sing Your praises and give You thanks, the closer we feel to You.*

*Omnipotent Father, we thank You that there is no limitations to the love and attention You can bestow upon us Your children. Lord we know that the more we know You and understand You, the more we learn to appreciate Your love for us. We pray Father that we will experience You more deeply so that our love for You will increase day by day. Thank You for listening to our prayer in Jesus' name we pray. Amen.*

## February

# God Our Strength and Song

*Day 28*

*The Lord is my strength and my song, and he has become my salvation; this is my God, and I will praise him, my father's God, and I will exalt him.*

*Exodus 15:2*

Whenever we are feeling weak and inadequate, let us remember that God is the One to whom we should look to take us through life's difficulties and challenges. He is the Author and Finisher of our faith and He never fails in taking care of those who have put their trust and faith in Him. The Lord always fulfills His promises and so we should never be afraid or reluctant to call upon His name and to give Him all the praise and glory for He is worthy of it all.

*Lord Jesus, help us to find our place of safety and rest in You. Father at times we find it very difficult to rest because sleep is sometimes elusive and so we ask You to allow Your Holy Spirit to turn our thoughts to You. Cause us loving Father to be filled with Your peace and to have an awareness of Your Holy presence. Continue Father to make us strong in our weakness and to praise You with our whole being.*

*Gracious Lord, we know that we are never alone because You are always with us and in this we find hope and courage for the uncertain times ahead. Thank You Father that You are indeed our antidote to our fear and hopelessness and for giving us the courage to praise You no matter what we may be going through. Lord You are our strength and our song and we will ever lift up Your most Holy and precious name at all times. We give You praise and glory for ever and ever. Amen.*

# March

# Variety In Praising God

## Day 1

*"I will also praise You with the psaltery, even Your truth, O my God: unto You will I sing with the harp, O You Holy One of Israel. My lips shall greatly rejoice when I sing unto You and my soul which You have redeemed."*

Psalm 71:22-23

God wants us to use everything at our disposal to praise, glorify and magnify His name. He is a God who likes variety and the resources we have are limitless so we should not limit ourselves as to how we can express our love for Him. Just imagine how we sing and clap our hands when we attend a secular or religious concert and all the energy we put into celebrating the occasion. Why do we become so reserved when it is God's time to really celebrate Him with all our hearts, souls and minds? After all His word declares that we should greatly rejoice when we sing unto Him.

Lord this is the day that You have made, let us truly rejoice and be glad in it. Father, we thank You for making so many things available to us to use in praising You. We thank You Lord for the sweet melody of music, the great songs that have been written, the musical instruments that provide different sounds and the melodious voices to sing Your praises. Help us merciful Father not to limit ourselves in our praise and worship of You.

Heavenly Father when we listen to the sweet melodious music and singing at church or at home, it fills our hearts with awe and wonder and a sense of being very near to You. Lord we thank You for all the many different gifts You have given to us and which You want us to use to praise You. Forgive us Lord for the times when we have failed to praise You as we ought to and enable us to be really sincere in our praise and adoration of You. We ask You Father to bless us in the name of Jesus Christ, Your Son. Amen.

## March

# All For God

### Day 2

*"O let not the oppressed return ashamed: let the poor and needy praise Your name."*

Psalm 74:21

It does not matter what our status in life is as to whether or not we are dark or white, rich or poor, educated or uneducated, we are not excused from giving to God what is truly due to Him and that is to praise His wonderful name. What a joy and a privilege it is to know that we have a God who cares and knows us to the very core of our being. Let us learn how to hold on to Him in every situation in which we may find ourselves. Thank God that even when we are feeling oppressed and down trodden, we should not give in to these feelings, because He is always with us.

*Unto You O God, do we give thanks, unto You Father do we give thanks, for Your name is ever to be praised and be lifted up. You have been good to us God despite our lowly estate and poor self-esteem. You have not discriminated against us Lord as people do because of the color of our skin or because we are poor and needy. Instead You have encouraged us to be the best we can be and to still praise You.*

*Father, we become so distracted by events that take place around us but when we turn our eyes toward You, we can see enduring the trials of this life are well worth where You are taking us. Lord, build in us Your assurance that You are sympathetic toward the matters that we bring before You each day. We know Father our comfort is only a prayer away and we thank You for listening to us. It is in Your name we pray. Amen.*

# March

# Taking A Stand For God

## Day 3

*"As for me, I will declare this forever; I will sing praise to the God of Jacob."*

Psalm 75:9

Just think of all the wonderful things God has done for us even though we are so undeserving of His mercy and goodness. The least then we can do is to show our gratitude to Him by thanking and praising His name. It is indeed a good thing for us as believers to recognize God for who He is and to demonstrate to the world how much we love and appreciate Him for having constantly blessed and prospered us. We can all agree that we should all give to God all glory and praise for He has done great things for us.

*You are worthy our God to receive all our praise, all our honor, all our thanks and all our gratitude because of what You have done for us. Your never ending and amazing love for us is more than we can handle. It is overwhelming and overpowering and we stand in awe of You. Father God we love You and we want to declare Your praises forever and ever.*

*Lord God, when we think of all the wonderful, marvelous and amazing things You have done for us, we are lost for words to thank You enough. Your love, mercy and grace are so sincere and overflowing to the extent that we find it very hard to appreciate You for showing us the great Father You are to Your erring children. Lord, You are indeed one of a kind and we thank You so much for everything You have so graciously blessed us with. Father we give You all the praise and adoration in the name of Jesus. Amen.*

# March

# Training and Nurturing Our Children

## Day 4

*"We will not hide them from their children, but tell to the coming generation the glorious deeds of the Lord, and his might, and the wonders that he has done."*

*Psalm 78:4*

One thing we all need to do as Christians is to impart the good news of salvation to our children so that they can pass it on to their own children in recognition of what the Lord has done for us. We should not fail in passing on the family values and morals that are so intricately intertwined with our beliefs as followers of God. The world we presently live in could be a much better place if we all inculcated into our children the importance of honoring God and following His commandments to love Him and to love others.

*Merciful Lord we thank You for the Bible and all its teachings. Through Your holy and inspired word Lord, we recognize that the lives of many can be touched and changed forever. Help us dear Father, never to fail in proclaiming the good news of salvation not only to our families and relatives, but to all with whom we come in contact. Lord we thank You for giving to us Your word so that we can discern between right and wrong.*

*Righteous Father, we read in Your Word about two roads and one of which leads to destruction and one to eternal life. We know Father that if we give heed to Your Word and follow Your commandments we will be on the road that leads us to eternal life. We pray Father that You will enable us to tell others who do not know You about You and Your plans for their lives so that they too will have the opportunity to know You by following Your Word and accepting You as their Lord. This we pray in Your precious name Lord and for Your sake. Amen.*

## March

# Following Our Shepherd

## Day 5

*" Then we your people, the sheep of your pasture, will praise you forever; from generation to generation we will proclaim your praise."*

Psalm 79:13

God is our Shepherd and we are His sheep. He provides water and food for us daily and in return we need to give to Him all the praise and all the glory for His protection and care. Like a good Shepherd, God's eyes are always watching us His sheep to make sure that no danger befalls us or we stray too far away from Him. His rod and His staff are always ready to pull us back whenever we seem to be losing our way and our focus. Let us continually thank Him for keeping a close watch on us.

Lord You are our Shepherd and as Your sheep as long as we stay close to the fold we will be safe and there is no need to worry. You are our God and we will sing praises to Your name forever and ever. Let us never be afraid Father to proclaim Your name abroad and to take a stand for what is right, honest and just. To Your glorious name be honor, praise, dominion and power.

Lord we thank You that You are the same yesterday, today and forever and that You will never change. We know Father that You are the only constant in our lives and we pray that You will continue to be there for us. Give us we pray Lord the zeal and the desire to want to praise Your name over and over again because it is the right thing for us to do. Help us never to fail in our worship of You. This we ask in Your name. Amen.

# March

# God's Name Be Glorified

## Day 6

*"All the nations you have made will come and worship before you, Lord; they will bring glory to your name."*
Psalm 86:9

When we worship the Lord we bring glory and honor to His name which is our reasonable service. Let us remember that when we worship God, everything that we do in the act must come from our hearts and not just from our lips. The Bible tells us that those who worship God must do so in spirit and in truth. This means that when we worship God in spirit and in truth it depends on a right mental grasp of the way God really is, truth.

*Lord please help us to bow down and worship You in order to lift You up and praise Your name forever and ever. Without Your presence in our lives Lord, there is no value or worth in living. To live for You and You alone Lord is to live with You for all of eternity. May we always seek to bring glory and honor to Your holy name Lord even as we worship You in spirit and in truth.*

*Father we thank You today for all the many blessings You have heaped upon us. Not only do You provide us with the physical things we need Lord, but our spirits feel Your goodness. Father how can we thank You enough for Your love and care each day of our lives? We can only offer up our thanksgiving to You Father in obedience and praise and allow You to have full control of our lives. Hear our prayer we ask Father, and let our cry come unto You. Amen.*

# March

# Heavenly Praise

## Day 7

*"The heavens praise your wonders, Lord, your faithfulness too, in the assembly of the holy ones."*

Psalm 89:5

God works in mysterious ways, His wonders to perform. He is ever faithful in delivering His promises and that's why we must constantly give Him thanks and praises. God's faithfulness is His unwavering trustworthiness and commitment to us His people and all the promises He has made. If we remain faithful to Him, He will remain faithful to us to the very end of our lives here on earth.

*My God, You are so big, powerful and mighty and there is nothing You cannot do. We are truly amazed at how well You created the world with all its minute details. You created the heavens and the earth and every living thing that lives on the face of the earth. Lord You are indeed just an awesome God and we can never refrain from praising and worshipping You.*

*Father we give You thanks for Your faithfulness in fulfilling all Your promises to us. We know Father that we can always depend on You to provide us with all that we need and for this we are very grateful to You. May You continue to help us to remain faithful to You even as You have always remained faithful to us especially in these challenges days we have been going through. We thank You that Your mercies are ever sure in the name of Jesus who is our Comforter, Friend and Confidante. Amen.*

# March

# God's Goodness To Us

## Day 8

*"It is good to praise the* Lord *and make music to your name, O Most High."*

Psalm 92:1

God has always been good to us and we should acknowledge His goodness by praising His name with hymns and music at all times. The Lord has always had our best interests at heart and He never misses a beat in ensuring that all our needs are met. As His children, all that He is asking us to do is to serve Him the best way we can and that should become a part of our daily routine. Let us never come up short or be found wanting in not giving to God what is due to Him, which is our praise and worship.

*Father in heaven, the greatest thing in our lives that we can do is to praise Your name. Lord You have given us everything to make us happy and You supply our daily needs. We are grateful to You Lord for Your love, peace and joy which You make available to us at all times. The more we praise You Lord is the more we are blessed and for this we give You thanks.*

*Our Father, our strength and our Redeemer, we cannot save ourselves from all the things that terrify us. We cannot Father save those who love us and look to us for protection. We thank You Father that we can call upon You for help and find You there, just waiting for us to ask. Lord we thank You for Your great power, Your mercy and Your love for which we give You thanks. This we pray in Your name. Amen.*

# March

# Joyful Singing

## Day 9

*"Come, let us sing for joy to the Lord; let us shout aloud to the Rock of our salvation."*

*Psalm 95:1*

God has demonstrated to us again and again that He is the Rock of our salvation and our future is secured in Him. We are reminded in Psalm 18 that the Lord is our Rock, our Fortress, our Deliverer and our God and we should call upon His name because He is worthy of our praise. With this great reassurance of who God is to us, we should always seek to shout His name loudly to all those with whom we come in contact so that they may come to know Him and accept Him as their Lord and Savior.

*Lord God, we thank You that You are our Rock, our Sword and our Shield. We thank You Father that You are our wheel within a wheel. You are our Lily of the Valley and You are our bright and morning Star. How can we not thank You for all the wonderful things You have done for us though so undeserving of Your love? Let us come before You today Father with singing and thanksgiving for that's the least we can do to show our gratitude to You.*

*Lord, without You in our lives, how could we face the many troubles and trials that come upon us so suddenly? We thank You for the strength You give to us to continue when troubles and trials assail us by filling our hearts with hope. All that we are Father are tied up in You and whenever we face hard times or good times, You are forever the focus of our lives. Help us Lord to feel Your holy presence always even as we pray in Your name. Amen.*

## March

# Down on Our Knees

*Day 10*

*"Come, let us bow down in worship, let us kneel before the Lord our Maker."*

Psalm 95:6

The Lord God is indeed our Maker and we owe it to Him to bow down and worship Him in Spirit and in Truth Worshipping the Lord is a personal and private activity as well as one we can engage in with fellow believers. We can worship the Lord through music, through our prayers, through reading His Word or we can just fall on our knees and reverence Him in silent meditation. Whichever way we choose to worship the Lord, He will listen to us.

*O Lord our God and Father in Heaven, we thank You that You are the Maker of heaven and earth and it is our duty to bow down and worship You every day of our lives. Lord there is no one else like You and so we give to You all the praise, all the glory and all the gratitude that we can ever offer to You.*

*Thank You Father for being such a wonderful and awesome God and we give You thanks today for all of Your magnificent creation. Father, every day as we look around us, we can observe the splendor and wonder of all that You have made. We cannot comprehend or understand how You made such a perfect world for imperfect people such as we are. We really thank You and praise You for this marvelous and amazing world You etched out of nothing and for having made us a part of it. We give You thanks Father in the name of Jesus. Amen.*

# March

# Declaring God's Glory

## Day 11

*"Sing to the Lord, praise his name; proclaim his salvation day after day. Declare his glory among the nations, his marvelous deeds among all peoples."*
Psalm 96:2-3

We are encouraged not only to praise the name of the Lord but to declare His glory and all the wonderful things He has done for us all. Our God whom we serve is certainly a good God who is always looking out for our best interests. At no time should we take our God for granted but rather we must instead show our appreciation to Him in songs and praise as often as we can. Remember that God always keeps His side of His promises and so we should also keep ours.

To Your name Lord be all the praise, glory, honor, dominion and power for having done so much for us Father. We cannot stop proclaiming Your word to the world to tell of Your goodness, mercy and love for us and for all humanity. We know Lord that we just can't do anything without Your help because we are helpless without You.

Thank You so much Lord for all the good times and bad times we have experienced in this life. Throughout it all Lord You have been good to us and You have always been faithful in every circumstance of our lives. We lift up our voices in thanksgiving and praise to You for all the many blessings You have bestowed upon us and we ask You Father to use us as You see fit to bring glory and honor to Your most precious and holy name. We ask You to bless us in the name of Jesus. Amen.

## March

# Celebrating God's Greatness

*Day 12*

*"For great is the* Lord *and most worthy of praise; he is to be feared above all gods."*

Psalm 96:4

The Psalmist tells us that the fear of the Lord is the beginning of wisdom. It is God and God alone that we must fear because He has the power to do to us as He pleases and that's why we are to constantly praise and magnify His name. Our fear of God is not the same as when we are afraid of someone who may cause us hurt. When we fear God, we show our love, respect and appreciation in praise of His providential care and goodness towards us despite of our failures.

O Lord our Lord, how excellent and majestic You are, sitting on Your throne high and lifted up. You and You alone Father have the power and the strength and might to do as You desire. There is no one else we need to fear but You Lord Almighty because You are God the Maker of heaven and earth. Let us praise and magnify Your name for ever and ever as we thank You Lord for Your goodness.

Lord, we cannot attribute our success in life to no other person but You and we thank You for constantly taking care of our needs. We recognize Father that in spite of our short- comings, You still love us with an everlasting love which will never go away. Father, we thank You that Yours is the only name that is worthy of our praise and so without hesitation, we give You our heartfelt gratitude and praise for all that You have done for us and what You will continue to do for us each and every day. We give You thanks Father in Jesus' name. Amen.

## March

# God Deserves our Worship

*Day 13*

*"Worship the Lord in the splendor of his holiness; tremble before him, all the earth."*

Psalm 96:9

    We are to worship God in holiness and come before Him with reverential fear and trembling because He is a Holy and Righteous God. It is so easy for us to forget who God really is in a world that is constantly competing for our time and loyalty. Let us always remember that it is God and God alone who carved out this great universe out of nothing and made us all uniquely His own. That is why we owe our very lives to Him because we are His creation and He deserves all the accolades we can heap upon Him.

    Lord we want to worship You this day in the beauty of holiness and bow down before You to proclaim Your glory and Your splendor. Because You are our God we want to praise You and adore Your name without fear. Help us to come into Your house with hymns of praise and just to lift up Your name for the world to see.

    Father, we thank You for all things bright and beautiful and for all creatures great and small. Thank You that You created all things and that through You life was breathed into us and we became living human beings. It is this gift of life You have given to us that You want us to use to worship You in the splendor of Your holiness. Loving Lord, help to truly worship You today in the name of the Father, Son and Holy Ghost. Amen.

## March

# Our Marvelous Heavenly Father

*Day 14*

*"Sing to the Lord a new song, for he has done marvelous things; his right hand and his holy arm have worked salvation for him."*

Psalm 98:1

Every day we are encouraged to sing a new song to the Lord for He has done great and awesome things for us. Consider that there is not a day in which the Lord has failed to do good for His people. No matter how much we may think He is not doing what He promises, we just have to look around us or listen to the ways in which He is working in the lives of individuals the world over. Our God is just an awesome God who is constantly in motion working out everything together for good for His children.

Father in highest heaven, help us to sing a new song to You today. You who perform mighty deeds and wonders, let us rejoice and tell of Your power and all the wonderful things You have done for us Your people. O God, help us to sing a new song to You as we lift up our voices in praise because You Lord are worthy of all our adoration and all our gratitude.

Merciful and loving Lord, help us to live lives that bring honor and glory to Your name. Help us never to become deceivers who try to live double standard lives. By so doing Father we know that we are giving the devil a foothold in our lives that would be contrary to how we should be living. Enable us Dear Father to make a concerted effort to live only for You and to never allow anyone or anything to separate us from Your love. This we pray Lord, in Your name. Amen.

## March

# Singing Joyfully to the Lord

### Day 15

*"Shout for joy to the Lord, all the earth, burst into jubilant song with music; make music to the Lord with the harp, with the harp and the sound of singing."*
Psalm 98:4-5

We are to worship the Lord joyfully and with hearts full of praise and adoration. Nothing should prevent us from really praising and lifting up His name through the songs we sing. God is a good and amazing God and He welcomes our songs of praises and adoration. The psalmist tells us to make a joyful noise unto the Lord because He enjoys our praise and worship of Him. The problem with us unfortunately is that we do not spend as much time with Him as we should when we compare the amount of time we spend doing other things.

*O Lord our God, how excellent is Your name in all of creation. We come to You today merciful Father with songs of praise and thanksgiving because You are worthy Lord God to receive more than what we can offer to You. Let us joyfully and jubilantly come into Your holy presence with songs and hymns of adoration which express our love for You.*

*Lord, give us the determination to renew ourselves spiritually every day. We pray Father that You will give us the strength of character to mitigate against those forces that are in the way of us truly and sincerely praising and worshipping You as ought to. May You continue Father to encourage and to guide us in the way we should go so that we will not depart from Your Word. This we pray in Your name. Amen.*

## March

# God's Overwhelming Presence

*Day 16*

*"The LORD reigns, let the nations tremble; he sits enthroned between the cherubim, let the earth shake."*
*Psalm 99:1*

One day God's might and power will be felt once again when He returns to claim His own. We must prepare ourselves for this great and awesome occasion. Every day we should be preparing ourselves by being immersed in God's word and doing what He has commanded us to do. We do not know how soon our Lord will return again and so it behooves us to be in that state of readiness so that when the trumpet sounds we will not be caught off guard.

*Father no matter what man may say, You continue to be the Ruler of heaven and earth. You are still in control because every day we see Your handiwork being expressed in so many different ways. When You speak and act the earth trembles and roars because You are all powerful, all knowing and You are Almighty God.*

*Father we pray that You will help us to take far more care in planning our trip to heaven. We do not know how much time we have to prepare for it, but while there is still time, help us Father to prepare ourselves in prayer, in Bible study to learn Your will and work to be faithful servants of Yours. We give You all praise, glory and adoration for Your faithfulness towards us. It is in Your precious and amazing name we pray. Amen.*

# March

# Appreciating God's Holiness

## Day 17

*"Let them praise your great and awesome name- he is holy."*

Psalm 99:3

Our Lord God is holy and because He is holy, it is our duty to consistently praise, adore and magnify His name. What would we do without the God we serve? He is indeed our all in all and without His presence in our lives, we find ourselves drifting further and further away from Him God's holiness is awesome and because He is such a holy God, He wants us His children to strive to become more like Him. This calls for full and total commitment in serving Him with all our heart, soul, body and mind and this can only be done if we take His word seriously and meditate on it day and night.

We praise You Lord, we adore Your holy name Lord, we sing praises to our God most high. Every single day Father You are deserving of our praise because of the wonderful and awesome things You have done for us. Help us never to neglect or become lethargic in our worship of You. May we give to You our all as long as we shall live on this earth.

Father in heaven, we give You thanks today for the storms and hurricanes that blow into our lives and we thank You for keeping us safe. Thank You Father that You are a God who understands us more than we understand ourselves. Give us Lord the zeal and desire to seek after Your word so that we will become well-grounded in what You want us to do and how to live in preparation to meet You one day. Hear this our prayer Lord, and let our cry come unto You. Amen.

## March

# Holy is His Name

### Day 18

*"Exalt the* Lord *our God and worship at his footstool; he is holy."*

Psalm 99:5

It is a good thing for all of us to lift up the name of the Lord and to bow down and worship Him with our whole being because he is a holy and righteous God. We have been reminded over and over again throughout the Bible how important it is for us to give thanks and praise to the Lord. There is no one else who can claim such honor, praise and adoration but the God whom we serve and worship, The most acclaimed name in the world is God because He is our Creator and Maker of the world and even though many call Him by different names, He is still God Almighty.

*Dear God, who are we that You are mindful of every detail of our lives? You provide us with food to eat. You put a shelter over our heads. You give us clothes to cover our bodies and shoes to wear on our feet. We are so very blessed loving Father and we want to praise Your name for ever and ever.*

*Lord we thank You for Your help in times of doubt and sorrow and for healing all our ills. Thank You for being a holy and righteous God who never fails or forgets Your promises to us. We thank You Father for all the blessings You have poured out upon us and for the ways in which You replenish our daily needs. We praise You Father for giving to us Your Son, Jesus, in whose name we come to You. Amen.*

## March

# Exalting God's Holiness

## Day 19

*"Exalt the Lord our God and worship at his holy mountain, for the Lord our God is holy."*
Psalm 99:9

When we exalt the name of the Lord and give to Him all the praise and all the glory, then others will want to emulate our standard and embrace Him as their God and Father. What does it really mean to exalt the name of the Lord? To exalt God, we need to raise Him to the highest place in our lives. To give Him first place in every thought in our mind, every spoken word and every deed we do. To achieve this, we must do it through His Son, Jesus Christ.

*Praise to You O Lord, the Almighty and King of all creation, our souls praise You Lord for You are our help in times of trouble; You are our help and salvation; You are our bright and morning Star and You are our Rock and Hiding-place. When we are weak and weary, You make us strong; when the going gets rough and the rough gets going, You are there for us.*

*Lord You are worthy of our praise and gratitude and we indeed exalt and lift up Your name on high. Thank You Father that You are our Unshakable, Unstoppable and Immovable God who firmly controls our lives and gives us hope for the future. We are so blessed Father to have You as our God and we thank You for making this all possible. It is to Your name we give You all the praise and glory. Amen.*

# March

# Gladness in Worshipping God

## Day 20

*"Shout for joy to the Lord, all the earth. Worship the Lord with gladness; come before him with joyful songs. Know that the Lord is God. It is he who made us, and we are his; we are his people, the sheep of his pasture."*

Psalm 100:1-3

For us to be able to shout for joy to the Lord, we must first experience what the joy of the Lord is. Many of us need to shake off our old selves and come to the Lord with a more joyful and effervescent attitude in serving and worshipping Him. Simply put the joy of the Lord is our strength and we should not be afraid to shout out to God with joy filled hearts. When we have the joy of the Lord, our whole lives take on a new meaning. We become stronger, bolder and more courageous in carrying out His will and purpose for our lives.

*Thank You heavenly Father that Your joy gives us the strength to carry on despite any obstacles we might encounter along the way. Let us worship You with gladness and come before You Father God with joyful songs of praise and thanksgiving. It is You O God who has made us in Your own image and we are happy that we are Your children. Help us to be obedient to Your word even as we seek to give You the best of who we are.*

*King of kings and Lord of lords, Your majesty exceeds our imagination and Your glory Father is beyond our wildest dreams. Thank You that You rule with authority and supremacy over all peoples on earth. We exalt Your name Lord, by bowing before You. As we go down on our knees Lord, You are lifted up higher and higher. We offer up ourselves to You Father as Your servants willing and ready to do Your will with all the gifts, talents and treasures with which You have blessed us. Lord we give You thanks in Jesus' name. Amen.*

# March

# Expressing Gratitude to God

## Day 21

*"Enter his gates with thanksgiving and his courts with praise; give thanks to him and praise his name. For the Lord is good and his love endures forever; his faithfulness continues through all generations."*

Psalm 100:4-5

It is a good thing for us to give thanks to Almighty God and praise His name for He is a good, faithful and compassionate God whose love for us endures forever. There will never be a dull moment in our lives when we are fully tuned in with the great I AM who will forever be our faithful and reliable Father. The Psalmist encourages us to enter into God's House with a sense of thanksgiving and praise because God is good and His love for us endures forever. What a wonderful, amazing and mighty God we serve!

Lord, help us to come into Your gates today with thanksgiving and into Your courts with praise. May we give thanks to You Father and praise Your name without ceasing for You are a good and faithful God and Your love for us never ends. Heavenly Father, we thank You that You are the same God today, yesterday and for eternity.

Help us Dear Father that all our thoughts, actions and deeds will always be keeping with Your will and purpose for our lives. We will do everything Father possible to be faithful and honest in all that we do so that others who are watching us, will find pleasure in also serving You and honoring You in all that they do. Thank You Lord that we can come to You confidently anytime to worship You and to know that You are always attuned to our prayers. Imprint Your word on our hearts Lord even as we lift up our praise to You in the name of Jesus. Amen.

## March

# A God of Justice

### Day 22

*"I will sing of your love and justice; to you, Lord, I will sing praise."*

*Psalm 101:1*

We are reminded by the prophet Micah that God requires us to do justly, to love mercy and to walk in humility with Him. When we do these things then we can truly praise and worship our King without fear or favor. We are living in a world where man's inhumanity to man is so terrible and where there is little or no justice. There are many people who are suffering at the hands of others and there is untold suffering and pain due to the atrocious treatment and cruelty meted out to the less fortunate and marginalized. As Christians we need to be different and show the world how to love and treat others with respect,

*Father for us to sing Your praises, we ask that You would search us and know our hearts today; try us and see if there is any wicked or evil ways or thoughts in us and then cleanse and purge us from all our sins and set us free. We know Father that we are not worthy to come even close to You because of our sins but due to Your unfailing love for us, we do not have to be afraid to let go and let You take over.*

*Lord we thank You that You are a just and righteous God who shows love, mercy and compassion for all peoples. It is so easy for us Father to condemn others and to treat them with disrespect. Forgive us Father for the times we have not been sensitive to the needs of others and for the bad attitude we display towards them. We are truly sorry for all the awful things we have done Lord and we ask You to forgive us in the name of Jesus. Amen.*

# March

# Passing on Our Legacy

## Day 23

*"Let this be written for a future generation, that a people not yet created may praise the Lord."*
Psalm 102:18

Let us give God thanks for the inspiration He gave to those who left a legacy behind for future generations to follow. The fact that God has heard the prayer of His people in a time of trial, shall be so recorded and remembered, that it may be referred to in similar circumstances in all times to come because God is an unchanging God. We need to keep on praising the Lord now and in the future so that the upcoming generations will not depart from the teachings and the heritage of the Bible.

*Dearest Lord God, we thank You for those holy men whom You inspired to record Your word and all the marvelous things You did from the beginning of creation. Father help us to use every opportunity we have in spreading Your word to all those with whom we come in contact and beyond.*

*Loving Father help us to do everything possible for the children of the world especially to guide them into the right path that leads to eternal life. If we Lord are to influence the lives of others in the Christian way of life, then we know we must work and bear the burdens of doing so. Give us we pray Father, the strength and courage to keep up the faith in touching the lives of the next generations to come. This we ask Father in Your name. Amen.*

## March

# Praising God From Within

## Day 24

*"Praise the L*ORD*, my soul; all my inmost being, praise his holy name."*

*Psalm 103:1*

Today let us give thanks and praises to our God with our heart, mind and soul for all the many blessings He has bestowed upon us. God is to be served with the best that we have as with the best of our gifts, talents, time and treasures. Our worship of God has to be more than superficial; it has to be offered as completely as possible. He wants us to praise Him with everything within us and not just halfheartedly as we so often do. So often we go to church to praise the Lord but we leave our minds at home. We hear about His grace, but our hearts become hardened by an unforgiving spirit. God requires our all when we worship Him in Spirit and in truth. In His precious and powerful name we pray. Amen.

*It is indeed a good thing our Father God to give You thanks every day and in everything for all the wonderful blessings You pour down on us even without deserving of it. Lord we thank You that You are greater than any other gods because of Your might and power and the mysterious ways in which You perform. We thank You Lord for anything, everything and for all things and we just praise You with our total being.*

*Thank You Father for all the opportunities You have given to us to serve You with our souls, bodies and minds. Help us Lord that we would always seek to worship You not only in Spirit and in Truth but with all the energy and emotions that we feel within us. We lift You up Father with our inmost being and we praise Your name for ever and ever. Father, let the words of our mouths and the meditation of our hearts be acceptable to You. Amen.*

# March

# Long and Lasting Praise to God

## Day 25

*"I will sing to the Lord all my life; I will sing praise to my God as long as I live."*

Psalm 104:33

Our God is truly the only one whom we should worship and give all our praise and gratitude for He has done great and marvelous things for us. In this psalm, the writer sees continuous praise and worship of the Lord to be the core cry within the depth of our inner being. God alone is worthy of such praise and worship. The Lord our God is indeed our great Creator and the Sustainer of the universe and so He is deserving of our honor and highly to be praised. It is God's will that we rejoice evermore, pray without ceasing and in everything give thanks to Him, for the joy of the Lord is our strength.

O Lord God Almighty, You have blessed us with life and we will never cease in praising and magnifying Your most holy and precious name. We love You Lord and we want to remain in Your shadow as we feel protected from all harm and danger. Lord You are exceptional in all that You do and we just want to thank You for being a holy and righteous Father.

Almighty Father of all creation, as we look around us and see all the good things You have provided, we realize that everything comes from You and that makes us more determined to give You thanks and praise. We thank You Lord that it is Your will for us to rejoice and be glad in You because in You there is fullness of life and joy forever more. We praise You Father and acknowledge Your constant presence in our lives and for this we give You thanks in the name of Jesus. Amen.

## March

# The Choice is Ours

### Day 26

*"But may sinners vanish from the earth and the wicked are no more. Praise the* Lord, *my soul. Praise the* Lord.*"*
Psalm 104:35

We are all sinners saved by God's amazing grace and we should never stop praising and thanking Him every day we live. God created and has control over every single created thing and they are stamped with His wisdom and artistry. Just imagine that every single blade of grass, water vapor, tree, animal, mountain and human being that ever existed was made to reveal the glory and majesty of God. It is with this perspective that the Psalmist speaks that the entire universe should join in chorus in praising God and that those who do not should be destroyed. We need to try and be among those who really praise and worship the Lord.

*Thank You gracious Father that it is through Your grace that we are saved from our sinful ways and not because of any good work that we have done. We realize Lord that we were born in sin and by nature we remain sinners Thank You Father that through the blood of Jesus Christ our sins are forgiven and we have the freedom to praise and worship You.*

*Lord we thank You that You have made us with a purpose and that is to love and serve You with all of our very being. Help us Dear Father to love, proclaim and reflect Your glory through the lives we live, always endeavoring to lift You up as often as we can. Thank You Lord that You remain a faithful, forgiving and merciful Father to us and for this we give You thanks in Jesus' name. Amen.*

# March

# Proclaiming His Greatness

## Day 27

*"Sing to him, sing praise to him; tell of all his wonderful acts."*

Psalm 105:2

Every day we can find myriads of things for which to be thankful to God and to sing our praises to Him. He is really an extraordinary God who goes over and beyond to provide our needs. The wonderful and marvelous deeds of God are the many interventions He has performed in the history of salvation from the creation of the world to the resurrection of Jesus. We are not short in finding things for which we ought to be thankful to God because He is always providing us with good things to satisfy our each and every need.

Lord Your word encourages us that in everything we should give You thanks for all the blessings You bestow on us on a daily basis. You have never allowed us to be without food or clothing or a roof over our heads. You have been merciful and gracious to us and You have given to us all that we need to live a wholesome and worthwhile life.

Lord it is truly a blessing when we can enjoy our work and the profits of that work. Father when we turn from thankfulness and begin to desire some of the things we do not have, remind us of the millions who suffer in poverty every day, no matter how hard they work. Remind us Lord of Your blessings that have little to do with wealth: love, peace, good health and the work of the Holy Spirit in our lives. We thank You that You are our Father who supplies all our needs and we ask You to continue to bless us in the name of Jesus. Amen.

# March

# God's Never Ending Love

## Day 28

*"Praise the L*ORD*. Give thanks to the L*ORD*, for he is good; his love endures forever."*

Psalm 106:1

God's love for us is from everlasting to everlasting and He is consistently pouring out His love for us even when we are so undeserving of it. The most satisfying thing that we can do as believers in God, is to place our lives into His hands and allow Him to lead us on the straight and narrow path. We should not allow anything to thwart our efforts in remaining faithful and resolute in our worship of Him because He deserves every praise and adoration we can render to Him. God is our only hope in a world where many do not recognize Him as our Supreme Leader and so it is critical that we continue to put Him first and foremost in our lives.

*We thank You heavenly Father that Your love for us is the same yesterday, today and forever. No matter how sinful and rebellious we are, we know Lord that You love us just the same. Help us not to take your love for granted but to give You all the thanks and praises that we can offer up to You for all that You do for us.*

*Dear Father God, we thank You for the opportunities You have given to us to help shape the lives of others. Show us, Dear Father, how to admonish, correct and inspire those who come to us for guidance, whether it be at work, at church or in the community. In our efforts to lead others to You Father, may we always remember to place everything in Your hands even as we give You praise and adoration. This we pray in Your name. Amen.*

# March

# Gathered in God's Name

## Day 29

*"Save us, Lord our God, and gather us from the nations, that we may give thanks to your holy name and glory in your praise. Praise be to the Lord, the God of Israel, from everlasting to everlasting. Let all the people say, "Amen!" Praise the Lord."*

Psalm 106:47-48

Our praise and thankfulness to God should be without any conditions attached. He is our God and Father and we are His children and so it is our duty to love, honor, adore and praise His name forever. We as a people have been privileged to have a loving God who takes care of His children by constantly providing their daily needs. Even as the children of Israel were encouraged over and over again to give thanks and praises to Almighty God, so we too are encouraged to keep on praising Him especially during these troublesome times.

*You O God art worthy of our praise and gratitude, because it is You who have made us Lord. Thank You Lord for being our Father and for the ways in which You have blessed and prospered us Your children. Help us Father to sing Your praises day and night and to lift up Your most precious and holy name.*

*Heavenly Father, we thank You for Your unwavering and unconditional love for Your children. Even though Father we have sinned and strayed far away from You, we thank You that You have always remained faithful to us. Forgive us Father for the many times we have failed to worship You as we ought to. Father, too often we have left the things we should have done and resorted to do other things that fail to bring glory and honor to Your name. Forgive us we pray Father in Your name. Amen.*

# March

# Let The Earth Praise God Our Father

## Day 30

*"Let them exalt him in the assembly of the people and praise him in the council of the elders."*

Psalm 107:32

Our God is a good and mighty God and all of us should constantly sing our praises and give thanks and honor to His great name. Remember we exalt God when we obey His commands because His ways are best. We exalt God when we line up what we do with His Word and in following His ways. When we help other people in their struggles by pointing them to God we are exalting our God. He is indeed our source of strength, comfort, peace and hope and for all these we need to be thankful.

*Our God, let us know how to truly praise You and worship You. Your love for us is from everlasting to everlasting and we thank You Lord for making us whom we are. We will always try to glorify and magnify Your name because You are the only one who makes the single most difference in our lives. Father we thank You today especially for those who put their trust in You.*

*Living Loving Lord, how we thank You for Your bountiful blessings upon us even in the darkest of times. You Father have been there for us through the good and bad times; during the times of hardships and difficulties and even when there was no way, You made a way for us. Thank You for Your abiding care, love and protection that You have so willingly lavished on us. This we pray Father in Your loving and precious name. Amen.*

## March

# Remaining Steadfast

### Day 31

*"My heart, O God, is steadfast; I will sing and make music with all my soul."*

Psalm 108:1

    As Christians we need to remain steadfast in our faith and not allow ourselves to be tossed to and fro by every wind of doctrine. We sing the praises of God out of season and in season. We should exalt God because He is the only one worthy to be exalted. Our God is the Creator of the heavens and the earth and all that fills it. God should be exalted because He created us and made a way for us to be reconciled to Him in and through Jesus Christ, His Son.

    Heavenly Father, help us to magnify and glorify Your name every day. Let us not waiver in our faith and help us to be consistent in our worship of You. It is so easy for us Lord to give up and to give in to sin especially when we take our eyes off of You. Remind us to follow in the path You have prepared for us and may we always do Your will.

    Lord, help us to remain steadfast in our faith and in our worship of You. Father we need You now more than ever before because of all the challenges with which we are faced and the threat that hangs over us from those who are challenging our beliefs. Continue Father to be the bedrock of our faith and help us never to let go of You. This we pray in the wonderful name of Jesus, Your Son. Amen.

# April

# High and Lifted Up is Our God

## Day 1

*"I will praise you, Lord, among the nations; I will sing of you among the peoples."*

Psalm 108:3

We cannot truly praise God enough given all that He has done for us. We must use every opportunity to sing songs and hymns of praise to the Most High God. The reason why we have been encouraged to praise the Lord so much is because of how good He has been to His people from the beginning of the world. In times of trouble, disasters, pandemics, wars and great need, God has always broken forth and delivered all those who call upon Him. Without His ever constant care and protection, we His people would not have been able to make it through the many challenges of life we have had to face.

Lord thank You that You are King of kings and Lord of lords and we need to sing praises to Your name with every breath we have. You are beautiful beyond description and our love for You will never be diminished. Loving Father, grant that we may ever do Your will and purpose for our lives and challenge us Father ever to lift up Your name even to the ends of the earth.

We thank You Father for the simplicity of life and for guiding us through Your Word as to how we ought to live our lives in order to serve and worship You. Father, we know that every word that comes from our lips should be words of praise and adoration. Forgive us we pray Father for the times when we have failed to sing Your praises instead of looking praise for ourselves. May we decrease and You increase in our worship of You. This we ask in Your name. Amen.

# April

# Watch Your Words

## Day 2

*"With my mouth I will greatly extol the Lord; in the great throng of worshipers I will praise him."*

Psalm 109:30

The Lord has blessed us with a wonderful body that He wants us to use and bless His name. We are to be careful with what comes out from our mouth as what we say can cause both good and harm. As God's beloved children, we need to be mindful that we are His voice on earth and so we should be diligent in proclaiming His Word to others in ways they can understand and process. We should avoid using any profane or filthy language because the world will judge us by what comes out of our mouths and that could be a hindrance in winning souls for the Lord.

O Living and Loving Father, it is in You that we live and move and have our being. You are indeed our Alpha and our Omega, the beginning and the end, the first and the last. Thank You Lord for giving to us mouths with which we can praise You in singing and in the spoken word. Help us Father to be watchful of our speech so that everything we say will be acceptable to You.

Lord, we thank You for the different parts of our bodies all of which we can use to praise and magnify Your name. We are grateful Father that You have not limited us as to how we must praise and lift up Your name. May we never be afraid Lord to express ourselves in worship of You with our entire being as that is what You desire of us. Forgive us we pray Father for the many times when we have failed in rendering our praise and gratitude to You and we just want to thank You in the name of Jesus for Your forgiveness. Amen.

# April

# The Heart of the Matter

## Day 3

*"Praise the Lord. I will extol the Lord with all my heart in the council of the upright and in the assembly."*
Psalm 111:1

How should we truly and sincerely give praise to the Lord? We should do so with all our soul, mind and body and it should be from the heart. The heart of worship is the matter of the heart and so when we worship the Lord, our hearts and relationships must be in sync with His Word. God wants us to worship Him in Spirit and in Truth and to do so we must purge ourselves of the things that get in the way of honestly worshipping Him so that our focus will only be on Him and none other. Too often we give to God the left over time and that is certainly not good enough. Jesus says that we are to render to Caesar what is Caesar's and to God what is God's but there is a tendency for Caesar to get it all. Let us put things into perspective and give God what He deserves.

*Father God when we praise You we must do so with our whole being. You are our everything and You are worthy of all our praise and gratitude. Without You we are nothing but with You we can do all things. Thank You Lord that we can always depend on You to supply all our needs and for never allowing us to think that You do not love us.*

*From the depths of our hearts Lord we want to give You our praises, so help us to empty ourselves of all that would prevent us from doing so. Forgive us Father for all the sins we have committed and which have often times separated us from You. We thank You Lord that You are a loving and forgiving God and so we beseech You to forgive us and to cleanse us from all unrighteousness. This we pray in Your name and for Your sake. Amen.*

# April

# True Wisdom is to Fear God

## Day 4

*"The fear of the* LORD *is the beginning of wisdom; all who follow his precepts have good understanding. To him belongs eternal praise."*

Psalm 111:10

If we are wise, we will learn to fear God and keep His commandments because this is the right thing to do. We acknowledge that it is our Father God who gives to us wisdom, knowledge and understanding so that we can discern between right and wrong, good and evil. Let us not be persuaded by anyone to stray away from the Word of God because God has equipped us with the tools we need in making right choices and remaining in His Word. We must seek at all times to bring glory and honor to God and we do so by following His precepts.

*Thank You dear Father that when we fear You it is the beginning of wisdom. We thank You Lord for the knowledge and understanding You have given to us to be able to discern between good and evil. May we always seek to praise and glorify Your name in all that we do. Lord we thank You for showing us the way we should go so that we will not depart from Your Word.*

*Father in heaven, we thank You that all wisdom, knowledge and understanding comes from You and we thank You for having blessed us with these so that we will avoid making mistakes which can be detrimental to our relationship with You. Help us Father, to depend upon You and not to lean unto our own understanding but that in all our ways we will seek Your favor to see us through this life and the one to come. All glory and honor be to You Father, to Jesus Your Son and to the Holy Spirit, our Comforter. Amen.*

# April

# Fear God And Be Blessed

## Day 5

*"Praise the Lord. Blessed are those who fear the Lord, who find great delight in his commands".*
*Psalm 112:1*

It is said that those who fear the Lord will be blessed and so it is our duty to fear God and to receive His many blessings. Today many people the world over live in fear of many things over which they have no control. People are fearful of wars, natural disasters, terminal diseases, hunger, loss of jobs, loss of homes, family separation and many other things, Many become petrified and paralyzed with fear and instead of looking to the One who says the fear of the Lord is the beginning of wisdom they look to others for help. May we always look to the Lord who has promised never to leave us nor forsake us and to supply all our needs.

*You and You alone Lord art worthy to be praised and adored and glorified. Your name is to be exalted and lifted up forever and ever because You are the Creator of the whole human race. Thank You for the many blessings we receive Father when we fear You and delight in Your commands. It is such an awesome feeling to have such a Father like You and we are indeed grateful to You Lord for securing a place in Heaven for us where we will be with You for ever and ever.*

*Lord, there is no other name under heaven deserving of our praise but You Lord God. Father, You created the heaven and earth out of nothing and from the dust of the earth You created man and blew into Him Your very own breath. Many have tried to imitate Your creation bur no one has come close to making anything such as You have created. We praise You and thank You for this wonderful and unique world You have created. In the precious name of Jesus, we pray. Amen.*

## April

# All Praise The Lord

### Day 6

*"Praise the Lord. Praise the Lord, you his servants; praise the name of the Lord."*

Psalm 113:1

We as God's servants are encouraged again and again to sing praises to Him for all the many blessings He has so lavishly and graciously bestowed upon us. We as mortals cannot thank God enough for all He has done and continues to do for us His children. It is truly amazing how God out of His love, mercy and grace has forever been good to us His children despite our own sinfulness. We owe Him a great debt of gratitude for never failing or forgetting us but He is always there when we need Him most. When we consider that no one in this big, wide world understands us as He does it should propel us even more to show our gratitude to Him with our songs of praise and thanksgiving.

Merciful Father, we acknowledge that we have sinned and fallen short of Your mercy and so we ask You to forgive us of all our sins. Even in our sinfulness Lord, You desire us to sing Your praises and to bow down and worship You. Lord we thank You for being an ever loving and caring Father and for really providing so much for us every day.

Almighty Father, we thank You that Your hands are not shortened towards us and that You give to us in abundance and over and above our asking. Lord we ask You to accept the praises and adoration we bring to You even as we try to express how much we appreciate Your loving-kindness and tender mercies towards us. Thank You for being a truly special Father to us and for never leaving us or forsaking us no matter how much we sin against you. Lord we ask You to shine Your light upon us in the name of the Father, Son and Holy Spirit. Amen.

# April

# From Beginning To End Praise

## Day 7

*"From the rising of the sun to the place where it sets, the name of the Lord is to be praised."*

Psalm 113:3

In our waking up and in our lying down, whatever we may do and wherever we may go, God's name is to be praised at all times. The Bible tells us that our God neither slumbers nor sleeps and so His eyes are always on us. We are indeed fortunate to have a God who is so concerned about His children that He does not take His eyes off us at any time. What an amazing, loving, kind, compassionate and gracious God we have and no wonder it is so important for us to give Him our undivided loyalty. The Psalmist tells us that God is so important that we are to praise Him from the rising of the sun even to the going down of it so there is no limit to our praise of Him.

Father we know that we must at all times and in all places praise and lift up Your name because You are the Author and Finisher of our faith and all that we do. We cannot do anything of value unless You are in our midst directing and guiding us and we owe it all to You Lord. Help us to keep on trusting and praising You Father, so that we may remain in Your favor.

Lord, we thank You that You fight our battles for us no matter what those battles are. Father, just as when the children of Israel went to war, You were there for them during the battle, so Lord we need You to be with us in our physical and spiritual battles. Whether we need to recover from an illness or fight off sin, we cannot do it alone and that is why we need You to be by our side constantly. Thank You Lord for the victory You give to us when we lean on You. This we pray in Your name. Amen.

# April

# Living Praise

## Day 8

*"It is not the dead who praise the LORD, those who go down to the place of silence; it is we who extol the LORD, both now and forevermore. Praise the LORD."*
Psalm 115:17-18

Certainly God gives us the breath of life so that we can praise Him at all times and in all places. We have to give Him all our praise and glory now while we are alive and not when we are snatched away. So many times we have heard others say that they are waiting until such and such a time to give their lives to the Lord because they are not ready yet. Sometimes it is too late to make a change especially when sickness or death comes suddenly and as the Psalmist says the dead cannot praise the Lord. It is those who are alive can praise Him and therefore the time is now for us to give God all our praise and undivided attention.

*Father God to You be the glory for great things You have done for us. Lord we thank You for giving to us the breath of life so that we are able to sing songs and hymns of praise and adoration to You. Your love for us is greater than any other love and Your banner shields us from all that is evil. Lord we thank You that we can rise above the ordinary things of life to the extraordinary.*

*Heavenly Father, we know that on our own we are incapable of keeping Your commandments perfectly, but Your mercy never ends and Your justice never fails. We ask Father that You would have mercy upon us and pour down Your Holy Spirit on us so that we can find comfort and joy in You no matter what season of life we may be going through. Thank You Lord God that You will never let go of us even when we fail to praise Your name. It is in the precious name of Jesus we pray. Amen.*

# April

# Beauty In Worship

## Day 9

*"In the courts of the house of the Lord-in your midst Jerusalem. Praise the Lord."*

*Psalm 116:19*

    When we come into God's house of worship, our sole purpose is to praise and adore His name and to give Him thanks for His goodness towards us. Our God is perfect and we His children are imperfect, yet He still cares for us no matter how far away we drift from His presence. The most important person in our lives and the One whom we should fear is Almighty God. He has proven Himself time and time again that He is in control of every facet of our lives and that He knows us inside out. The task is ours to try and serve Him in the beauty of holiness and to give to Him all that He desires of us.

    *Father God, help us to enter into Your gates with thanksgiving in our hearts and in Your house with songs of praise on our lips. May we never stop praising You O God because that is what You require of us. We have not always expressed our gratitude to You Lord but we know that You understand. Give us the grace to love You more and to follow in Your footsteps day by day so that we can become more like You.*

    *Father, help us to examine the way in which we use our time in Your service. Lord we know that we spend so much time doing other things and with other people rather than developing a deeper relationship with You. We stand as guilty Father when we put into perspective how very little of the twenty-four hours we really spend with You. Forgive us we pray Lord and help us to do the right thing from now on even as we pray in the name of Jesus. Amen.*

# April

# God's Endless Faithfulness

## Day 10

*"Praise the* LORD, *all you nations; extol him, all you peoples. For great is his love toward us and the faithfulness of the* LORD *endures forever."*

Psalm 117:1-2

God does not only love us but He is faithful in all that He does for us. We can never thank Him enough for supplying all our needs and more and that's why praising Him daily is so important. The whole world belongs to the Lord and everything in it He has created. Even though there are those who do not believe in our Creator and try all they can to discredit Him, God does not have any equal on earth and so no matter how hard man may try to suggest that we are here by chance, it is something that believers in God will never accept because there is really no god like Jehovah.

To You our Father be honor and praise and thanksgiving for all of Your benefits towards us. You have proven Lord time after time how much You love and care for us and that is why You are truly and sincerely deserving of all our praise. Lord, no matter what others may say about You, we will always recognize You as our Lord and Creator because there is just no one else like You,

We thank You Father that Your faithfulness is from everlasting to everlasting and that Your love for us endures forever. Father when the world tries to beat us down and box us in, You are there for us and we are so grateful to You for caring so much for us. Grant Lord that we will always endeavor to serve and follow You and to give You our praise and glory in the name of Jesus, our Lord and Savior. Amen.

## April

# Unending Praise

### Day 11

*"Seven times a day I praise you for your righteous laws."*
*Psalm 119:164*

How much is enough for us to praise the Lord? It really cannot be too much considering all that He does for us day after day. There is this tendency for us to set certain times to read and study God's Word and pray to Him which is indeed a good thing for us do. However, we should never limit ourselves as to how often we should read His Word or pray to Him because He has not given us a limit. In fact I believe that the more we read the Bible and pray to God, the better understanding we will have about what we read and the closer we will be drawn to our Heavenly Father.

*Righteous and Holy Father, thank You for doing so much for us. We really have not done anything to be deserving of the love You have for us and all the many blessings You keep on showering down on us. We just cannot thank You enough Lord for all Your goodness and mercy and so we will praise You night and day, with thanksgiving in our hearts for all Your blessings upon us.*

*Lord, we know that we cannot thank You and praise You enough because You have done awesome and wonderful things for us and You have never ceased from blessing us daily. We promise You Father that as often as we can, we will make the effort to pray to You and to praise You since there is no limit on how often we can approach You in prayer and adoration. We thank You Lord for Your generosity and the ways in which You have provided our daily needs. To You Father, be honor and praise in the name of Jesus. Amen.*

# April

# Lips of Praise

## Day 12

*"May my lips overflow with praise, for you teach me your decrees."*

Psalm 119:171

Let us use our lips to praise the Lord continually with our whole being even as we obey His commands. As followers of the Lord, we need to devote much more time in studying and applying His Word to our lives. It is so easy for us to get into our busy schedules to the expense of spending time in God's Word and with God Himself. When you love someone, there is always that desire to spend more and more time with that person and so it should be with us yearning to spend time with the Lord in prayer, praise and adoration.

With our lips Lord we will sing songs and praises to You without ceasing. We will praise You in the daytime and in the night even before we go to sleep. Lord, we thank You for teaching us Your precepts and we ask You to help us to walk in the straight and narrow way as we try to follow You daily.

Thank You Heavenly Father for opening our eyes to see Your righteousness and for raising us from our sin to a new life in You. Without You Father, we would be blind and lose our way but thank You that Your love for us has changed and transformed our lives. Father we have so much for which to give You thanks so let us begin by thanking You today for the beauty of the earth and for all that You have created. It is in Your name we pray. Amen.

# April

# Living Life for God

## Day 13

*"Let me live that I may praise you, and may your laws sustain me."*

*Psalm 119:175*

We live daily to praise our God for all His mercy and love shown towards us. Let us be guided by His Holy Word that we have at our disposal. As we live our lives each day, let us remember that God has provided us a blueprint by which to live and how to live. His Word is the foundation on which we build our faith and so we must hold on to His Word and live it out in our everyday lives. There is no book so precious and profound with the truths we need to know than the Bible. It is indeed the Book of all books and it is holy because God is holy.

*In times like these Lord we need to praise You knowing that our very lives depend on praising Your holy and precious name. As we study Your word Lord, may it be a blessing to us and sustain us as long as we live. You are indeed worthy of all our praise and gratitude and so Lord we ask You to guide us as we seek to meditate more and more on Your Word and applying it each and every day in love.*

*Father God, we thank You that Your Word is a lamp unto our feet and a light to our path and that we do not have to walk in darkness because Your light is always with us. We thank You Father that Your Word is the foundation of our faith and we ask You to help us to feast upon Your Word so that we may not sin against You. Loving Father, we know hat You do not only want us to know Your Word but also to apply it daily as we live out our lives here on earth. Lord, it is in Your name we pray. Amen.*

## April

# God's Footstool

### Day 14

*"Let us go to his dwelling place, let us worship at his footstool."*

Psalm 132:7

As we enter into the house of the Lord, let us do so in reverence and adoration on bended knees for our God is holy. God's dwelling place is where we worship Him in Spirit and in Truth. True worship of God begins with the condition of our hearts. If our hearts are not pure and in sync with the Word of God, then our worship of Him is just futile. God wants us to come to Him with clean lips and pure hearts so that we can enjoy a wholesome relationship with Him. It is important for us to really be honest, purposeful and intentional about our worship of the God whom we serve. He is a jealous God who demands our undivided attention.

*Holy, holy, holy, Lord God Almighty, we come to You today in the precious name of Your Son, Jesus Christ whom we worship and adore. Help us to bow down in silence and in humility to worship the King of kings and Lord of lords. We are grateful to You Father that we have the privilege of worshipping You in a free society but help us not to take this for granted because things can change so quickly.*

*Gracious and loving Father, help us to get our perspectives clear as well as help to train us in the art of spiritual warfare so that we will be able to resist the attacks of the devil and come through victoriously in following You. Grant us Father the ability to trust You with all our hearts and to love You more dearly day by day. Father in lowliness and humility we come before recognizing that You are our Father and we acknowledge that You want us to worship You at Your footstool. This we pray in Your name. Amen.*

# April

# All Praises to God

## Day 15

*"Praise the Lord. Praise the name of the Lord; praise him, you servants of the Lord, you who minister in the house of the Lord, in the courts of the house of our God. Praise the Lord, for the Lord is good; sing praise to his name, for that is pleasant."*

Psalm 135:1-3

God is good and loving and His mercies extend to all generations. He is worthy to be adored and lifted up because He is a holy God and we should sing His praises from now until eternity. Have you ever wondered why we have been encouraged so much to give praise and thanks to our Almighty God? It is because our lives are wrapped up in God and because He is at the center of our universe. Without Him we are indeed nothing and since He is our everything, then that is why it is so important for us to really and truly give Him what is due to Him.

*We will praise You Lord in Your Sanctuary. We will praise You Lord in Your mighty heavens. We will praise You Lord for Your greatness and Your power. We will praise You Lord for Your healing touch and for Your anointing which flows to heal our wounds. We will praise and thank You Lord for turning our thorns to roses.*

*Father, help us to see and to know how important it is for us to put You first and foremost in all that we do. We thank You for Your goodness Lord and the way You fill our lives with joy and happiness. Help us Father that as we seek to worship You, we will do so with a sense of praise and adoration recognizing that You are God and God alone who is worthy of our praise. Let heaven and earth praise You Father and give You thanks for all your bountiful blessings that You have bestowed upon us. We pray all of this in Your name and for Your sake. Amen.*

## April

# Let's Just Praise The Lord

## Day 16

*"Praise be to the L*ORD *from Zion, to him who dwells in Jerusalem. Praise the L*ORD*."*
Psalm 135:21

It is right to sing praises and to give thanks to our Almighty God for all the wonderful blessings He has poured out upon us wherever we may be and in all that we do. There is nothing in this world that we should allow to prevent us from giving to God all of our time, talents and treasures to His will. If the world is going to know about the God whom we serve, then we have to use every opportunity at our disposal to spread the good news of salvation that He gives to all those who seek Him. The more we talk about His goodness and loving kindness and sing His praises, the more others will learn about Him and will want to accept Him too.

*Gracious and ever loving Father, maker of heaven and earth, giver of every good and perfect gift, we give to Your most holy and precious name all our praise and heartfelt gratitude for every blessing with which You have seen fit to bless us. We just cannot help thanking You Lord for meeting all our needs and more. You are an awesome God and for that we give You our thanks.*

*O God our Father, we are so thankful to have a God like You to come to our rescue when we are under attack from Satan's forces. We know Lord the devil does not like us when we come to You in prayer and praise and resist his constant beckoning for us to follow him. You are our God and Father and we will ever give You all of our loyalty as we come to You each day with singing and thanksgiving in our hearts. Father for all the many things You have done for us and will continue to do, we give You thanks in Jesus' name. Amen.*

## April

# God Our Great I Am

### Day 17

*"I will praise you, Lord, with all my heart; before the "gods" I will sing your praise."*

Psalm 138:1

There is absolutely no other god but the true and living God whom we worship and to Him alone we should sing songs of praises with all our heart, mind, soul and body. The God of Abraham, Isaac and Jacob is the same God of Matthew, Luke and John and all of us who call upon Him in Spirit and in Truth. Of all the gods people serve and worship, there is none like our God Jehovah who is the only true and living God. We should have no fear in talking about the God whom we serve, worship and adore because He has no equal.

*God of grace, mercy and compassion, we come to You today with songs of praise and adoration in our hearts for You. There is truly no other God like You who is deserving of all our praise and thankfulness. Today we will praise You O God with our whole being and we pray that You will accept our praise of You. Lord, we thank You for the ebb and flow of life and for remaining faithful to us even when we are not.*

We thank You Father that when the world is asleep, You are awake keeping watch over us. We thank You Lord that You have set standards by which we rise or fall. We realize Father that when we fulfill them we rise and when we break them we fall. Give us Your strength Lord, to fulfill all Your laws especially the one to remain always truthful to You. Lord, help us to understand how different You are from all other gods because You are alive and well and You are indeed the Creator and Sustainer of life. We give You thanks in Jesus' name. Amen.

# April

# Sing a New Song to the Lord

## Day 18

*"I will sing a new song to you, my God; on the ten-stringed lyre I will make music to you."*

Psalm 144:9

Every day gives us a new opportunity to just praise and adore the name of our God in songs, music and the spoken word. Let us never fall short in our effort to praise the name of the Lord. Let us give thanks to God for having gifted us with the various gifts He has given to all of us and to use those gifts to honor and worship Him joyfully and willingly. So many people have received special gifts from God and yet instead of using these gifts to give Him thanks and praise, they used these gifts to their own advantage. Sometimes we lose our blessings especially when we use them selfishly so we should serve the Lord with what He has blessed us with at all times.

Lord You have shown us what You require of us: to do justly, to love mercy and to walk in humility in Your holy presence. Help us Lord that as we seek to walk with You that we will always praise Your name and give You thanks for Your continuous blessings upon us. Lord, we give You thanks for helping us to remain positive in everything that we do and for Your faithfulness towards us.

Father we know that on our own we are incapable of keeping Your commandments as You would have us to, but we know also that Your mercy never ends and Your justice never fails. Have mercy upon us Lord and pour out Your Holy Spirit upon us so that we will continually praise and magnify Your name. Remind us Father that You will never let us go far from Your side for You desire our presence even more than we desire Yours. In Your name we pray Lord. Amen.

# April

# Our God is Great and Mighty

## Day 19

*"I will exalt you, my God the King; I will praise your name for ever and ever. Every day I will praise you and extol your name for ever and ever. Great is the Lord and most worthy of praise; his greatness no one can fathom. One generation commends your works to another; they tell of your mighty acts."*

*Psalm 145:1-4*

God depends on us to share the good news we have received with others so that His will for the world to know about Him can be fulfilled. We do so by exalting His name day and night and giving thanks and praises to Him at all times and in all places. Our God is a great and mighty God and most worthy of our praise and His greatness is unfathomable. It is our duty as His followers to pass on His Word to succeeding generations so that His goodness and His mercy will never be forgotten. Our God is good all the time and all the time our God is good and that is why we should not fail in talking about His goodness day in and day out.

*Lord, we will exalt and praise Your name for ever and ever. Every day we will praise You and lift up Your holy name. We will tell the world of Your love and mercy and all the wonderful and amazing things You have done for us and for others. Great is Your faithfulness O Lord our Father and we thank You that You will never turn away from us.*

*Lord, we give You thanks for the unity we have in Christ Jesus our Savior and our Lord. Wherever we may go we cannot separate ourselves from Your Holy Spirit. We thank You Lord that You have given us the opportunity to worship You in Spirit and in truth and we thank You that You have not prevented us from truly worshipping You as we ought to. You are indeed a good, loving and gracious God and for this we give You thanks in the name of Jesus. Amen.*

# April

# Forever God Alone

## Day 20

*"My mouth will speak in praise of the* Lord. *Let every creature praise his holy name for ever and ever."*
Psalm 145:21

God is the Creator of everything in the universe and He is to be praised and lifted up for His mighty act of creation. All creatures great and small must praise the name of the Lord even to the end of the earth. Nothing is more important than for us to give to God what He deserves and that is our praise and gratitude. When we consider how mighty and powerful God is and the mysterious ways in which He works, we cannot help but to magnify and adore His name. He is absolutely unique in all His ways and there is no one else like Him.

*Lord, we thank You for creating us and for having breathed into us the breath of life to make us living souls. O loving Father, help us to ever praise and worship You all the days of our lives because You are worthy of all our gratitude and thankfulness. Without You Lord our lives would be meaningless and all our efforts would be in vain.*

*Lord, we thank You for not giving up on us in spite of and despite our sinfulness and for having declared Your unconditional and everlasting love for us. We are Yours Father and You are our Father and in the same way You love us, we want to tell You that we love You too. Forgive us for the times when we failed to worship You as we should and to express our gratitude to You for all the many blessings You have blessed us with. As we lift up our praise and thanks to You, we do so in the name of Jesus Christ, Your Son. Amen.*

## April

# Giving God our Utmost

*Day 21*

*"Praise the Lord. Praise the Lord, my soul. I will praise the Lord all my life; I will sing praise to my God as long as I live."*

Psalm 146:1-2

As long as we live and have the breath of life in our body, we must praise the Lord with our utmost as He has done great and marvelous things for us. From Genesis to Revelations we recognize how much God is feared and revered and all the accolades that have been heaped upon Him from all generations. We have benefited so much from the lives of others and the legacy they have left us and we in return should also leave our own legacy behind for others to follow. We owe it to Almighty God to praise and magnify His name all the days of our lives because of the great and marvelous things He has done for us.

*Lord our whole being- body, soul and mind just want to praise You for whom You are. You are absolutely the best and greatest Father in the entire universe and You are indeed deserving of our praise and adoration. When we consider what You have done for such wretched people like us, we just fall on our knees and cry holy to You the Most High God. Lord ,You are unparalleled in all of history and You certainly have no equal on earth.*

*Heavenly Father we are struck by references in the Bible that we are the apple of Your eye and we realize how precious we are in Your sight. If we are the apple of Your eye then we must replicate Your characteristics to be true offspring of Yours and to compare our righteousness to Yours and not to others. Help us Father to grow in Your likeness and try to become more like You in everything that we do. Grant us Father the capacity to be able to praise and glorify You in the name of Your Son, Jesus Christ, our Lord and Savior. Amen.*

# April

# Our Sovereign Heavenly Father

## Day 22

*"The LORD reigns forever, your God, O Zion, for all generations. Praise the LORD."*
Psalm 146:10

One generation after another must take responsibility for giving to God what is due to His name. We must praise, honor, adore and glorify His precious name for ever and ever. Our God is not slack or His hand short in dealing with us His children. He has always given to us the best of His blessings and this He will continue to do for as long as we shall live. It is our obligation as His followers to show our appreciation to Him in everything we do and at all times by offering up our sincerest gratitude and appreciation to Him for His continued blessings upon us.

*Glorious Father, we exalt Your holy and immortal name. We worship, honor and adore You Lord. We delight Lord to be in Your Holy presence forever. We magnify and adore Your holy name and we invite You to come into our hearts today and reside there forever. Lord, how we thank You for that place which You are preparing for us where we will live with You forever and ever.*

*Help us Lord that when others speak ill of us because we tell them of Your love, that we will glorify You. We thank You Father for Your amazing promise to never leave us nor forsake us and for reassuring us to remain steadfast in our faith. Lord, we have every reason to give You all the praise and glory because of Your dedicated and consistent love for us and because no one else besides You can fill our hearts with joy, peace, love and happiness like You do. We give You thanks Father for all Your constant care and protection and we glorify Your name through Jesus Christ, Your Son. Amen.*

## April

# Praises Fitting for a King

### Day 23

*"Praise the Lord. How good it is to sing praises to our God, how pleasant and fitting to praise him!"*
Psalm 147:1

We acknowledge that it is certainly a good and pleasant thing to sing praises to God our Creator for without Him, there would be no reason for living. In times of crises such as we experience from time to time, it is important that we rely on Almighty God to sustain, protect and see us through these dark periods of our lives. We are to give Him thanks for everything, anything and for all things because the Bible tells us that in everything we must give thanks. Sometimes we find ourselves dealing with issues that are overwhelming to us and it is only God who can help us through it all, hence our trust and faith in Him. Let us never take our eyes off the Lord because His eyes are always on us.

*Father God, we come to You in the name of Your Son, Jesus Christ. With the divine help of Your Holy Spirit and by Your grace so freely given to us, we join with the heavenly host in making a joyful noise to You, serving You with gladness and come before Your presence with hymns of praise and thanksgiving from our lips. Loving Lord, what a sense of joy we feel when we spend time in Your presence, praising and magnifying Your name. We cannot truly express our feelings to You as we ought to but we just want to thank You for making us feel the way we do.*

*Gracious and Living Lord, we thank You for the victories and achievements which we have experienced in spite of all our failures. Lord, we cannot look good into Your eyes by glorifying ourselves. When we try to do that we only become self-righteous. Forgive us Father for our tendency to put ourselves before You and we thank You that we can glory in Your righteousness despite our own shortcomings. How we thank You Father for journeying with us through the difficult periods in our lives and for this we give You thanks and praise in Jesus' name. Amen.*

# April

# God Our Providential Provider

## Day 24

*"Sing to the Lord with grateful praise; make music to our God on the harp. He covers the sky with clouds; he supplies the earth with rain and makes grass grow on the hills."*
Psalm 147:7-8

It is God our Father who supplies us with all our basic needs for survival and so it is appropriate for us to get down on our knees to give Him all the praise and all the glory due to His name. It is God our Father who sends the rain and replenishes the earth with His goodness. Everything on this earth, was created by God, and so everything owes a debt of gratitude to Him for His goodness and mercies towards us all. We are thankful to God for not holding our sins against us and despite all the wrongs we have done, He still showers His many blessings on us just the same.

Thank You for Your grace Lord which is teaching us to trust ourselves and others more and more. Thank You Lord for all the material blessings You have bestowed on us to meet our daily basic needs. Lord, we just want to sing praises to You for having given us so much. You are a loving, kind and compassionate Father who wants the best for us at all times and for this we are indeed grateful.

We thank You Lord for supplying the earth with rain that makes the grass grow and the plants flourish. We are truly indebted to You Father God for all of Your bountiful blessings upon us Your unworthy children. Help us we pray loving Father, to express our gratitude to You at all times for all Your myriad of blessings You have so lovingly blessed us with. Father, remind us that we owe it all to You because You have never disappointed us or failed to provide our daily needs. To You be honor and glory, dominion and power for ever and ever. Amen.

## April

# Our All Powerful God

## Day 25

*"Praise the LORD, O Jerusalem! Praise your God, O Zion."*
*Psalm 147:12*

What a wonderful thing it is for us to sing praises and to give thanks to Almighty God for all His mercies so freely given to us. Let us give Him our praise and thanksgiving every day He blesses us. God is calling on all peoples the world over to acknowledge Him as Creator, Provider, Sustainer, Protector and as our Father who has carved out this world in which we live out of nothing and placed us here to be His stewards to take care until He comes again. We should all endeavor to be the best stewards we can in taking care of God's beautiful creation

*Father, in the name of Your Son Jesus Christ, You have become our light and our salvation and there is absolutely nothing of which we should be afraid. You are indeed the strength of our lives and we can do all things through Your Son Jesus. We thank You Father for giving us Your strength each day to praise and magnify Your name.*

*Today we thank You Lord for being our Provider and we bring our sacrifices of praise and thanksgiving to You as we bow down and worship You as our Lord and King. Grant us Your grace Father to remain humble and steadfast in our faith even as we carry out that which You have called us to do. Lord, You are truly an awesome and magnificent God and to You we owe a debt of gratitude for Your loving kindness and tender mercies towards us. This we pray in none other name than the name of Jesus. Amen.*

# April

# Let Everyone Praise the Lord

## Day 26

*"Praise the LORD! Praise the LORD from the heavens; praise Him in the heights! Praise Him, all His angels; Praise Him, all His hosts! Praise Him, sun and moon; Praise Him, all stars of light! Praise Him, highest heavens, and the waters that are above the heavens! Let them praise the name of the LORD, for He commanded and they were created."*

Psalm 148:1-5

The Lord's name is to be praised by everyone and everything He has created for He is the Creator and the Ruler of all that is in the heavens and on earth. The Psalmist here is encouraging everything and everyone to become engaged in praising and honoring the Creator and not the created. So many people today tend to worship material things that can only give them temporary satisfaction instead of worshipping the Almighty Father who is from everlasting to everlasting. Today let us stand firm in recognizing God as our Creator and the Lord of our lives especially when so many are rejecting Him.

*Father help us not to be anxious about anything, but in every circumstance by prayer and petition with thankful and grateful hearts, we will make our wishes known to You. Let us not hold back in praising You Father God for everything You have created. You desire of us to sing praises to Your name and that we will do for as long as we live.*

*Lord, we thank You that in everything that we have encountered in this life, we are overcomers. With You Father in charge of our lives, nothing will have a stranglehold on us because You have formed a wall around us and You have hemmed us in on every side. We give You all the praise and glory Father from now to eternity in the name of Your Son, Jesus, our Lord and soon coming King. Amen.*

# April

# He is Worthy to be Praised

## Day 27

*"Praise the LORD from the earth, Sea monsters and all deeps".*

*Psalm 148:7*

    Let everything God has created sing praises to His name because He is good and His mercy endures forever. Have we ever stopped to think of the teeming number of creatures God has created and He has a name for everyone! It is truly amazing how God formed the earth out of nothing and spoke everything into being. When we look at every form of animals, plants, fruit bearing trees, herbs, the rivers, seas and oceans and human kind, it boggles our minds of the minute details of every created thing on earth. God is certainly an awesome God and so day in and day out, we must celebrate His goodness and greatness with praise and thanksgiving.

    *Father in the name of Your Son, Jesus Christ, we come before Your throne of grace to receive mercy and to find grace in the time of need. We laud, praise and magnify Your name Lord for You have blessed us in Christ with every spiritual blessing in the heavenly realm. Lord God, we give You thanks for the indwelling of the Holy Spirit in our lives and for the joy we receive from praising You.*

    *Father, so many of us stumble through our lives in darkness afraid of what we might touch and what we might become. Give us the assurance Father that You are our light and with Your presence in our lives there can be no darkness and no evil can overcome us. We keep on praising You Father for Your banner that You have placed over us to protect us from all that is evil. We give You thanks Father for Your unconditional love for us and for constantly blessing us through Your Son, Jesus, our Redeemer. Amen.*

# April

# One and Only God

## Day 28

*"Let them praise the name of the LORD, for His name alone is exalted; His glory is above earth and heaven. And He has lifted up a horn for His people, Praise for all His godly ones; even for the sons of Israel, a people near to Him. Praise the LORD."*

Psalm 148:13-14

It is no secret that our God is a good and noble God and so we need to praise and adore His holy and mighty name for all the unimaginable things He has done for us day in and day out. May we always praise His name forever and ever because of His constant love and goodness towards us His erring children. No matter what our status in life is as it relates to color, class, race, ethnicity, creed, religion or being rich or poor, God loves and cares for us just the same and that is why it is so important for us to sincerely pour out our hearts to God in praise and adoration.

Heavenly Father, You chose us in Christ even before the foundation of the world that we should be holy and blameless in Your sight. You created us with a purpose to praise, adore and glorify Your awesome and wonderful name. Help us Lord to be faithful and genuine in our worship, praise and adoration of You constantly and consistently. Too often Father we slip up and become too busy and neglect to give to You our praise and thanksgiving and for this we seek your forgiveness.

Father, at times Your purposes seem to run contrary to our interests, but the more we ponder and think about them, the more we see that You always have our highest interests at heart. Help us loving Lord to trust You more and to think less of ourselves by surrendering our all to You because without You in our lives, we feel like a ship that has lost its rudder and is just drifting aimlessly. We offer up our praise and gratitude to You and thank You for always being there for us. This we pray in the name of Jesus. Amen.

## April

# Let the Godly Praise the Lord

### Day 29

*"Praise the LORD! Sing to the LORD a new song, and His praise in the congregation of the godly ones."*
*Psalm 149:1*

What a wonderful thing it is for God's people to constantly bless the name of the Lord and to thank Him for His loving kindness and tender mercies towards us. There has never been a time when God has not delivered what He promises on time although we become so impatient with Him. One of the things from God's holy Word we have been encouraged to do, is to wait upon God because He is never in a hurry but He delivers on time. Can you recall those times when we became so anxious to the point of giving up, when God broke through and satisfied our desires just at the right time? That is the God whom we serve and to Him we owe our loyalty.

Father Almighty, Maker of heaven and earth and Giver of every good and perfect gift, in love and humility we open our hearts to You and offer up our thanks for the brightness You have shed so steadily upon our earthly way. For the world in which we live Lord and for all that You have created, we give You thanks and praise this day for all Your goodness to us and to all peoples.

Lord, You have been our mainstay throughout all facets of our lives and we acknowledge You for all Your wonderful and tremendous blessings You so kindly and lovingly bestow upon us. Father, we are sorry for not praising and worshipping You as we ought to, and so we ask You to help us to make the effort in utilizing our time better to give to You what is Yours. Forgive us of all our shortcomings Lord even as we lift up our prayers to You in the name of the Father, Son and Holy Ghost. Amen.

## April

# God Loves Variety in Worship

## Day 30

*"Let them praise His name with dancing; let them sing praises to Him with timbrel and lyre."*
Psalm 149:3

We should never be afraid to praise the Lord with all the resources He has given us to do so. Whatever gift or talent we may have, let us use it to lift up the Most High God who loves to hear us give Him praise and sing songs of joy. The Lord loves when we make joyful noises to Him with all the musical instruments He has made available to us. When we enter into God's holy presence, whether in our quiet place alone or in cooperate worship, we should bring sacrifices of praise to Him including dancing and singing. Our God loves variety in our worship of Him and we should certainly not be afraid to express our praise of Him in whatsoever way we can.

*Father God of truth and goodness, grant that we may fasten our eyes on You and call You God and You alone. Lord we pledge our loyalty to You and none other and to You we will always be faithful and sing Your praises day and night. We thank You Lord for Your still small voice that speaks to us when we are listening to You. Help us Dear Father never to be afraid to worship You and to praise You with whatever gifts or talents we have at our disposal as long as it is pleasing to You.*

*Father God, we are so thankful to You that You have made it possible for us not to be enslaved by fear, but that we can be free to come to You as we are and to worship You individually and collectively. Touch us we pray Father in the deepest parts of our being and fill us with Your holy Spirit. May we never be afraid Father or reluctant to express our deepest feelings to You through songs, instruments or dancing. We thank You for accepting our expressions of love shown to You in the variety of ways we worship You. We ask Father that You continue to bless us in Jesus' name. Amen.*

## May

# Be Ready to Defend

### Day 1

*"Let the high praises of God be in their mouth, and a two-edged sword in their hand."*

Psalm 149:6

As people of God, we must always be prepared to defend and praise His name continually. While we worship God, it is also important that we are to be mindful of those who will harm us because their beliefs are different from ours and there are many persons who are opposed to the Christian faith and doctrine. We must constantly remember those who have left their homes and countries to take the good news into remote areas of the world and where many are faced with hostility. We must always pray for God's mercies and protection upon them.

*Almighty and eternal heavenly Father, we thank You this day for supplying all our needs and more. You are the only one on whom we can call and depend and when we make our requests known to You, no one else knows because whatever we ask of You in secret remains in secret. We thank You Father for all those who put themselves in harm's way to spread the good news about Jesus and pray that Your protection will be with them always.*

*Lord we thank You and praise Your name for all the leaders of the world whom You have chosen to lead Your people. We pray Father that You will endow them with wisdom, knowledge and understanding and the fear of God so that they can lead their people wisely and with compassion. We thank You Father for those leaders who seek Your guidance and who acknowledge You as their God and Father. Lord, we pray for all those who call upon You for help and to seek Your guidance and protection. May You bless them in the wonderful name of Jesus we pray. Amen.*

# May
# Tumultuous Praise to God
## Day 2

*"Praise the LORD! Praise God in His sanctuary; praise Him in His mighty expanse. Praise Him for His mighty deeds; praise Him according to His excellent greatness. Praise Him with trumpet sound; praise Him with harp and lyre. Praise Him with timbrel and dancing; praise Him with stringed instruments and pipe. Praise Him with loud cymbals; praise Him with resounding cymbals. Let everything that has breath praise the LORD. Praise the LORD."*

*Psalm 150:1-6*

There are so many ways in which we can praise the Lord. We are not limited to any one way and we need to seize the opportunity to praise Him in whatever ways we can. The Psalmist outlines for us the various ways in which we can praise the Lord and there should be no excuse for us not to be able to praise the Lord wherever we may be. Music is very important in our praise of the Lord and we are thankful for all those who use this medium to show their gratitude and adoration for God who has blessed them with this special and awesome gift. All of us can use our voices to make joyful praises to the Lord and that we should do as often as we can.

*Lord we will praise Your name at home, at work, in the church and wherever we may be. We will praise You and thank You for Your mighty deeds and excellent greatness. Father we will sing praises to You in the morning and in the evening and whenever we can. You are a great God and greatly to be praised forever and ever. We give You thanks even for the birds that sing sweet melody in praising You.*

*We thank You Father for challenging us through Your Word to use everything possible in our lives to worship You and to raise Your name on high. We thank You Father for opening our eyes to see Your righteousness and for raising us from our sin to new lives in You. Lord, sometimes we just cannot understand why You love us the way You do and why You want us to be faithful in our praise of You. Forgive us Father for the many times when we have not lived up to our expectations. This we pray in the name of Jesus. Amen.*

## May

# Go And Tell God's Word

### Day 3

*"Praise the LORD in song, for He has done excellent things; let this be known throughout the earth."*
Isaiah 12:5

All peoples and nations on earth who have received God's blessings and prosperity should give Him thanks and praise for being such a gracious and generous Father. The more we think about what the Lord has done for us is the more determined we should be in showing how much we appreciate and are grateful to Him. We do so by reading, studying and applying His Word to our lives on a daily basis so that non-believers can be drawn closer to Him. As His people, we need to go into all the world and tell others what the Lord has done and is doing for us.

O Lord our God, let us walk in the way of love that knows not how to seek self in anything whatsoever. Thank You Lord for first loving us and for sending Your only Son into the world to redeem us from our sin. We cannot thank You and praise You enough Father for all that You have done for us and for all the love You have shown us. May we learn Father to share this love with others with whom we come in contact daily.

We thank You this day Father for Your great love for mankind and for all the excellent things You have done for all of humanity. Please help us Lord to be brave and bold enough to take Your Word to the uttermost part of the earth so that everyone will have knowledge of it. Thank You Father for the responsibility You have placed upon us to proclaim Your Word to every land. Help us Father never to be afraid or timid in telling others about You especially when we do so in the precious name of Jesus, Your Son. Amen.

## May

# For Time and Eternity

## Day 4

*"O LORD, You are my God; I will exalt You, I will give thanks to Your name; for You have worked wonders, plans formed long ago, with perfect faithfulness."*
Isaiah 25:1

The Lord our God is mighty and powerful and we need to exalt and give thanks to Him for all His wonderful works and for His faithfulness to all generations. Throughout the history of the world since time began, God has been working His plans out for His people. He has never failed in providing for and protecting His people even at times doing what we would consider the impossible. Truly God has demonstrated in no uncertain terms His love for us and we should in return express our love for Him.

*O Lord our Lord, we recognize that there is no other god like You and we owe all our allegiance to You and You alone. We will ever praise and thank You Father for Your absolute power and might and for all the wonderful things You have done for us and the entire world. Thank You Lord God for Your faithfulness to us and for never letting go of us no matter how much we sin against You.*

*Lord, You know we want our ways to please You and serving You is the greatest thing we can do. You have promised Father that because we obey You, You will smooth our path and even those who do evil against us will become peaceful to us because of You. Thank You Father for Your peace that goes before us every day to bless our lives. In the name of Jesus, our Prince of Peace we pray. Amen.*

## May

# Only One God

### Day 5

*"I am the LORD, that is My name; I will not give My glory to another, nor My praise to graven images."*

Isaiah 42:8

We should be careful not to worship any false gods as can so easily happen. All our allegiance, praise and gratitude should be to Almighty God and Him alone. In today's world, many people try to find substitutes to fill the emptiness in their lives that is often short lived. Only God can fill that void we have through a relationship with Him. He alone can give us a purpose for living and a life filled with peace, joy, love and hope. Let us look to the One who has the answers to all our problems and seek His guidance.

*Dear Father God as we begin this journey of faith into a prayer filled life, we ask You to guard, guide and protect us from all that is evil. We know that You have promised never to leave us nor forsake us as long as we sing praises to Your name. We thank You Father that You are our strength and defense and for becoming the Rock of our salvation. Thank You for being our God and we will praise and exalt Your Holy name forever and ever.*

*Almighty Father, today we ask You for the blessing of peace and tranquility on the peoples of the world and that in our life time we will never have to face the ravages of war. Help us Father to put our faith and trust in You and to seek You alone and not the things of this world that are just temporal. May we learn to trust You every day of our lives because there is no one else like You. Father, You are majestic in holiness, awesome in glory and a wonder working God. Lord we give You thanks for all Your goodness in the name of Jesus our Savior and Lord. Amen.*

# May

# Praise to the Lord Almighty

## Day 6

*"Sing to the LORD a new song, sing His praise from the end of the earth! You who go down to the sea, and all that is in it you islands, and those who dwell on them."*
Isaiah 42:10

To God be the glory, honor and praise for all the great things He has done for humanity. Every day we need to sing new songs of praise to Him because without Him we can do nothing. The greatest thing we can do as followers of Christ is to acknowledge that He is Lord of our lives and to do His will and purpose. God's will is to spread His Word to every corner of the earth so that everyone will have the opportunity not only to hear about Him but also to have a personal and intimate relationship with Him.

*Ever loving and ever giving heavenly Father, we pray that this day You will put a new song on our lips to sing to You and give to us a new zeal and desire to praise and lift up Your name. You are a holy and righteous God and we shall not fail to praise and glorify Your name for as long as You allow us to live on this earth. Lord our God, help us to praise and adore You among the nations on earth. May we Your people sing the praises of your mighty and powerful name.*

*Father God, we praise You from everlasting to everlasting for You Lord art great and powerful and glorious and everything in heaven and earth is Yours. Lord we thank You for the many times You have encouraged us to sing Your praises and to surrender our all to You. We thank You Father that the whole world is Yours and You made everything in it. As Your created beings Lord, help us to show our appreciation to You at all times and in all places for all that You have done for us. Forgive us where we have failed to sincerely honor You and to truly acknowledge You for who You are. Let our cry come unto You Father as we pray in Your name. Amen.*

## May

# God is Worthy of Praise

### Day 7

*"Let them give glory to the LORD and declare His praise in the coast-lands."*

Isaiah 42:12

Even in the most remote areas of the world, God's name is to be praised and so it is our duty to ensure that His word reaches to every corner of the globe. Let us remember all those who risk their lives to take the gospel to all corners of the globe. Because of them, so many people who would not have heard about the Lord have been able to receive the Bible in their own languages and because of this, many have come to accept the Lord. Let us ask the Lord to protect and guide all those who have made themselves available to proclaim His Word throughout all the earth.

O Spirit of the living God, fall afresh on us today and fill us with the desire to serve and to follow You all the days of our lives. Precious Father, enable us to sing Your praises and give You thanks in season and out of season. Help us that wherever we may go we will praise Your name and spread the good news of salvation abroad. Father in heaven, we pray for those who have dedicated their lives in the spreading of Your Word in all corners of the globe. May You protect them and keep them safe from all harm and danger.

O Lord, day by day we are catching little glimpses of what You are trying to teach us that the more we depend on Your righteousness and the less on our own, the better off we will be. Help us Father to humble ourselves before You and to declare Your praise as much as we can to all the people we can for as long as we can. Blessed be Your glorious name Father and may it be exalted above all blessing and praise. We praise You for making the heavens and all their starry host, the earth and all that is on it and the seas and all that is in them. To You Father be all honor and praise, dominion and power forever and ever. Amen.

# May

# We Belong to God

### Day 8

*"The people whom I formed for Myself will declare My praise."*

Isaiah 43:21

    The Lord expects those whom He has called to be faithful in expressing their gratitude to Him and praising His name for His bountiful blessings. The Bible tells us that those who will humble themselves and confess their sin and seek God's forgiveness, He will forgive them and heal their land. How our lands need forgiveness and cleansing for all the wrongs and sin we have committed. God our Father is always ready and willing to forgive and to cleanse us from all unrighteousness. He stands in waiting and willingness to come to our rescue and to transform our lives for His glory.

    *Thank You for calling us O God and for blessing us with privileges and opportunities to do Your will. We thank You Lord for making us in Your image and placed within us Your likeness. Thank You Father for giving to us so many blessings and for all these we are eternally grateful. We thank You Lord that You are our Rock, our fortress and our Deliverer and for being the stronghold of our lives.*

    *We will exalt You Lord, for You lifted us out of the depths and did not allow our enemies to trample upon us. Lord in our distress, we called out for help and You delivered us. Gracious Lord and Master, how can we sufficiently thank You for all the many gifts You have given to us. Show us Lord how to effectively spread Your Word and declare Your praise to as many people as we can. You require of us Lord to do our best in preaching Your Word and in remaining faithful and loyal to our faith. This we pray in Your name Father. Amen.*

## May

# No Evil Shall Overcome Us

### Day 9

*"Sing to the LORD, praise the LORD! For He has delivered the soul of the needy one from the hand of evildoers."*
Jeremiah 20:13

Thanks and praises should be given to God for having delivered us time and time again from the snares of the devil. Without the Lord's intervention we would be crushed and destroyed by the evil one. Every day we are in a spiritual warfare as our enemy the Devil keeps on prowling to see who will fall prey to his tricks. We need to attach ourselves to the Lord in such a way that His hold on us will keep us safe from the constant attempt by the Devil to pull us away from Him. Remember the Word of God will keep us away from the Devil or the Devil will keep us away from God's Word.

*We are grateful and thankful to You Lord for all the impulses which come into our hearts to praise You. Even at times when we feel discouraged, helpless and inadequate, we feel the urge to just praise and magnify Your name because we know You are always aware of our circumstances and our feelings. Lord, please help us always to seek You and when we have found You, we will share Your goodness with others.*

*O God of mercy, God of might, teach us more and more to depend on You and to live our lives in accordance to Your Word. We know Father that the Devil is always trying to put things in our paths for us to stumble and to fall out of grace with You. Strengthen our faith Lord so that we will be able to resist the Devil and remain steadfast in our worship of You. Grant to us we pray Father, Your grace which surpasses all understanding through Your Son, Jesus our Lord and Savior. Amen.*

## May

# God's Remnant People

## Day 10

*"For thus says the LORD," Sing aloud with gladness for Jacob, and shout among the chief of the nations; proclaim, give praise and say, 'O LORD, save Your people, the remnant of Israel."*

Jeremiah 31:7

It is when we cry out to God that He hears us and responds to our cries for help. He never slumbers or sleeps so we can depend on Him to hear us. The Lord wants us to pray for those who have been chosen to be leaders of nations and to seek His guidance and protection upon them. Too often we fail to lift up those in authority including the God we serve. Our God is Leader of leaders and He is the One who rules and therefore it is our duty to elevate Him at all times. He does not forget His remnant people but He draws them unto Himself and saves them from all their troubles and it is His desire for them to praise Him.

O God our Creator and Redeemer, our Bright and Morning Star, from the deep recesses of our hearts, we lift up our praise and thankfulness to You for the great things You have done for us. We cannot explain adequately enough Lord how grateful we are, but we know that You understand when we say we thank You. Father, we know it is always a good thing to give thanks to You because not only do You deserve it but as Your people it is our duty to proclaim Your mighty and powerful name to all people.

Father, we sing praises to You because You are our Almighty God and the King of all creation. Lord all that is within us adore You and all that has life and breath give You thanks and come before You with singing and thanksgiving. Father we thank You that Your mercy and goodness will always be with us as long as we will serve You. We thank You Father that we can indeed make Your name known throughout all the earth so that men and women and children will not only hear Your name but will surrender their lives as well to You. This we pray in Your precious and wonderful name. Amen.

# May

# God Grants our Requests

## Day 11

*"To You, O God of my fathers, I give thanks and praise, for You have given me wisdom and power; even now You have made known to me what we requested of You, for You have made known to us the king's matter."*

Daniel 2:23

It is Almighty God who has blessed us with wisdom, knowledge and understanding and who has given us the ability to think and to act in keeping with His will and purpose for our lives. We praise the Lord at all times for His mercies extended to us. We must acknowledge our Lord for giving to us wisdom and power to be able to discern between what is right and what is wrong. In this present world, we need to as Christians to be alert and sharp in making decisions that are life threatening or life transforming. Too often we fail to do what is right and so we lose our way in impacting the lives of others.

Lord You have said that we should not lean unto our own understanding, but in all our ways we must acknowledge You for having blessed us with Your wisdom, knowledge and understanding. Lord we know that we cannot achieve anything on our own, as it is You Father who makes all things possible. We thank You Father that You have made known to us what we ask of You and once we ask, You always respond to our requests.

Father, we thank You that You are rich, merciful and kind and we come now to You with minds and hearts that are grateful for Your continuous blessings on us. Lord, without Your constant care and protection we would find it hard to survive in these troubling and difficult times. We thank You that despite everything, we can still sing Your praises and call upon Your name. You have been so, so good to us and we thank You for blessing us over and above that which we deserve. We give You thanks in Jesus' name. Amen.

# May

# Godly Recognition

## Day 12

*"But at the end of that period, I, Nebuchadnezzar, raised my eyes toward heaven and my reason returned to me, and I blessed the Most High and praised and honored Him who lives forever; for His dominion is an everlasting dominion, and His kingdom endures from generation to generation."*

Daniel 4:34

Even leaders are expected to praise and extol the name of the Lord. It is the Lord who has chosen them and so they have a responsibility to show honor and reverence to Him. The Bible reminds us that where there is no vision the people perish and so it is incumbent upon our national leaders to put God first before self. When they do this, the Lord will guide and direct them in the ways they should go and they will realize success in what they do. Our responsibility as followers of Christ is to pray for our leaders and to seek God's guidance on their lives.

*Almighty and eternal God, You whom have appointed men and women to serve as leaders of nations, we pray that You would make them bold to confess and accept You as their Lord and Saviour. In troublesome times such as these, we pray that You will grant each leader wisdom and understanding and the humility to admit that they cannot succeed without Your help. May they learn to praise and glorify Your name Lord in the good times and in the bad times.*

*We thank You Father for those leaders who fear You and put their faith and trust in You. Help them Father never to lean unto their own understanding but in all their ways may they acknowledge You as their Lord and Creator. As your people Lord, help us to play our part in lifting up our leaders in our prayers and to never be afraid to call them out when they do wrong. It is in your name we pray. Amen.*

## May

# Humility in Leading

*Day 13*

*"Now I, Nebuchadnezzar, praise, exalt and honor the King of heaven, for all His works are true and His ways just, and He is able to humble those who walk in pride."*
Daniel 4:37

The hallmark of a great person is humility. Let us pray for all those who lead to humble themselves before Almighty God and seek His guidance and wisdom. Too often leaders become arrogant and haughty and take things into their own hands instead of depending on the Almighty God. Soon they realize that their power is limited and so they often have to swallow their pride and seek help. We are thankful that God is merciful and forgiving and so when we mess up, He is quick to forgive us and set us on the right path.

*Lord may You endow the leaders You have chosen to lead nations with patience, love, compassion and integrity. We thank You Father that we have a responsibility to pray for all our leaders. Loving God we pray for all our local leaders both spiritual and secular that You would bless them with a double portion of Your grace. Give them hearts of mercy and love and help them to truly acknowledge You as their Lord.*

*We thank You for those leaders past and present who have made a difference and who have left an indelible mark on the lives of their countrymen. Lord help us to so live our lives that we too may leave a lasting legacy for those who will come after us. This we pray in Your mighty and Holy name. Amen*

# May

# No Shame in Serving God

### Day 14

*"You will have plenty to eat and be satisfied and praise the name of the LORD your God, who has dealt wondrously with you; then My people will never be put to shame."*
Joel 2:26

It is a good thing for us to recognize all that God has done for us and all the blessings He has showered on us. He is truly deserving of our praise and our honor because He has blessed us with so much and yet at times we still complain. Let us never fail in admitting how much God has really reached out to us and we should seize the opportunity to give Him thanks and praise at all times.

*Spirit of the living God fall afresh on us today. Melt us, mold us, shape and use us. Spirit of the living God fall afresh on us. To Your name O God be glory, honor and praise because of the wonderful things You have done for us. Loving Father we just cannot thank You enough for all the blessings You have bestowed on us and we want You to know how much we appreciate You.*

*Father we know that we cannot obtain absolute perfection in our lives because only You are perfect. We ask You Lord to have mercy on us and we know that Your forgiveness is without limit, provided we exercise the same forgiveness with others. In our failure Lord to thank You as we should, we seek Your forgiveness and ask You to never leave us or forsake us. This we pray in the precious name of Jesus. Amen.*

## May

# Blessed is God's Name

### Day 15

*As soon as He was approaching, near the descent of the Mount of Olives, the whole crowd of the disciples began to praise God joyfully with a loud voice for all the miracles which they had seen, shouting: "Blessed is the King who comes in the Name of the Lord; peace in heaven and glory in the highest.*

*Luke 19:37-38*

Today we can join with those who shouted, "Blessed is King Jesus who comes in the name of the Lord." Because of Him we can find peace in a world that is everything else but peaceful. The world is in mess and people all over are going through hard and difficult times. At the time of Jesus, things were not so different from what we are experiencing today. People were sinning left, right and center and every one was doing his own thing. Our world is in a serious state and we too need Jesus to return to bring peace on earth good will to men.

*Lord we thank You that today we can sing Your praises because of what Jesus has done for us. He has brought peace, love and joy to our hearts and has set us free from the bondage of sin, shame and degradation. Lord May we continue to praise and magnify His holy name. Precious Jesus we thank You that because of Your entry into this world we can live life and live it more abundantly.*

*O God, save us from our insistent and demanding spirit. You are always Father God reaching out to us in love and awakening us, but yet we fail to show our appreciation to You for all Your goodness towards us. We thank You Father for Jesus who is our King of kings and Lord of lords. Lord we ask You to bless us in the name of Jesus, our Lord and Savior. Amen.*

# May

# Imprisoned But Free

### Day 16

*"But about midnight Paul and Silas were praying and singing hymns of praise to God, and the prisoners were listening to them; and suddenly there came a great earthquake, so that the foundations of the prison house were shaken; and immediately all the doors were opened and everyone's chains were unfastened."*

Acts 16:25-26

The greatest force on earth is that unleashed by God. No prison walls or chains can contain us when God is in the midst of us. No matter what situation we may find ourselves in, it is important that we pray and offer praises to Almighty God who is our Deliverer. What looked like an impossible situation for Paul and Silas, God entered their space and freed them as they prayed and sang hymns of praise to God. This action impacted the lives of their fellow prisoners and many must have turned to the Lord.

*Lord we thank You that Jesus is our Liberator, Conqueror and Deliverer. He is always there for us when we need Him most and He never fails in demonstrating how powerful and mighty He is. You alone Father God can calm the storms in our lives and set us free from the shackles of sin that enslaves us.*

*Father we thank You that we can depend on Your Son Jesus to always be by our side especially when we are tested and tried. Thank You O Father God that we can call upon You to deliver us from the things that imprison us. Give us the faith of Paul and Silas Lord to remain hopeful and trusting in the face of being locked away or imprisoned. This we ask in Your wonderful and precious name. Amen.*

## May

# On Bended Knees

### Day 17

*For it is written," As I live, says the LORD, every knee shall bow to Me, and every tongue shall give PRAISE to God."*
*Romans 14:11*

For us to be in the holy presence of God, we need to become knee weary and tongue tired in praising, praying and worshipping Him. We should not do less but more as that is the only way we can get to know Him better. Our world would be a much better place if more of us spent at least ten per cent of our time in prayer and praise to God instead of devoting so much time to things of lesser importance. We are all guilty as Christians of shortchanging God in the time we spend with Him and so we need to make the effort in giving to God what is due to Him.

*Lord we thank You that we can come into Your presence on bended knees praising You and lifting up Your name on high. We know Father that we are guilty of not praising and thanking You enough. We spend so much time Lord doing other things without feeling exhausted but when we are to spend quality time with You we find it so onerous. Forgive us Father for failing You.*

*We know Father that this world in which we live could be so much better if we would just spend more time with You in prayer. Forgive us Father for our lethargy and the nonchalant way in which we worship You. We thank You for being so good to us despite our failures and shortcomings. Help us Father to praise You at all times no matter the situation we may find ourselves in. To You Father we give all the praise and glory in the name of Jesus. Amen.*

## May

# All One In Christ

### Day 18

*"For I say that Christ has become a servant to the circumcision on behalf of the truth of God to confirm the promises given to the fathers, and for the Gentiles to glorify God for His mercy; as it is written, "Therefore I will give praise to You among the Gentiles, and I will sing to Your Name." Again he says, "Rejoice, O Gentiles, with His people."*

Romans 15:8-10

God is no respecter of persons and so what He demands from the Jews He also demands it from the Gentiles since with God we are all one in Christ Jesus. Therefore we all need to praise and thank God from whom all blessings flow. Every one of us is precious and valuable in the sight of God because He created us all in His own image. We should not feel discouraged or belittled when others frown at us or try to knock us down since God loves and cares for us and what He does matters more than anything else. Let us learn to cherish and appreciate who we are and how God has made us.

*Righteous and everlasting Father, thank You for accepting us for who and what we are. We realize that we are sinners saved by Your grace which is a gift from You. Lord we thank You that we do not have to be afraid to praise and magnify Your name because we are children of King Jesus and we are heirs to His kingdom.*

*We thank You Father so much for creating us in Your own image and that is why we are to be proud of what You have made us to be. Forgive us Father for the times we have complained about how we look or what the color of our skin is. Remind us Father that we are all precious in Your sight and that we should never be ashamed of being who we are. We magnify and praise Your name O God in the name of the Father, the Son and the Holy Spirit. Amen.*

# May

# Claiming Our Spiritual Blessings

## Day 19

*"Blessed be the God and Father of our Lord Jesus Christ, who has blessed us with every spiritual blessing in the heavenly places in Christ."*

Ephesians 1:3

We must be reminded again and again that all of our blessings come from God and we must acknowledge Him as often as we can. Our blessings from the Lord are not only physical but spiritual and we must learn to feast upon these spiritual blessings. God has seen fit to send into our lives His Son Jesus Christ so that we can remain connected to Him. The more connected we are to God, the more we will feel His holy presence in our lives and the more we will learn how to appreciate His blessings.

*Lord You have said in Your Word that whoever believes in You will have rivers of living water flowing from their hearts. Father we believe in You and we desire this living water to flow in and through our hearts today so that we may praise Your name for ever and ever. We thank You Father for blessing us with every spiritual blessing in the heavenly places through Jesus Christ Your Son.*

*We thank You Father for sending Your Son Jesus into our lives so that we can have a mediator to intercede for us. Help us Lord to become connected to You through Christ so that we can constantly feel Your presence. Father we know that the more connected we are to You, the more we feel safe and protected from all harm and danger. This we pray in Your name and for Your sake. Amen.*

## May

# God In Our Midst

### Day 20

*... saying," I will proclaim Your Name to my brethren, in the midst of the congregation I will sing Your praise"*
*Hebrews 2:12*

Doubt and uncertainty about our faith often prevents us from truly praising God as we ought to especially in the company of others. When we take a stand for God He makes us bold and brave and we are able to face up to anyone who would challenge our faith. We should never be afraid to share the love of Jesus with those around us because by so doing we can draw others to know Christ. Every opportunity we get, we should use it to praise the name of the Lord especially for His abiding and unwavering love for us.

Father Your Word says that ,"the Spirit also helps us in our weaknesses. We do not know what we ought to pray for, but the Spirit Himself intercedes for us with groans that words cannot express." (Rms. 8:26). Help us Lord never to be afraid of praising and thanking You for all Your blessings upon us. We thank You Lord for guiding and protecting us through all the challenging and difficult years we have been through.

Lord Jesus, we pray that You will help us to remain faithful and sincere believers and followers of You. Lord it is so easy for us to become distracted by the many voices that are appealing to us to listen to their messages. Help us Dear Lord to stand firm in our faith so that we will not yield to those competing voices but to keep focused on You. It is in the mighty name of Jesus we pray. Amen.

# May

# Ever Abiding in Praise

## Day 21

*"Through Him then, let us continually offer up a sacrifice of praise to God, that is, the fruit of lips that give thanks to His name."*

Hebrews 13:15

Our sacrifices of praise to God can be offered through His Son Jesus Christ as they are both one and the same as Jesus Himself said, "I and my Father are one."(John 10:30). When we think of the many sacrifices God has made for us including that of sending His Son Jesus to the cross to die on our behalf, it should not be so difficult for us to make sacrifices for Him in return. We can give of our time to become involved in helping others or we can use the one or many talents God has given to us to bless others or we can use the financial blessings to help those who are really in need. Whatever we do for others remember we do so unto the Lord.

*Lord God we will offer sacrifices of praise to You in Your sanctuary. Thank You Father that through Jesus we can come to You boldly to the Throne of Grace where we will find comfort for our souls. Father our lips will ever praise You even as we lift up our hands in Your name in praise and adoration to You.*

*Almighty Father, help us to use all that You have given to us in terms of gifts, talents and material resources to honor You and to be a blessing to others. Father, there are so many people in the world who are desperately in need and some of these do not live far away from us. Help us Lord to reach out to them in love by expressing our love in tangible and profound ways. It is in Your name we pray Father. Amen.*

## May

# In Everything Give Thanks

### Day 22

*"Is anyone among you suffering? Then he must pray. Is anyone cheerful? He is to sing praises."*
James 5:13

Whether in sickness or in health we can sing praises to the King of kings and Lord of lords as He is the one who heals us from all our wounds. Sickness does not always mean an end to all our joy or happiness. Sometimes it is necessary for us to become more focused on the One who wants us to depend solely and completely on Him. Many times when we are going through periods of suffering or any traumatic experiences in our lives, it is usually at that point when we really call upon God to help us especially when we have sought help from others to no avail. God is always near us hearing what we say and He knows about all our thoughts and feelings and that is why He tells us to just leave all our burdens at the foot of the cross and He will take care of them.

*Father in heaven we thank You for being willing and able to bless us whether in sickness or in health. Help us Father to be appreciative of all You do to make our lives abundant and to count our blessings and give You the praise and glory You so well deserve. We thank You Lord that You have promised to be with us through the good times and the bad times, in sickness and in health and in every other situation over which we have no control.*

*Father forgive us for the times when we have left You for the last having exhausted every other option for help before turning to You. We know Lord that You are the only One who can help us in any situation and yet we still turn to other sources before coming to You. Forgive us we pray Father and help us at all times to seek You first in everything we do and to leave our burdens at Your feet. This we pray in Your name. Amen.*

# May

# Well Rooted and Grounded

## Day 23

*"So that the proof of your faith, being more precious than gold which is perishable, even though tested by fire, may be found to result in praise and glory and honor at the revelation of Jesus Christ."*

1 Peter 1:7

The Lord allows us to be tested in order for us to exercise our faith and trust in Him. He has promised never to give us more than we can cope with and we can depend on Him to honor His promise. One thing that we should always bear in mind as Christians is that the Lord will never go back on His Word even when we fail to adhere to His teachings. Let us not forget to pay homage to God who has been there for us throughout all situations that have tested and tried our faith. Our praise, glory and honor of Him should be an automatic response to His goodness towards us.

*Lord please help us to remain faithful to You no matter what may befall us. We know that You will allow our faith to be tested and tried, but You will provide a way of escape for us. Thank You Lord that You have given to us Your Son Jesus Christ whose praises we sing night and day because of what He has done for us.*

*We thank You Father that in the midst of our darkness there is Your marvelous light to guide us along the way. Father, we ask You to help us to remain faithful to You no matter what challenges or hardships that may confront us. We know Lord that You are always there for us and therefore all we need to do is to continue to trust You and to honor and glorify You with our entire being. We lift up our voices Lord to You in praise and gratitude and we give You thanks in the name of Your Son, Jesus Christ, our Lord. Amen.*

## May

# Jesus Is Worthy To Be Praised

*Day 24*

*"Worthy is the Lamb that was slain to receive power and riches and wisdom and might and honor and glory and blessing."*

Revelation 5:12

The God of heaven whom we worship is worthy to receive all of our praise, gratitude and thanksgiving for His goodness and kindness towards us His unworthy children. Every day we must count the many blessings God has bestowed upon us and we will be surprised how much He has really blessed us. No praise or adoration can be too much to offer to the Lord when we consider how much He has lavished on us. Our God is certainly worthy of our constant loyalty and devotion to Him considering the myriads of ways in which He has been faithful to us.

*Father God, Your Son Jesus Christ our Lord is worthy to receive all power, riches, wisdom, might, honor, glory and blessing for dying on a cross to save wretches like us from our sin. We cannot repay You Lord for all that You have done for us but we promise to just bless and praise Your name for ever and ever.*

*Father how we thank You for being truly present in all areas of our lives. We really struggle without You Father and that is why we feel so compelled to lean on You and not on our own understanding. Help us Dear Father that in everything we will acknowledge You and give You praise because You are indeed worthy. We lift up Your Holy name Lord and thank You for blessing us in the name of the Father, the Son and the Holy Spirit. Amen.*

# May

# Everything or Nothing

## Day 25

*saying, 'Amen, blessing and glory and wisdom and thanksgiving and honor and power and might, be to our God forever and ever.' Amen.*

*Revelation 7:12*

Everything that we do in this life as Christians must be centered on worshipping, praising, thanking, honoring and blessing God. He is our Alpha and Omega, our Beginning and the End. There is no one else who possesses the characteristics of God except His Son, Jesus and so it is our duty to serve and worship Him only. God is a good, loving and forgiving God and only He has the power to transform our lives and make it possible for us to go to heaven. This is however not an automatic thing as we must live and abide by His Word and do what He commands us to do in this life in order for us to inherit eternal life with Him.

*Father God, we thank You for the gift of Your Son Jesus Christ to us and to the world. Because of His coming into the world, we have had a new lease on life for which we are very grateful. Thank You Lord that Jesus experienced the ultimate suffering to deliver us from any suffering we experience in this world and that is why we will always sing His praises and honor and magnify His name.*

*Lord we want to thank You for the suffering Christ endured for our sake. Through His death and resurrection Lord, we have hope of being able to see Jesus face to face again when He comes to claim His chosen ones. Forgive us Father for the times when we have failed to give our undivided attention to Your Son and help us to become more dedicated in our worship and praise of Him. This we pray in Your name and for Your sake. Amen.*

# May

# God Reigns in Heaven and on Earth

## Day 26

*And a voice came from the throne, saying, "Give praise to our God, all you His bond-servants, you who fear Him, the small and the great."*
*Then I heard something like the voice of a great multitude and like the sound of many waters and like the sound of mighty peals of thunder, saying, "Hallelujah! For the Lord our God, the Almighty, reigns."*

Revelation 19:5-6

When God speaks to us we must heed His voice as He is the one who reigns forever and ever and one day we will all appear before Him to give Him praise and glory and to bow down and worship Him. We can only imagine what it will be like when Christ returns to gather together all those who served and remained faithful to Him. As Christians we should be ready at all times because we do not know the time or the hour when He will return. Let us have our lamps trimmed and filled with oil and ready so that we will not be caught off guard because the Bible says He will come like a thief in the night.

*We bow down Lord and worship You from the depths of our heart. You are our God the one in whom we trust and can share all our dreams and aspirations. Thank You for being such a mighty and powerful God who is the Ruler of this vast universe. Father we adore You and come into Your holy presence with singing and thanksgiving in our hearts.*

*Father we thank You that You are our reigning King and we owe You our allegiance. Help us Dear Father to be ready by paying heed to Your Word because we do not know the time or the hour when Your Son, Jesus is coming again. You have given us enough warning Father to put our house in order so that when Jesus comes He will not find us wanting. In the precious and mighty name of Jesus we pray. Amen.*

## May

# Freely Receive, Freely Give

### Day 27

*"And when you offer a sacrifice of thanksgiving to the LORD, offer it of your own free will."*
Leviticus 2:29

God does not force us to do anything against our will. He has given us the opportunity to make our own choices. When we make our own choices, we must remember that there are consequences. Those who refuse to accept and follow the Lord Jesus Christ will ultimately have to answer on judgment day. Those who accept and follow the Lord Jesus Christ will also be judged on how they have kept God's Word and the lives they lived while on earth. Let us so live our lives that God will be pleased with us.

*We come to You freely Lord God in humility to offer unto You our sacrifices of praise and thanksgiving. You are a holy and righteous Father and You are deserving of whatever sacrifices we make to bring honor and glory to Your name.*

*Lord we thank You for never failing to walk with us and to talk with us and to tell us that we are Yours. We thank You Father for giving us the opportunity to make our choices. We choose Lord to follow You and to serve You because this is the right thing to do. Grant unto us O Lord Your grace which is always sufficient to take us through any and all situations we may have. Father we ask You to bless us in the name of Your Son, Jesus, our Lord and Savior. Amen.*

## May

# Every Nation, Every Tribe Give Praise

### Day 28

*"Therefore I will give thanks to You, O LORD, among the Gentiles, And sing praises to Your name."*
2 Samuel 22:50

We must give to our God and King all the praise and glory for all the marvelous and great things He has done for us and continues to do. Our desire to serve and worship God must come out of our love and acceptance of Him as being our Father who is the Creator of all human beings on earth. God made us all equal and so no one has superiority over anyone else. We are all precious in the sight of Almighty God and He has no favorites. He requires of all of us to recognize Him as Lord and King of all heaven and earth.

Omnipotent, Omniscient, and Infinite God, thou who art King of kings and Lord of lords, once again we come to You in the name of Your Son Jesus Christ to express our thanks of praise and gratitude for all that You have done for us. You O God have supplied all our needs and more and for these we give You thanks.

Lord we thank You for the challenges that we have had to overcome to be what we are today. Father without Your help and direction, it is so easy for us to lose our way in this busy and demanding world of ours. Continue Father to be there for us as we seek to lift You up in everything we do. May we always sing praises to You in the name of the Father, the Son and the Holy Spirit. Amen.

## May

# The Lord's Name is a Strong Tower

### Day 29

*"Oh, give thanks to the LORD! Call upon His name; Make known His deeds among the peoples!"*
1 Chronicles 16:8

All peoples on earth from every tribe and every nation should praise and give thanks to Almighty God for His goodness, mercy and kindness that are new every morning. We are called upon to make sure that God's goodness must be made known to all peoples the world over. It is our duty to use all the gifts, talents and treasures God has blessed us with to impart His holy Word to as many people as we possibly can. If we do not assume the responsibility of spreading the gospel then many will continue to live in ignorance.

*Mighty God and Merciful Father, how we thank You for this bright and beautiful day which You have made. As we look around us Lord and behold the beauty of Your creation, we can't help but to thank You and to praise You and to bow down and worship You.*

*Lord we thank You for the seasons of life that we go through and for going through these seasons with us. Lord we ask You to help us to be prepared to go out in the highways and byways to tell others about You because unless we do so many will not be able to hear about You. Help us Dear Lord not to be afraid to testify to others about Your love for all of human and all the provisions You have made to ensure that no one is lost. We give You thanks and praise in the name of Jesus. Amen.*

## May

# God's Goodness and Mercy Needs Repeating

### Day 30

*"Oh, give thanks to the LORD, for He is good! For His mercy endures forever."*

1 Chronicles 16:34

God's mercy is from everlasting to everlasting and every day presents us with an opportunity to render our thanks and praise to Him. God is good all the time and all the time God is good. This cannot be said of any other person because the Bible tells us that only God is good. As Christians we should strive to be good and walk into the footsteps of our Father God. When we try our best to emulate our Father then we will become more like Him in the way we treat others, as they will see Him in us.

*Thank You gracious and loving Father that Your mercies endure forever and ever. You are never short in doling out Your mercy upon us no matter what we do and for this we are very thankful. So often we take You for granted precious Lord and we just cannot understand why You keep on blessing us despite our many sins.*

*We truly thank You for blessing us over and over again even though we have fallen short so many times. Lord Your name will continually be in our mouths because You are deserving of our praise and adoration. We ask You Father to forgive us for failing You so many times and yet You keep on loving us. You are truly an amazing Father and we thank You for being in charge of our lives. This we pray in Your name. Amen.*

# May

# Praising God At All Times

## Day 31

*"stand every morning to thank and praise the LORD, and likewise at evening."*

1 Chronicles 23:30

Our Father God certainly does not place a limit on how often we should sing His praises. The least we can do is to praise Him as often as we can wherever we may find ourselves. We are encouraged to stand every morning and evening just to praise the Lord because great things He has done for us over and over again. As long as we live, we should devote some of the time we have been blessed with in praise and thanksgiving to Almighty God who has always been generous to us in so many ways.

*Creator God and Sovereign Lord, we thank You for the wonderful versatility of Your creation: for the birds of the air and the beasts of the field; for the fish of the sea and for trees and flowers and vegetables and all created things. Most of all Lord we thank You for having created us in Your own image and for all the blessings You have bestowed upon us.*

*Father we are so fortunate to have a God like You who is consistently blessing us and providing our daily needs. We thank You for Your love and generosity that You have been showering on us. Sometimes Father we are confused and truly cannot understand how You can really love us the way You do knowing how wayward and ungrateful we have been. We praise You Father for Your mercies that endure forever and we give You thanks in the name of Jesus. Amen.*

## June

# God's Powerful and Mighty Hand

### Day 1

*"Both riches and honor come from You, And You reign over all. In Your hand is power and might; In Your hand it is to make great And to give strength to all. "Now therefore, our God, We thank You And praise Your glorious name."*

1 Chronicles 29:12-13

Giving to the Almighty God our thanks and praise is not optional. It is mandatory and one that we should all take seriously and honor. Unfortunately so many choose not to worship the Lord but instead seek after other gods to fulfill their earthly cravings. It is a decision each and every one of us has to make and God has given us a free choice in either following Him or the way of the world. May we all seek to follow Him because our reward awaits us in heaven where Jesus has gone to prepare a place for all those who call Him Lord.

*Heavenly Father we thank You that in Your hand is power and might and from You come all riches and honor and You reign over us all. Thank You that You have not placed a limit on us as to how we should worship and praise You or how many times we should sing Your praises. Lord we want to thank You and praise You for Your glorious and majestic name.*

*Gracious and loving Father God, we thank You for the gift of today and we ask You to refresh and renew us each and every day to do the work You have called us to do. Help us Dear Lord that when things are going well to rejoice and when it grows difficult and challenging, please surprise us with new possibilities. May we Father ever continue to lift up praises to You in the name of the Father, the Son and the Holy Spirit. Amen.*

# June

# United in Praise

## Day 2

*Indeed it came to pass, when the trumpeters and singers were as one, to make one sound to be heard in praising and thanking the LORD, and when they lifted up their voice with the trumpets and cymbals and instruments of music, and praised the LORD, saying: "For He is good, For His mercy endures forever," that the house, the house of the LORD, was filled with a cloud.*

2 Chronicles 5:13

The more God's people sing His praises in this world, the greater the impact it will have on those who do not believe and the more blessings we will receive from the Lord. The problem with us today is that we are afraid to give to God what is truly His and that is to honor, laud and praise His name all the time and forever. God is worthy of all our praise because it is He who has made us and not we ourselves. Sometimes we spend too much of our time seeking praise for ourselves or giving it to others instead of giving it to God.

*It is not always easy for us to give You thanks Father. Not because we have so few blessings for which to be thankful, but because we have so many. Many of our prayers seem to be praising You because we are not hungry or homeless or poor or sick or in need and then we feel guilty and find it less painful to stop all our praising and thanking You. Lord we thank You for Your incredible providence, Your inconceivable diversity, Your incomprehensible abundance and Your unimaginable generosity.*

*Thank You Father for proving to us time and time again of Your endless and unconditional love. Father, You left the portals of heaven and came to earth in human flesh through Your Son Jesus Christ so that we could have a second chance after we had all messed up to be able to come into Your holy presence and give You praise. It is with heart felt gratitude in our hearts that we give You thanks and praise in the name of the Lord Jesus Christ. Amen.*

## June

# Our Wonder Working Father

### Day 3

*"That I may proclaim with the voice of thanksgiving, and tell of all Your wondrous works."*
Psalm 26:7

We are encouraged to proclaim God's word with the voice of thanksgiving so that all people on earth will hear of the good news of salvation. God has given to us His Word and He has challenged us to take His Word to every corner of the earth. Failure to do so could prevent millions of people from hearing about Him and accepting Him as Lord and Savior of their lives. It is a good thing for us as God's followers to study His Word so that we can effectively tell it to others. God is depending on us His followers to execute His mandate.

*Eternal and Everlasting God, we thank You for being the great I AM. We thank You Father for making us feel and know that You are God and that in You we can live and move and have our being. We thank You Lord God for the times when we have been persuaded that You exist and You are indeed the Creator of heaven and earth.*

*May we use our voices to praise You our Lord and to thank You for all the wonderful and amazing works You have performed all over the world. We thank You Lord for the renewing power You have given to each and every one who believes and we pray Father that You will help us never to forget to give You thanks and praise continually. It is in Your name we pray. Amen.*

## June

# Forever and Ever Praise

### Day 4

*"To the end that my glory may sing praise to You and not be silent. O LORD my God, I will give thanks to You forever."*

Psalm 30:12

Let us not be silent or nonchalant in our praise and worship of our Father God. He deserves all the accolades we can heap on Him because of His goodness and faithfulness. Praising God forever doesn't mean now and again or sometime. It means that every day for as long as we live we will lift up His name at all times and in every situation. There's the tendency for us not to acknowledge our Father God when the going is good as often as we should. We wait until the going gets rough before we give Him our praise and this is not good enough. We are encouraged to praise Him forever.

*O God our Creator and Sustainer, we cannot breathe another breath of fresh air unless You provide that oxygen which sustains life in all of its fullness. Help us dear Lord not to be silent in our praise and worship of You because in giving ourselves to You, we need to surrender our all. May we Father ever seek to lift up Your holy name forever and ever.*

*Father we thank You for the limitless opportunities we have of demonstrating our thanks and gratitude to You. Lord, You have blessed us with all the time, talents and gifts we need for doing so and yet we tend to fall short because we are too busy doing other things, Forgive us we pray Father for our nonchalant attitude and help us to really make the effort in praising You more. This we pray in Your wonderful and awesome name. Amen.*

## June

# Paying Our Vows to God

### Day 5

*"Offer to God thanksgiving, and pay your vows to the Most High."*

Psalm 50:14

We are to render to God what is truly His even as we render our vows to our earthly leaders. God is the Creator and Ruler of us all and we ought to acknowledge Him for that. In the same way we can become so loyal in our following of our political leaders and our allegiance to our political parties, we should even be more loyal in acknowledging the God who made heaven and earth and everything in it. We live a double standard life when we say that we are followers of God but yet do not show our loyalty to Him in the same way we do for our earthly leaders. God should be first and foremost in all our doings.

*Most Holy and Triune Father God, we give You thanks for the privilege of being able to pray to You. Without this medium Lord, we cannot communicate with You. We feel at peace Father when we pray to You and know that we have someone above who listens over and over again to our daily repetitions of words.*

*Father sometimes we absolutely feel exhausted when we are praying and yet You always help us through this period when we are at our lowest. Lord we thank You for watching over us day and night even when we fail to honor You the way we should. Forgive us Father for falling short so often and for failing to give You more of our time. Help us Father to be diligent in paying our vows to You in the name of Your Son, Jesus Christ, our Lord. Amen*

## June

# God Is Always Near Us

### Day 6

*"We give thanks to You, O God, we give thanks! For Your wondrous works declare that Your name is near."*
*Psalm 75:1*

We give thanks and praise to God not only for what He does for us but because He is our Creator and the One who has made us and not we ourselves. No matter how unbelievers may want to discredit His existence, we as believers know that His Word is authentic. We know that God inspired men to write all they could about His existence and that is why we believe in the Bible. It is better for us to believe that God exists because we have nothing to lose even if that were not so. But consider how worst it will be if He does exist and we do not believe. Let us hold fast to our faith and continue to believe in a God who is for real.

*Your name is worthy Lord God to receive our praise and thanksgiving because You are the only true, wise and living God who created the world and everything in it. Nothing will ever prevent us Father from thanking You for all Your mercies and blessings You have given to us. We thank You for the written word and for all the teachings we receive from the Bible.*

*Lord today we thank You for the splendor and majesty of the mountains You have formed and for all the beauty of Your creation. You are indeed a wonderful and awesome Father and no one can truly understand Your ways and Your thoughts. We will ever continue to praise and adore Your name forever and ever. Amen.*

**June**

# An Offering of Praise

### Day 7

*"Let us come before His presence with thanksgiving; Let us shout joyfully to Him with psalms."*
Psalm 95:2

Every time we come before God's throne of grace, we must bring an offering of praise and thanksgiving to offer to Him. What would we do without the God whom we serve and the God who provides all our needs? We would certainly be like lost sheep without a shepherd and going our own way and doing our own thing. Thankfully, we have a God who is consistent in all He does and is always available and accessible to us His children. We should always seek God's guidance and protection even as we walk through this world of ours.

*Loving and Eternal God, today we bring our sacrifice of praise and thanksgiving to Your house to worship, adore and glorify Your name. The earth is Yours Lord and everything in it. You made the world Father and all who live in it. You founded it upon the seas Lord and established it upon the waters. God Almighty You are truly and sincerely to be praised and adored for there is no one else like You.*

*We thank You Lord for speaking to us through the ordinary things of life. Help us Father to love and adore You and to shout joyfully to You with psalms and songs of praise. Living, loving Lord, we thank You for being so good to us and for the ways in which You have provided all our needs. We will always give You praise and adoration because You are good and Your mercies endure forever. Amen.*

## June

# Rejoicing in the Lord Always

### Day 8

*"Rejoice in the LORD, you righteous, and give thanks at the remembrance of His holy name."*

Psalm 97:12

People of God must always rejoice in Him and continually lift up His name in thanksgiving and praise as He is worthy of it all. As children of God, we must not become captives of our circumstances no matter what those might be, but we must rejoice always. We as Christians have more valid reasons to rejoice about rather than not having enough and we should let our rejoicing be independent of our circumstances. Let us not allow our negative circumstances to control our lives because they are temporary but let us instead engender a positive attitude which will help us to overcome the issues that confront us.

Lord we want to thank You for enabling us to respond to the many voices which have called us and have influenced our lives. We thank You for the voice of love, for the voice of faith, for the voice of hope, for the voice of wisdom and understanding and above all for the voice of Your Son Jesus Christ.

We thank You Father for the richness of life that has resulted because we rose to the moment and responded to the opportunities. Help us dear Lord never to allow our circumstances to prevent us from rejoicing in You because these are temporary but to be in Your holy presence is eternal. This we pray in Your name. Amen.

## June

# Developing An Attitude of Thanksgiving

### Day 9

*"Enter into His gates with thanksgiving, and into His courts with praise. Be thankful to Him, and bless His name."*

Psalm 100:4

When we enter into the holy presence of God, we must do so with thanksgiving and praise and blessing from our hearts. We are to be always thankful because we have a relationship with our Father God through His Son Jesus Christ. God has not left us alone and because of His great love for us, He gave us His Son so that we would have a second chance to enter into His kingdom. We must always seek to give God all our praise and gratitude for His continued goodness towards us.

O God Almighty, Creator of Heaven and Earth, Lord and Giver of Life, we pause to give You thanks for Your uninterrupted blessings and mercies You constantly shower down on us. Thank You Father for being our Protector, our Provider, our Providence and our High Priest. No one else on this earth Lord can match Your power and might and greatness.

Lord God Almighty, we thank You for having invested so much in us and for Your constant love and compassion. Help us Father to enter into Your house of worship with thanksgiving and praise and may we ever seek to proclaim Your name throughout the world. Cause us Oh Lord to develop an attitude of gratitude even as we give You thanks in the name of the Father, the Son and the Holy Spirit. Amen.

## June

# Calling on God's Holy Name

### Day 10

*"Oh, give thanks to the LORD! Call upon His name; Make known His deeds among the peoples."*

*Psalm 105:1*

God wants us to call upon His holy name at all times and in all places so that His greatness will be known throughout the world. Unless we make the effort to mobilize ourselves and take the message to all corners of the globe, there will be many who will not have knowledge of God's transforming power and ability to touch lives. Our world can only be a much better place in which to live if more lives are being touched by God's Word and there is much more love than being exhibited now. May God give us the courage and strength as Christians to arm ourselves with His Word and make it known to all the nations of the world.

*God of all ages and Lord of all time, Creator of all things in perfect design, we lift up our voice in praise and adoration to You the Most High God. When we call upon Your name Father, You hear and You answer our prayers. Help us Lord to tell of Your goodness and greatness to the world so that many people will come to know You and accept You as their Father.*

*Lord we thank You that Your love for us endures forever and that it will never end. We acknowledge Father that we have not always lived and behave as we ought to and we have fallen short many times. We thank You Lord that despite our failures You still accept our praise and gratitude to You for all Your benefits towards us. This we pray in Your name. Amen.*

## June

# God's Enduring Goodness

## Day 11

*"Oh, give thanks to the LORD, for He is good! For His mercy endures forever."*

Psalm 107:1

Let us thank the Lord at all times for His goodness and for His plenteous mercies that last forever and ever. God has given so much to us and we need to give back to Him as much as we can. Throughout our lives we should give back to Him cheerfully and with the right attitude. We must remember that God loves cheerful givers so we must give Him all the praise and adoration we can for as long as we can. Two marks of our lives as Christians are giving and forgiving and we should practice these each and every day.

*Father in Heaven, we give You thanks because You are good and Your mercy and love for us endure forever. Lord we give You thanks because You are indeed the only true and living God of all gods whose love endures forever. We give to You thanks and praise O God because You are Lord of all lords and because Your love for us endures forever.*

*Loving Father we thank You today for the wonderful inheritance You have given to us through Your Son Jesus Christ. We thank You Father for blessing us with so much and we will remember that we are stewards over what You have given to us and we will give back to You even as You have directed us to. It is in Your name we pray. Amen.*

# June

# People of God Praise the Lord

## Day 12

*"Oh, that men would give thanks to the LORD for His goodness, and for His wonderful works to the children of men!"*

Psalm 107:8

What a fantastic and awesome thing it would be if we would all give thanks and praise to Almighty God for all His goodness and kindness towards us. This world would certainly be an entire different place in which to live. Instead of us fussing, fighting and quarreling over what does not belong to us, we should spend more of our time thanking God for all His goodness and for all the wonderful and unimaginable works that He performs from day to day. Surely goodness and mercy will follow us all the days of our lives when we give praise and thanks to our God most high.

*We give to You thanks O Merciful God for Your gentleness, goodness and kindness that You have shown to us day after day. Father, we thank You so much for speaking to us through the ordinary things of life and for allowing us to do the extraordinary things for You. Lord we thank You for the revelations of Yourself through Your Son Jesus Christ and we thank You today for the continued guidance of Your Holy Spirit in our lives.*

*We thank You Father for filling us with Your Holy Spirit who spreads Your love throughout our innermost being. We realize Father that without the Holt Spirit in our lives we cannot praise and magnify Your name as we ought to. Thank You Father for loving the world so much that You gave us Your most precious gift- Jesus our Savior in whose name we pray. Amen.*

## June

# Offering a Sacrifice of Thanksgiving

### Day 13

*"I will offer to You the sacrifice of thanksgiving, and will call upon the name of the LORD."*

Psalm 116:17

When we call upon God's holy name and offer to Him our sacrifices of thanksgiving and praise, He blesses us even more than we can think or imagine. Let us bless His name as often as we can because we cannot do enough to show our gratitude and appreciation to Him. Consider how much God has blessed and prospered us, not because we are deserving of all His blessings, but because of His love for us He never stops loving and blessing us.

*Gracious and loving Father, in the midst of our confusion, doubt and hopelessness, we come to You knowing that You are the all-powerful, all-embracing, all-knowing and all-forgiving God who understands us more than we understand ourselves and who is the only one to help us when we seek Your help.*

We thank You Father that You are our Rock, our Shield and our Fortress and that You will take care of all our needs. Father we thank You for being there for us when we need You most. We know Lord that we can always depend on You even when we fail You. We worship You Father and adore You for being such an awesome and wonderful God. This we pray in Your marvelous and adorable name. Amen.

## June

# God's Mercy Endures

### Day 14

*"Oh, give thanks to the LORD, for He is good! For His mercy endures forever."*

Psalm 118:1

All of us can testify of how God has extended His hand of mercy upon us and how He has saved us many times from the brink of disaster. One thing we know about God is that His good promises to us never fail. He is our faithful Father and He promises to fulfill His Word in our lives. In everything we do, God must be at the center of it all because without His presence in our lives, we cannot make it through the difficult periods that we will encounter along the way. We are encouraged to give God thanks not because He asks us to, but because He deserves it.

*Almighty God, Creator, Redeemer and Lord of our lives, whose word and love endure forever and ever; we adore You Lord and thank You that in Your infinite goodness You have spared our lives to see another bright and beautiful day. May we Father offer unto You our gratitude of praise and adoration for all that You do for us.*

*Father we thank You that even in our faithlessness and disobedience, You have continued Your loving kindness and tender mercy towards us. Thank You Lord for sustaining us in our weakness and when things seem to be going out of control. Lord, we know that we can always depend on You to deliver even when we fail to praise and thank You for Your goodness towards us. We give You thanks Lord for all things in the name of Jesus Christ. Amen.*

# June

# Repetition is Good For Remembering

## Day 15

*"Oh, give thanks to the LORD, for He is good! For His mercy endures forever."*

Psalm 118:29

Every new day God pours out His mercy upon us thou undeserving of it, because He is a good and loving God who cares for His children. God is our Potter and we are the clay and He is shaping and molding us each day after His will. Once we walk in the footsteps God wants us to follow, our lives will be shaped in His image. His goodness and mercy will continually be with us as long as we chose to keep His commands and abide in His Word. Once we do this, then giving Him praise and thanks will become a part of who we are.

*O Lord our God, the Author and Giver of all good things, we thank You today Father for the manifold blessings with which You have continually blessed us. Help us dear Lord ever to be sincere and faithful in our praise and worship of You. Your love for us has just been wonderful and we thank You Father that nothing will change that.*

*Lord, we thank You for being the Potter in our lives and we pray that You will continue the workmanship You have begun in us so that we can truly become more like Your Son, Jesus Christ. We surrender our lives to You Lord and ask You to shape us according to Your will and pleasure. This we ask in the mighty and precious name of Jesus. Amen.*

## June

# Right Judgments

### Day 16

*"At midnight I will rise to give thanks to You, because of Your righteous judgments."*

*Psalm 119:62*

No matter what time of the day it is, we can give thanks to the Almighty for He never slumbers or sleeps. God is omnipotent, He is omniscient and He is omnipresent so He spans time and eternity. The God whom we serve is here, there and everywhere and so wherever we may be or wherever we may go, He is there with us. All we need to do is to keep our trust in Him and give Him our undivided attention in our praise and worship of Him.

*Heavenly and eternal Father who has constantly and consistently provided all our needs and given to us our daily bread, grant us Your grace Lord to receive all Your gifts with gratitude that they may be consecrated with thanksgiving to Your glory. Give us today Father the gift of love so that we will always be mindful of the needs of others and to freely give even as we have freely received.*

*Lord, we thank You today for all those who suffer in one way or another and for whom You are concerned. Help us Lord to constantly pray for those who are less fortunate than we are and who find themselves in uncompromising situations. May we Father always give thanks to You on behalf of others who are unable to express themselves as we can. This we pray in Your name. Amen.*

## June

# Dwelling in God's Presence

### Day 17

*"Surely the righteous shall give thanks to Your name; The upright shall dwell in Your presence."*
Psalm 140:13

The Lord blesses those who have clean hands and pure hearts and who lift up His holy name in praise and adoration. They will live in His presence always and He will never forsake or forget them. God will respect those who are upright and allow them to dwell in His presence forever. It is our duty as followers of God to remain connected to Him through His written Word that is our guide on how to prepare ourselves for His kingdom. Surely those who live in accordance with the will of God will be rewarded when He comes again to judge the world. Let us never fail in giving Him thanks for all His benefits towards us.

*O Lord our God when we in awesome wonder consider all that You have made, we can only praise and thank You for Your unique and splendid creation. Thank You Father for the delicate way in which You have created and formed us in Your own image. Lord we thank You that no one can pluck us from Your hand because we belong to You.*

*We give You thanks today Father for every fiber and blood vessel in our bodies. We praise You for having made us and placed within our bodies all our organs to live and function as Your creation. O God, You are so special and wonderful and we give You thanks for who You are and for how You have made us. It is in Your wonderful and precious name we pray. Amen.*

# June

# Offering Praise of Thanksgiving

## Day 18

*"Sing to the LORD with thanksgiving; Sing praises on the harp to our God."*

*Psalm 147:7*

It is right and mete for us always to give thanks and sing praises to God the Almighty, Creator of heaven and earth who has made all things well. We should use all our gifts, talents and resources to glorify God in every way we can because nothing that we own belongs to us but it is God's. As good stewards, we should learn how to use wisely all the blessings God has bestowed on us to honor Him and to edify others. We should not take God's gifts for granted but rather we should use them to glorify and honor Him and to be a blessing to those who are less fortunate than we are.

*Lord the earth is Yours and the fullness thereof; the world and all who live in it. We thank You Father God for Your manifold works, for in wisdom You have created all creatures both great and small. Father God thank You for sending us the rain from heaven and for the fruitful seasons You have given us, providing our hearts and souls with food and gladness.*

*Lord we thank You for the many gifts, talents and resources You have blessed us with. Help us Father to use these to honor and glorify Your name and to use them to be a blessing to others especially those who are less fortunate than we are. We realize Father that all that we have belong to You and we should never take Your bountiful blessings for granted. Father accept this our prayer and let our cry come unto You. Amen.*

## June

# Constant and Consistent Praying

### Day 20

*He [Daniel] knelt down on his knees three times that day, and prayed and gave thanks before his God, as was his custom since early days.*

Daniel 6:10

Men and women of God must be bold and fearless in standing up and defending their faith no matter the circumstances and consequences. Daniel was unafraid to pray to His God even though he was a captive in pagan Babylon. His faith in God was unrelenting and surpassed all worldly concerns even those for his own safety.

We learn from Daniel that it is ok for us to pray as often as possible and not only when we are confronted with problems and challenges. Daniel was fearless in His worship of God because he knew that his God would deliver him no matter what the situation might be. God will also deliver us if we remain true and faithful to Him.

*Lord we pray that You would dare us to be like Daniel in standing firm against the evil which is so pervasive in our society today. Help us Lord never to be afraid or act cowardly in demonstrating our belief and faith in You because we know Father that You honor those who honor You and You deliver them from all that is evil.*

*We pray Lord that we will ever remain true and faithful in serving You and You only. Help us Father that when we face challenging and insurmountable problems as Daniel did, we will remain faithful and steadfast in our faith knowing that You will deliver us and we will come out victorious. This Father is our prayer in the name of Jesus. Amen.*

## June

# Our Salvation Comes From God

### Day 20

*"But I will sacrifice to You with the voice of thanksgiving; I will pay what I have vowed. Salvation is of the LORD."*

Jonah 2:9

Our salvation comes from God through His Son Jesus Christ who paid the price on a cross to save us from our sin and the sin of the whole world. It is our duty to show our appreciation to the Almighty by thanking and praising Him for this great sacrifice. Jonah prayed when he was in trouble in the belly of the fish and so we too need to pray when we are faced with diverse afflictions or challenges. Not only did Jonah prayed to God but he acknowledged that salvation comes from God and none other. The bottom line is that no matter what the situation in our lives might be, we must remember to give God our praise and thanksgiving.

*Holy Father, Almighty and Everlasting God, we give You thanks this day for the gift of salvation You have given to the world through the sacrificial death of Your Son Jesus Christ on a cross. You secured our salvation Lord by Jesus becoming flesh and dwelt among us full of grace and truth. Father God we cannot thank You and praise You enough for this great sacrifice You were willing to make to save us from sin.*

*We give You thanks today Lord for the life and ministry of Jesus and for the way He has been able to transform our lives. Like Jonah Lord, when we tried to run away from You, You pursued us and brought us back to You. Thank You Father that no matter where we try to hide from You, we cannot escape Your presence because You are indeed everywhere. This we pray Lord in Your name. Amen.*

## June

# An Attitude of Gratitude

### Day 21

*And one of them, when he saw that he was healed, returned, and with a loud voice glorified God, and fell down on his face at His feet, giving Him thanks. And he was a Samaritan.*

Luke 17:15-16

Expressing our gratitude to God for all that He does for us should not be taken lightly or for granted. It is the right thing for us to do irrespective of our race, class, creed or status in life. Our sense of spiritual leprosy should make us very humble whenever we draw near to God even as this leper was. Only one of those who were healed returned to give thanks to God and so we too should become more like this leper to be very humble in thanksgiving as well as in our prayers. This leper was sensitive to the power of God and grateful for His mercies and did the right thing in returning to express his gratitude to God for His goodness. This is an example that we should all follow as Christians.

*Most gracious and forgiving God, help us to pour out the desires of our hearts to You today. We know that we cannot hide any secrets from You O Father because You are God and You know everything we do. Thank You for granting to us healing and full pardon and remission of our sins.*

*Please accept us dear Father as we dedicate ourselves anew to You and help us to be ever thankful and grateful to You for healing us of all our infirmities. Lord we thank You for Your divine intervention in the affairs of all Your people and for responding to all those who call upon Your name for healing. It is in Your awesome name we pray. Amen.*

## June

# Christ Our Victor

### Day 22

*"But thanks be to God, who gives us the victory through our Lord Jesus Christ."*

1 Corinthians 15:57

    To our God be glory, praise, dominion and power for giving us victory through His Son Jesus our Savior and Lord. The victory Paul is referring to here is that over sin and death that Christ has taken care of on our behalf. The Bible tells us that all of us have sinned and have fallen short and that the wages of sin is death but the gift of God is eternal life through Jesus Christ.

    None of us has done anything worthy of God's love because we are all sinners, but God not wanting any of us to perish sent His only Son into the world to pay the ultimate price for the sin of us all by His death on a cross. Our duty and response to this great sacrifice is to give our lives in return to Him.

*    Lord we want to serve You with gladness and come into Your presence with singing. Father we want to enter Your house with thanksgiving and into Your courts with a song of praise. We thank You Lord and bless Your name because of Your goodness and steadfast love for us. Father we thank You for the victory You have given us over the devil's hold on our lives.*

*    Thank You Lord Jesus that through Your death on a cross we have victory over sin and the grave. We thank You Father for paying the price for our sin so that we all can be saved. Lord Jesus we cannot thank You enough for this great sacrifice You made to set us free from the clutches of sin and to give us a second chance to be reconciled with You. For all these blessings we give You thanks Lord in the name of Jesus. Amen.*

### June

# God's Awesome Gift To Us

## Day 23

*"Thanks be to God for His indescribable gift!"*
2 Corinthians 9:15

We cannot truly comprehend God's gift of His Son Jesus Christ to a lost and sinful world. It's just mindboggling when you think that we did absolutely nothing to deserve such a gift and yet we find it so difficult to consistently thank Him for what He has done for us. We all like to receive gifts especially on special celebrations and we appreciate the gifts that we receive. However, no matter how beautiful or expensive those gifts might be, they will get old and deteriorate and are replaced in time by something else. The indescribable gift of which Paul writes is that gift of His Son, Jesus Christ whom He gave to humanity- a gift with eternal consequences that will never grow old or lose its value. John 3:16 tells us that:

*"for God so loved the world that He GAVE us His only Son, that whosoever believes in Him, would not perish, but will have everlasting life."*

Heavenly Father, You who have delivered us from the bondage of sin through Jesus Christ our Lord, we offer up ourselves to You in with humble and contrite hearts. . We confess that we have been unworthy of the perfect redemption You have secured for us in Jesus who died on a cross for our sin. Lord we thank You that today we can rejoice because You have set us free and we can sing praises to Your name and thank You for all Your goodness towards us.

Father, we give You thanks for the death and resurrection of Jesus Christ Your only Son who died on Calvary's cross to save us from the pit of hell. To You Lord Jesus we give all honor, praise and adoration for this indescribable gift of Yours that You have given to us so freely and without any conditions attached. You are truly an awesome God and we just give You all our praise and adoration in the name of the One who died to set us free, Your Son, Jesus Christ. Amen.

## June

# Asking and Receiving

### Day 24

*"Be anxious for nothing, but in everything by prayer and supplication, with thanksgiving, let your requests be made known to God."*

Philippians 4:6

Prayer is the medium through which we make our requests and petitions known to God. The thing is we do not pray and thank Him enough because of our busy life-style. The verse exhorts us not to be anxious for nothing. That is a command and so every time we become anxious about life we are actually sinning against God. Notice the verse says that in everything by prayer and supplication we must make our requests known to God. Sometimes there is the tendency for us to rely on our own wisdom and understanding instead of taking all our concerns to God in prayer. So often we do the exact opposite of what the Bible tells us to do to our own detriment. Let us always heed God's holy Word and do as we have been commanded to do.

*Lord so often we become anxious and worried about life that often times leave us sick. You have reminded us Lord that in everything we must give You thanks and that means Lord even when we are under the weather. We thank You Father that Your eye is always on us and we can depend on You to provide all that we need.*

*Forgive us Father for the many times when we have allowed the cares and concerns of the world to truly rob our joy and to lose our focus on You. Even though You tell us Father that You will supply all our needs, we still spend countless hours worrying about life. We pray that You will help us to turn to You in prayer and thanksgiving when we are tempted to do otherwise. This we ask in Your wonderful name. Amen*

# June

# God's Wonderful and Lasting Peace

## Day 25

*"And let the peace of God rule in your hearts, to which also you were called in one body; and be thankful."*
*Colossians 3:15*

    The only true and lasting peace we can have is that which comes from God. We are to seek His peace daily so that we may live a more ordered and peaceful life. Our world is longing for real and lasting peace that can only come from God. Any form of peace on earth is temporary since lasting peace comes from God and God alone. Peace of course begins in our hearts since if we are not at peace with ourselves we cannot be at peace with others. Jesus Himself declares that His peace passes all human understanding and if we are to experience true peace on earth it must come from God. According to the Word of God, we are to allow the peace of God to rule in our hearts.

*    God of peace and Father of love, grant that we would seek Your peace today which passes all understanding and which we can only receive from You. All that the world has to offer us is brokenness and strife but You O Lord can make something beautiful of our lives.*

*    You have said Lord in Your Word that You leave us and give us Your peace and not the peace that the world offers. We pray Lord that You will help us to pass Your peace to others so that the world will become a more peaceful and better place in which to live and move and have our being. Father help us to receive the peace of Christ today as we pray in His name. Amen.*

# June

# In Word and Deed

### Day 26

*"And whatever you do in word or deed, do all in the name of the Lord Jesus, giving thanks to God the Father through Him."*

Colossians 3:17

As Christians we must be careful with our speech and our actions for whatever we do or say must glorify and bring honor to the name of the Lord. At times we dishonor Him with our words and our deeds when we should be showing our gratitude to Him. Let us not forget that God is the source of all things both living and inanimate and we therefore need to be constantly proclaiming our praise and gratitude to Him out of love and appreciation for all His goodness towards us. Certainly He will continue to bless and prosper us even as He sees fit to do.

*Almighty and most merciful Father, we confess that we have sinned against You in our thoughts, in our deeds and in our actions and we have not loved You with all of our heart and soul, with all of our mind and strength and we have not loved our neighbors as ourselves.*

*Forgive us dear Lord of our sin and we promise that we will learn how to love, praise and adore You more. Father we thank You in the name of Jesus for cleansing and drawing us closer to You through Your Word. Thank You Father that Your Word is a lamp to our feet and a light to our path and that with You we shall never walk in darkness. Hear our prayer Oh Lord, and let our cry come unto You. Amen.*

# June

# Vigilant and Earnest Praying

## Day 27

*"Continue earnestly in prayer, being vigilant in it with thanksgiving."*

*Colossians 4:2*

The devil is always on the prowl like a roaring lion seeking whom he may devour. The only way we can defend ourselves is to entrust all our cares to God through our faithful prayers of thanksgiving and supplication. The apostle Paul exhorts us to continue earnestly in prayer and to be vigilant in it with thanksgiving to God. Earnest praying is for us to learn to walk in prayer daily. It is important for us to pray when we get up, when we are on our way to work or wherever we may be going as well as to pray for those we encounter. Earnest praying is a lifestyle that is consistent throughout every day of our lives and as Christians we all should make an effort so to do.

*Teach us dear Lord, to serve You with a loyal and steadfast heart; to give and not to count the cost; to fight and not to heed the wounds; to toil and not to seek for rest and to labor and not to ask for any reward. May we always seek to follow You and to praise and thank You for supplying all our needs and requests.*

*Lord please help us to be committed to the task of following our prayer routine as it is so vitally important for us to be consistent and earnest with our prayer life. Father when we fail to pray, we are giving the devil a foothold on our lives and that is when we have the potential to stumble and fall. Strengthen our faith Father so that we can live a well-disciplined life of prayer that is acceptable to You. It is in Your name we pray Father. Amen.*

## June

# Unconditional Gratitude

## Day 28

*"In everything give thanks; for this is the will of God in Christ Jesus for you."*
1 Thessalonians 5:18

Life has its ups and down and so no matter what card is dealt to us, we must always give thanks to the Almighty because things could have been worse. To the Christians who trust God's providence and believe that our prayers are heard every time we pray to Him, must remember that God constantly and consistently fulfills His will and purpose for our lives. It is for this reason why we should always be thankful to God when we pray to Him. All of us can always find something for which to be thankful and there may be reasons why we ought be thankful for even those things that may be dark and dismal in our lives. God is always willing and ready to come to our rescue when we reach out to Him.

*O holy Father, almighty and everlasting Lord, we would at all times and in all places give thanks to You through Your Son Jesus Christ our Savior and Lord. We thank You Father that through Jesus You fashioned us in Your own image and when we were lost in trespasses and sin, You sent Him into the world to rescue and to save us.*

*Thank You Lord that we can rejoice today because of Jesus and what He has done for us. Help us Father that each day we would not forget to give You thanks and to get on our knees to praise and magnify Your name. Father, when we think of all the good things You have done for us and yet we have still failed in not thanking You enough for these bountiful blessings. Forgive us we pray Father and help to do what is right and pleasing to You always. It is in Your name we pray. Amen.*

# June

# Our Varied Prayers

### Day 29

*"Therefore I exhort first of all that supplications, prayers, intercessions, and giving of thanks be made for all men."*
1 Timothy 2:1

When we pray we do not only pray for ourselves but we should pray for all peoples. God is Father of us all and He is concerned about every one of us and so we in turn must show love and concern for our fellowmen. It is so easy for us only to think about our own welfare and not that of others. As a community of faith, we need to be concerned as well about the needs of those who are less fortunate than we are. When we pray, we are encouraged to lift up everyone whether known or unknown to us through prayers of adoration, confession thanksgiving and supplication to God on their behalf. God will listen to our prayers and answer them in His time.

*Eternal Father the Creator and Maker of mankind, we give to You our humble and heartfelt thanks for all the peoples of the world. You know Father all those who are suffering and are going through difficult and challenging times. Help us Father always to keep them in our prayers and to reach out to as many as we can with love and compassion as You would.*

*We thank You for all the blessings You have bestowed upon us and we pray that You will enable us to be a blessing to others as well. You have been a merciful and compassionate Father to us and You want us to reach out to those who are so desperately in need. Help us Lord always to be ready and willing to give to those who will ask of us.*

*We thank You Jesus for the rich and diverse heritage You have given to us as a people and may we learn how to be at peace with all men. This we pray in Your loving and holy name. Amen.*

# June

## Words of Blessings

### Day 30

*"The Lord bless you and keep you; the Lord make His face to shine on you and be gracious to you; the Lord turn His face toward you and give you peace."*

Numbers 6:24-26

Words are powerful indeed especially when God speaks to us. In the beginning, God spoke and the world came into existence. Jesus, God's only Son, spoke through His life and all that He did including being crucified on a cross, thus giving life to all those who trust in Him. The Bible that contains God's holy Word, continue to speak today by revealing the way to all those who believe and His promise of eternal life. What words will we speak today to bless and challenge others to become followers of the Lord Jesus Christ?

*Father God, You spoke and the world came into existence. Your Son Jesus spoke Father, and all those who listened and are listening to Him, receive forgiveness and remission of their sins. Lord, we ask You to help us that the words we speak today will not only bless others but will also point them to You.*

*Heavenly and merciful Father, we pray that as we come to the end of another day, You will spread Your protective arms over us Your children and keep us safe from all harm and danger. We ask Father that You will continue to bless us and to cause Your face to shine upon us and to grant us Your peace. All these and other mercies we ask in Your name Father. Amen.*

## July

# God Our Great I Am

### Day 1

*.. saying: " We give You thanks, O Lord God Almighty, The One who is and who was and who is to come, Because You have taken Your great power and reigned."*
Revelation 11:17

We acknowledge that Jesus Christ is the same yesterday, today and forever. Before the beginning of time He was and He came in human flesh and lived amongst us and He will return again to claim those whom have remained faithful. The name of Jesus is the most preeminent name in the entire universe. One day every knee will bow to Him and every tongue will confess Him to be Lord. This indeed will bring glory and honor to our Father God in heaven. Jesus Christ is our Lord and Savior and one day He is coming back to reign over all of heaven and earth. So let us get ready to welcome His coming again into our world and into our hearts.

*O Jesus our Lord and Savior, we thank You that before the foundation of the world was established, You were in the world reconciling lost humanity so that we could all find our way back to God. Thank You Jesus that even though You came to Your very own and they rejected You, You made Yourself available to all those who believed that You are truly the Son of God.*

*We thank You Father for Your Son Jesus Christ and for the power of His name. Heavenly Father, we know that when we pray in the name of Jesus, even demons have to take flight and we experience joy and our prayers are answered. Thank You Lord for making a positive difference in our lives and in the lives of all those who have surrendered their lives to You. We give You thanks and praise in the name of Jesus. Amen.*

# July

# Living in God's Presence

## Day 2

*"I know that the LORD secures justice for the poor and upholds the cause of the needy. Surely the righteous will praise your name, and the upright will live in your presence."*

Psalm 140:12-13

Those who heed and live according to God's Word, will one day live in the presence of the Almighty. It is God who rewards us for the good or evil that we have done in this life. The Lord is always concerned about the poor and needy because they are the ones who are often forsaken and forgotten. As people of God, we too should be sensitive to those who are in need and are really experiencing hardships in life. Our response is to seek out those who are in need and provide whatever help we can give to them. That is why we are told that the Lord upholds the cause of the needy and He secures justice for those who are poor. As Christians we are being challenged to do the same even in our daily walk with God.

*Lord help us to rely on You alone and may we always be thankful for your overflowing blessings in our lives. Father we thank You for maintaining every thought we think and every word we speak and everywhere we walk. We thank You Father for those who are righteous and who praise Your name for we know that one day we will live in Your holy presence.*

*Almighty and loving Father God, we ask You to help us to always consider those who are less fortunate than we are. Lord we think about the poor and needy who live among us. Help us Father, never to turn a blind eye on their condition or to pretend that they are only victims of circumstances. We know Lord that there are many who are suffering around us and so we pray that You will enable us to be of help to those who come knocking. It is in Your name we pray. Amen.*

# July

# Ever-Enduring Love

### Day 3

*Give thanks to the God of heaven. His love endures forever.*

Psalm 126:36

No matter how much others may say they love us, there is no love like the love of God our Creator and Maker of heaven and earth. God's love for us is from everlasting to everlasting and it has no conditions attached. We are compelled to love God with all of our souls, minds, and bodies as well as to love others. Giving thanks to God at all times should become an everyday thing and not only when we need God's favor. In the same way God loves us unconditionally, we too must love Him and others as He has called us to do. When we demonstrate our love for God and for others, we are setting the right examples for those who would make a commitment in following our footsteps of which God will be pleased.

*Our Father we thank You that Your plans for us are good and You have a future for us that is full of hope and opportunities. Thank You Lord that You are always restoring our lives to greater dimensions and that You will never let go of us. Lord we thank You that You are our everything. You are indeed our Comforter in times of grief; You are our Provider when we are in need; our Healer when we are sick; our Deliverer in times of trouble and impending danger and our Redeemer who saves us from our sin. Thank You Lord that we can depend on You because Your word is unfailing.*

*Lord God we thank You for loving us the way You do and without condition. Father, no one has ever expressed their love for us as You have done because You love us forever. Grant unto us Father the capacity to love others in the same way You love us and help us never to be afraid to express our love for others. We know Father that to love is the greatest action in the world and if we truly love others the way You love us, then what a difference it would be in the world. Flood our hearts Father with love and help us to share this love with all those around us and beyond. It is in Your wonderful and precious name we pray. Amen.*

## July

# Our Wonder Working Father

### Day 4

*"To him who alone does great wonders. His love endures forever".*

*Psalm 136:4*

    Who can understand the wonders and great mysteries of our Father God? No one really can. The things He does and how He does them to say the least is often mindboggling. Still His love for us will never end. No matter what man's achievement may be in this world, nothing can compare to what God has done and continues to do. When we look around us and see His handiwork, we cannot help but to acknowledge how great and mighty and powerful our God is. He made the heaven and the earth and everything in it and yet nothing falls out of place. Every day when we look around us and observe the beauty of God's creation, it is such an awesome feeling to know that He is in charge of this great universe and despite all that is happening around us, we do not have to be afraid because God is indeed in control.

    *We will praise You O God with our whole heart. Before other gods we will sing praises to You because You are the only true and holy God. We will worship You Lord in Your holy temple and praise Your name for Your lovingkindness and Your truth. Thank You for magnifying Your word above Your name. Thank You Lord that in the day we cried out to You, You answered us and made us bold with strength in our soul. We thank You Father that Your love for us endures for ever and ever.*

    *Father in Heaven, we thank You that we serve a God who is powerful and mighty but yet compassionate, loving and kind to all Your children. Loving Father, we magnify and lift up Your most holy and precious name because Your love for us endures forever. Thank You Father for having invested so much in us to the extent of sacrificing Your only Son to redeem us from our sin. We owe it all to You Father and we ask that You will forgive us for all the wrongs we have done and to cleanse us from all our unrighteousness. This we pray in the name of the Father, the Son and the Holy Spirit. Amen.*

# July

# God's Mindboggling Creation

## Day 5

*"Who by his understanding made the heavens, His love endures forever."*

Psalm 136:5

The earth is the Lord's and everything in it. He is the Creator of heaven and earth and he knows all of us by name. We cannot hide from Him because He is God and He is all-knowing. God through His wisdom created this beautiful world in which we live to declare His glory and to show forth His handiwork. Consider how marvelous His creation is that nothing is there to hold all the celestial bodies in place. Everything just moves around freely in space ever changing but never changed. To say that there is no god is certainly an understatement given the magnificent splendor of this vast universe with all of its unique beauty and mindboggling details. Our God is indeed a great and powerful God and to Him we attribute all our praise and gratitude for having created the heavens and the earth.

*O Lord our Father, help us to set aside a time each day to meet with You alone. Help us to resist and remove everything that would prevent us from doing so. Lord we thank You for making the heaven and the earth but above all we thank You for making us in Your very own image. Thank You Creator God for having made us in Your own likeness and for giving us Your very breath of life. We realize that we are very special and we want to thank You for that.*

*Father God, we know that Your love for us endures forever and ever and it has no limit. Lord we thank You for the immeasurable splendor and beauty of the world in which we live, and move and have our being. No one else Father could have created such a perfect and awesome world with all its intricate and precise details. We thank You Father that even though there are those who do not believe in You or Your creation, that You love them just the same and You send the same blessings on them as well. Thank You Father that Your love for us endures for ever and ever. It is in Your name we pray. Amen*

# July

# Truly Our Lord is Great

## Day 6

*But may all who seek you rejoice and be glad in you; may those who long for your saving help always say, "The Lord is great!"*

Psalm 40:16

The God whom we serve is a great and mighty God. All those who serve Him must rejoice and be glad that we have such a wonderful and loving Father who is always mindful of our needs and never fails in supplying them. The psalmist here is not only concerned about mere prayer for himself but he extends his supplication to cover all those who are faithful to the Almighty. All of us are encouraged not only to focus on our own needs or wants but also on those of others especially the least fortunate ones among us. When we remember others, we are doing God's will and God's will can only be done through those who make themselves available to be used by Him.

*You are worthy O Lord our Father to receive all honor, glory and praise because You are our God and it is You who have made us and given to us the gift of life. We thank You Lord that we are living beings with a brain to think and to make decisions for ourselves. Help us dear Father, never to be presumptuous as to lean on our own understanding but rather in all our ways may we acknowledge You so that You can direct our path.*

*Lord we thank You that amidst all the changes taking place around us, You remain the only constant in our lives. Help us Father, always to remember those who are less fortunate than we are and to extend our hands of love and fellowship to them. We thank You Father that those who seek You can rejoice and be glad in You because of Your goodness and greatness. May we always Father give You honor and praise for all Your continuing blessings and protection upon us and even upon those who do not recognize You as their Lord. Bless all the peoples of the world Father and may You grant them Your peace in Your name and for Your sake we pray. Amen.*

## July

# Sing the Goodness of God

*Day 7*

*I will sing the Lord's praise, for he has been good to me.*
Psalm 13:6

God is good all the time, and all the time God is good and that is a fact. He never fails or disappoints us. He can be trusted and depended on to deliver His promises. That is why He is deserving of our praise and we should at all times recognize Him for all His benefits towards us. When the Lord has shown us kindness and favor as He did for the psalmist, this should provoke us in responding to Him with our gratitude and praise. Whatever situations we might be going through in life, let us remember that in everything we are to give thanks to God because only He alone can take us out of the mire clay and save us. Giving thanks to Almighty God is not optional but something that we must do because of His faithfulness towards us His wayward children.

*Creator God and Sovereign Lord, You who still create and still hold everything together in the palms of Your hands, we praise and thank You for the wonderful diversity and versatility of Your creation. We thank You Lord for the birds of the air; for all plants and animals both on land in the mighty seas and oceans; the sky, and clouds and for the bountiful showers of rain that replenish the earth. Above all Father, we thank You for creating even us to serve You and to give praise and honor to Your name.*

*Lord we thank You for Your promise never to leave us nor to forsake us but to be always there for us. We thank You Father that no matter what trials or tribulations we might be going through, You want us always to trust You to guide us and to protect us. Thank You Father for having been so good to us even when we mess up and turn away from You. We cannot do without You Father and so we ask You to stay beside us always. This we pray in Your Holy and precious name. Amen.*

# July

# A Sacrifice of Adoration

## Day 8

*"Those who sacrifice thank offerings honor me, and to the blameless I will show my salvation."*
Psalm 50:23

The sacrifice that we make to God should come from the heart and not merely out of compulsion or from feeling guilty for the sins we have committed. He is a God who rewards those for being faithful and trustworthy. Thank God that we no longer have to offer animal sacrifice to appease Him for our sins. His Son Jesus Christ became the ultimate sacrifice for us and because of His shed blood on a Cross, our redemption from sin was paid for. Our faith in God pleases Him while our thanksgiving glorifies Him and when we glorify God, it testifies that we are true worshippers of God in spirit and in truth. The sacrifices we make to God must come from our love for Him and when we love Him, it becomes a sweet-smelling fragrance to the Lord our God. Let us always lift up a sacrifice of adoration to our God who is worthy.

*Almighty and Eternal Father, giver of all that is given and maker of all that is made, we know that Your love for us is everlasting and Your care is without ending. You do not change Lord and we thank You for having been the same yesterday, today and forever. Help us dear Father to come into Your presence with a sacrifice of thanksgiving and adoration and may we ever seek to honor and love You all the days of our lives.*

*Loving God, we thank You for securing our salvation through Your Son, Jesus Christ who was sacrificed for our transgression. We confess Father that we have not been deserving of Your love because we have all sinned and fallen short. We thank You for not punishing us as You should do and we thank You so much for Your great expressions of love for us Your sinful children. Grant to us loving Father the ability to praise and adore Your name continually and may we seek to worship You in Spirit and in Truth. This we pray in Your name. Amen.*

# July

## All Praise The Lord

### Day 9

*I will give you thanks in the great assembly; among the throngs I will praise you.*

Psalm 35:18

No one who has ever paid respect and honor to Almighty God has ever been disappointed in the blessings received. God is gracious, kind and plenteous in His mercy and so wherever we may be, it is our duty to express our gratitude to Him. As Christians we should all make a promise to give thanks to God in every situation be it good or bad, God delivers His people from their enemies and those who seek to cause harm and to destroy. Whether the going gets rough or the rough gets going, God is our ever present help in times of trouble and challenges. It is very important that as believers we support one another and gather together as often as possible, as there is great strength in numbers.

Lord God Almighty, it is only sometimes when we are faced with challenges or sickness or some malady, that we choose to seek You because we need Your help. Forgive us Lord where we have taken so much of You for granted and enable us to demonstrate our praise and gratitude to You in everything we do and whatever we may say. You are truly our God and early will we seek You so that we may be spared from Your wrath.

Lord we are ever thankful and grateful to You for entering into our hearts and making us whole. Lord, we are dedicating our lives to live for You because we do not know what the future holds for us but You know. Father God, we thank You for giving us wisdom to discern between right and wrong and we ask You to help us to choose to love, obey and cling to You with our whole body, soul and spirit. This we ask in Your name and for Your sake. Amen.

# July

# Saintly Praise To The Lord

## Day 10

*Sing to the Lord you saints of His; praise His holy name.*
*Psalm 30:4*

    Those whom have served the Lord with all of their heart, soul, mind and body and have kept the faith, they are called His saints. It is indeed a very pleasant thing for God's people to offer sacrifice of praise to Him. When we think of what God has done for us throughout our lives, it is imperative that we devote much of our time in blessing His name with our prayers and praise. God requires us to worship Him both inward and outward because He sees our inner being while those around us look at our outer appearance. Let us not become weary in praising the name of the Lord because as His chosen people, we have an obligation in making the world know that we are His and He is ours.

    Lord we pray that You would reveal to us what work You would have us do if we are not doing what You want us to do. Whatever it is Father that You have called us to do whether now or in the future, give us the strength and courage to do it to the best of our ability. Father, we thank You that in all our labor, there is profit of one kind or another. We know Lord that You will reward us according to Your will and purpose for our lives.

    Today we thank You Lord for the gifts and abilities You have given to us and for the way in which You have been using us to do Your will. Help us dear Lord never to be afraid to witness about You and to tell the world of Your goodness and love for all of humanity. Father God help us to remain steadfast and immovable in our faith and may we always seek to praise and to magnify Your name at all times and in all places. We give You thanks Lord for all those who have served You relentlessly and have been called Your saints. May we learn to walk in their footsteps doing so in the name of the Father, Son and Holy Spirit. Amen..

# July

# Our offering of Thanksgiving

## Day 11

*I will sacrifice a thank offering to You and call on the name of the Lord.*

Psalm 116:17

What can we render to the Lord in return for all His many, continuous blessings on us? We can give to Him our praise and thanksgiving with grateful and contrite hearts. Over and over again we have been encouraged by the Word of God to offer our sacrifices of praise and thanksgiving to Him because God is at the center of everything that we do and without Him we cannot do anything that is worthy of His praise. The sacrifices that we offer are according to the will of God and are pleasing to Him when offered through His Son, Jesus Christ. We are thankful to God for no longer requiring of His people the old way of offering sacrifices to appease Him for sins committed, but now we have a Savior who has paid the price with His life for our sins.

Lord we pray that You would search our hearts today and see if there is any wickedness in us that is preventing us from worshipping and praising You as we ought to. Replace all that is wrong in our lives Father with Your goodness so that we may feel free and unhindered to truly offer our thank offering to You and to call upon Your name. We thank You that You are a holy and righteous God and to You we owe our very lives.

Lord we want to thank You for the opportunity to be of service to others and to use the gifts and talents You have given to us to glorify Your name and to edify others. We thank You Father that when we call upon Your name, You will hear and answer us. Lord we thank You that You are pleased with us when we offer up to You our sacrifices of praise and thanksgiving and so we ask You to help us to be consistent in our worship of You. Forgive us of all our shortcomings Father in the wonderful name of Your Son, Jesus. Amen.

## July

# Witnessing for the Lord

### Day 12

*Therefore I will praise You among the nations O lord; I will sing praises to Your name.*

*Psalm 18:49*

    As God's chosen elect in this world, we should never be afraid or ashamed to let the world know that He is our God and it is He who made us. That's why we must sing praises and give thanks to Him for His love endures forever. In this verse David expressed His adoration for God and vowed to praise Him among the nations. We too must praise God among those with whom we come in contact so that they may know who the true and living God is. Remember before Jesus ascended into heaven, He commissioned believers to go into all the world and proclaim the good news about His death, burial, resurrection and the promise of His return. This is good news and we all should be spreading it especially in these dark and challenging days.

    Father God, You have said in Your Word that You did not call us to uncleanness but in holiness. Father You chose us to be holy and blameless before You. Help us to strive at all times to be holy even as You are holy O God. Enable us dear Father to do what it takes to get rid of everything out of our lives that is not Your best for us. If we are to truly and sincerely praise You and thank You, we must make the effort to live a pure and holy life.

    Lord we thank You that You will keep us pure and holy so that we can fulfill that which You have ordained us to do. Father help us to so live our lives that others will be drawn to You and surrender their lives to You too. Remind us Father of the charge You have given to us to go out into the world and tell the good news about Your Son, Jesus Christ who gave Himself as a ransom by dying on a cruel cross to rescue us from our sins. Lord we know that You have no voice but our voice; no feet but our feet and no tongue but our tongue here on earth, so help us to go and do as You have commanded us to do in the name of the Father, Son and Holy Spirit. Amen.

# July

# A Matter of the Heart

## Day 13

*That my heart may sing to You and not be silent. O Lord my God I will give You thanks forever.*

*Psalm 30:12*

 Let us not fail in our daily walk with God to show Him how much we appreciate all that He does for us by remembering to lift up and praise His name. We just cannot thank God enough for all His blessings and protection for us His erring children. As Christians we cannot remain silent in our praise and worship of God because He is deserving of all our gratitude and thanksgiving. For as long as we shall live, we must give thanks to God for without Him in our lives, we are nothing. It would be a shameful thing, if, after receiving God's mercies, we should forget to praise Him. God would not have our tongues lie idle while we have so many things for which to express our gratitude to Him so let us not fail in doing so as often as we can.

 O Lord You have done great and marvelous things and we will praise You. Father in Heaven, we will extol You and magnify Your name forever. We will sing praises unto You O God and remember Your goodness. Thank You for forgiving our past and for giving new life to us through Jesus Christ. Lord, we thank You for crowning us with Your steadfast love and tender mercies. We promise Father that we will do Your will and bless and praise Your name always.

 Lord we thank You that You have promised to take care of us even as You take care of the sparrow and so day and night we will praise and magnify Your name for all the good things You have done for us. Father, You have blessed us with all spiritual blessings and everything we have in our possession is a trust from You and we want to thank You for truly blessing us the way You do. Lord we owe our very lives to You and we ask You to accept us even as we are and all that we bring to You in the name of Jesus, our Lord and Savior. Amen.

# July

# God's Exceptional Creation

## Day 14

*Let the heavens rejoice, let the earth be glad; let the sea resound, and all that is in it; let the fields be jubilant and all that is in them. Then all the trees of the forest will sing for joy.*

Psalm 96:11-12

Isn't it amazing how God created the heavens and the earth and everything in it and no living thing is excluded from giving thanks to the Creator? Our God is certainly a wonderful and awesome God and that is why it is so important for us to honor Him not only with our lips but from the bottom of our hearts and our total being. Notice the psalmist says that both things in heaven and on the earth must rejoice together in acknowledging the blessing of the Lord upon the earth. This indeed is a testimony that God created the heavens and the earth and therefore He owns everything and we cannot deny this fact no matter how hard we try to disclaim it. Our duty is to ensure that we give Him all the honor and praise that He deserves because He is God and God alone.

*Invisible, infallible, incomprehensible and indescribable Father God, no one else can perform the great and mighty works that You have performed since the creation of the world. Everything in heaven and on the earth that You have made, recognize that You are God and in their own way express their praise and gratitude to You. Dear Father help us not to become weary in thanking and praising You because if we do, we would have failed You.*

*Lord, we thank You that You are an inclusive Father who shows care and concern for all of creation. We thank You that You have no favorites and that You have given to each and every one of us opportunities for making a difference in this world. Even though Father many of us have messed up and have fallen short, You still provide us with a second chance to change our ways and be reconciled to You. Give us the strength Father to try never to fail You again but to remain steadfast and well rooted in our faith. May You see fit Father to bless us in the most precious and holy name of Your Son, Jesus Christ our Lord. Amen.*

# July

# The Lord is our God

## Day 15

*You are my God and I will give You thanks; You are my God and I will exalt You.*

Psalm 118:28

Over and over again the psalmist recognizes that the Lord is His God and that he would do everything to lift up His name. Every day we need to re-enforce our zeal and desire to serve the Lord in ways that express our thanks and gratitude to Him. We cannot thank Him enough for His unconditional love and for the ways in which He cares for us. We must all accept Him as our God and Father and pay our dues in really honoring and demonstrating through our worship of Him how much we love and adore Him. As believers we cannot be afraid to declare to the world who God is by proclaiming the good news about His Son Jesus and how He is able to transform lives. If we fail to declare the Word of God to the world, then we would not be carrying out God's command.

*Almighty God, Creator, Redeemer and Lord of our lives, we thank You that Your love never fails and even in our unfaithfulness and disobedience, You continue Your kindness towards us. We thank You Father for Your strength which sustains us when we are weak; Your patience which bears with us in sin; Your guidance which leads us when we are perplexed and Your comfort which helps us in times of distress.*

*Loving Father, we pray that You would give us the courage and the boldness to take Your Word into every corner of where we live and by extension to every corner of the earth. You have invited us Father to become fishers of men and the only way we can do so is by spreading Your Word. Forgive us for the many wasted opportunities we have thrown away by not using the occasion to testify to others about Your love and forgiveness. Help us Dear Father God to walk in the ways You have commanded us to so that those around us may be influenced by the lives we live and as a result, many would come to accept You too as their Lord. We ask that You will grant us this favor through Your Son, Jesus Christ. Amen.*

# July

## Love Forever

### Day 16

*Give thanks to the Lord for He is good. His love endures forever.*

*Psalm 136:2*

God's love for us is never ending and is new every morning. He loves us in spite of whom or what we are and the sins we have committed and for this we should always express our thanks and gratitude to Him. There is nothing in this whole wide world like the love of God for His children. God loves us so much that He was willing to sacrifice His only Son on a cross so that lost humanity would have a second chance of being saved. No wonder the psalmist keeps on reminding us about our Father's love for us and the need for us to give thanks to Him always. It is good to know that God's love for us is endless and we do not have to worry about Him forgetting His promise that He will never leave us nor forsake us.

O Lord our God, we thank You that Your love for us is unconditional. Thank You Father for loving us no matter what we do, or say, or how we behave. Thank You for always giving us a second chance and for never giving up on us. We know loving Father that we can depend on You at all times for Your blessings which are new every morning. Lord help us to love You as much as You love us even though we know we will fall short in trying to do so.

Today we thank You Lord for Your abundant life that we have through Jesus Christ, Your Son. We thank You Father that there is nothing else in this whole wide world like the love You have for us which is forever. We thank You that we have this great privilege of being called Your children and all the investment You have in us. We just want to praise and magnify Your name Father and to thank You for all Your many blessings You have poured out upon us. Father, it is hard for us to comprehend or even imagine the depth of Your love for us and for this we give You thanks in the precious name of Jesus who made it all possible on our behalf. Amen.

# July

# Love That is Certain

## Day 17

*Give thanks to the Lord of lords. His love endures forever.*

Psalm 136:3

Forever and forever, God's love is ever certain, ever sure. We do not have to fear or worry about anything because the Lord is our Provider and Sustainer and He is in charge of our lives. There is absolutely no God like Jehovah who is Lord of lords and King of kings. He is our great I AM and will ever be so from everlasting to everlasting. We must praise God for His work of creation and His provisions, His deliverance and care of His people, His justice on those who have done wrong and His goodness to us all. Everyday let us count our many blessings, name them one by one and the surprise we will have to know how much we have been blessed.

Lord we thank You that You give wisdom to the wise and knowledge to those who have understanding. Increase our knowledge and wisdom Father so that we may learn how to praise and thank You more. Lord, help us to always seek after godly counsel and not look to the world and ungodly people for answers. Thank You that You will give us the counsel and instruction we need each and every day and thank You that You will show us the path of life to follow.

Father we thank You today for the ability to think and act in accordance with Your will and purpose for our lives. You have been our stronghold Lord throughout the tough and difficult times in our lives and we thank You for the way You have brought us through. We give You thanks Father for Your deliverance and care and for all Your continued goodness towards us. You are indeed worthy of all our praise and gratitude and for all that You do for us Father, we want to give You our thanks in the name of Jesus, Your Son. Amen.

## July

# Love That Never Fails

### Day 18

*Give thanks to the Lord for He is good. His love endures forever.*

Psalm 136:1

Our God is a good and faithful God and He never fails in supplying our every need. His love for us is wide and deep and broad and high. His name is truly to be praised and magnified at all times and in all places. Let us never grow weary in praising the Lord for He has done great and marvelous things throughout all generations. God's goodness, love and mercy will be with us His children even until the end of the ages and therefore we need not fear for He will be with us always. As His children, we should dedicate more of our time tuning in to Him through His Word so that we can have a more intimate and personal relationship with Him.

*Heavenly Father, we thank You that You have promised to deliver us from every evil work and preserve us for Your heavenly kingdom. We know Father that we do not wrestle against flesh and blood, but against principalities, against powers, against the rulers of darkness of this age and against spiritual hosts of wickedness in the heavenly places. We thank You Lord that You have put all of these enemies under Your feet and there is nothing covered that will not be revealed, and hidden that will not be made known.*

*Father we thank You that Your love for us will last forever and ever and that we can depend on You to keep Your promises. Thank You loving Father that Your love, mercy and goodness will be with us throughout this life and in the next. Gracious Lord, we thank You for seeing us through all the confusion in our lives and for guiding us along the right path. We honor and adore Your name Father and we thank You for revealing Yourself to us through Your Son, Jesus Christ our Lord, in whose name we pray. Amen.*

## July

# Rejoice with Joy

### Day 19

*Rejoice in the Lord you who are righteous and praise His holy name.*

*Psalm 97:12*

Let us remember that the Lord's name is a Strong Tower and those who run into it should not only praise His holy name but they also shall be saved from the enemy. Our God is a righteous and holy God and He requires us to become more like Him in our thoughts, words and deeds. We are exhorted to rejoice in the Lord always and come into His holy presence with praise and thanksgiving because it is He who has made us and not we ourselves. There is much to be sad about in life but there is even more to rejoice about. When we think about the goodness of God and all the trials and tribulations He has brought us through coupled with all the spiritual and material blessings He has bestowed upon us, there is indeed more than enough for which to rejoice and be thankful.

*O Righteous and Gracious Father, in the midst of our despair, depression, doubt and distress, help us to cry out to You Lord for You will hear and answer us. We thank You that You are always there to deliver and to save us from all that may beset or befall us. You are our God and early in the morning we will sing songs of praises and thanksgiving to You. Blessed be Your name Lord and to You we give all honor and glory, dominion and power.*

*Father God we thank You for being a holy and righteous God and who desires Your children to walk in Your footsteps and to follow Your precepts. Lord God when we think of Your goodness towards us and having been with us through the good times and the bad times, we just want to give to You all the praise and glory which is due to Your name. Merciful Father You are certainly a very special God and we will always love and serve You for the rest of our lives. Lord we ask You to accept our prayer and let our cry come unto You in the precious name of Your Son we pray. Amen.*

## July

# Beholding God's Glory

## Day 20

*The heavens proclaim His righteousness and all the people see His glory.*
Psalm 97:6

Everything that God has created in heaven and on earth will proclaim His righteousness and His glory will be seen by all nations of the world. Even though there are those who do not believe that God exists, we are happy and confident that one day every knee will bow and every tongue will confess Him to be Lord. We are in the waiting period now and sometimes we become overly anxious about the future and the return of Christ. When the time comes for Jesus' return to claim those who have remained faithful to the Father, it will be a day of rejoicing as the sheep will be separated from the goats and the dead in Christ will rise up and those who are alive will be caught up in the heaven. Let us not ease up our watching but keep on doing what the Lord wants us to do until He comes.

*Eternal God our heavenly Father, You who have seen fit to create us in Your own image, help us this day Lord to bow down and worship You in spirit and in truth. You are a righteous and holy God and one day everyone in heaven and on earth will experience Your glory because You are the only true and living God. We thank You Lord for filling us with Your Holy Spirit when we are empty; for giving us strength when we are helpless and for making us whole when we are broken.*

*Heavenly Father, we thank You that we can run to You for safety and protection and that You are our Sword and Shield to keep us safe from our enemies. Lord we thank You that we are the apple of Your eye and that we are engraved in the palms of Your hands. Help us Dear Father never to fail in singing Your praises and for expressing our love and devotion for You and for Your word. Grant us Your peace which passes all understanding and which only You can give. This we pray in the awesome and marvelous name of Jesus. Amen.*

# July

# One of a Kind

## Day 21

*For You O God are the Most High above all the earth; You are exalted far above all gods.*

Psalm 97:9

There is absolutely no other god like Jehovah. There is none beside Him. Neither is there any Fortress like our God and there is none holy as He is. The heavens and the earth declare that He is God who is exalted above every other god. Only God who is self-sustaining and self-sufficient can boast about anything that He has made or created. We as mere mortal human beings cannot comprehend or understand the mind of God. Isaiah declares in Isaiah 55:9 that as far as the heavens are higher than the earth, so are God's ways higher than our ways and His thoughts than our thoughts. This indeed should cause us to humble ourselves before Him and to call upon His name continually because there is just no one else like our God Jehovah.

Father in heaven, we thank You that there is no other love like Your love for us. Your love does not fade or fall and thank You that Your love is boundless and free. Lord help us to harken to Your voice each and everyday so that we may not roam but become firmly fastened to You. Let us this day learn how to exalt and magnify Your name because You are indeed the most high God above all the earth.

Loving and Adorable Father, we thank You for giving to us Your Son and leaving Your Holy Spirit with us until the work on earth is done. We praise You O Lord because Your ways are perfect and Your Word is true. Father we thank You that You are our shield once we take refuge in You and no one is able to pluck us out from Your mighty and powerful arms. We know Father that once we are fully rooted and grounded in You, no one will be able to pluck us away from You. We ask You Lord that You will continue to build a hedge around us through Your Son, Jesus Christ, our Lord and Savior. Amen.

## July

# Musical Praise

### Day 22

*Make music to the Lord with the harp, with the harp and the sound of singing, with trumpets and the blasts of the ram's horn-shout for joy before the Lord the King.*
Psalm 98: 5-6

We should not limit ourselves as to how we praise and magnify the name of the Lord. Whatever means we can use, God accepts what we offer as long as we do so with a humble and contrite heart. There are those who do not believe in the use of musical instruments during their cooperate worship of God. However, throughout the Bible, we read of the various musical instruments that were used by people of God to bring praise and glory to Almighty God. He has gifted many people with the ability to play musical instruments and all these gifts must be used to make music to the Lord as often as we can. The Lord has also blessed us with our voices to be used as instruments of praise to Him. Therefore let us all use our God given musical abilities to honor our Lord the best ways we can.

*Lord we are grateful to You for who You are in our lives and what You have done for us. Help us never to take for granted the people, the opportunities and the success You have blessed us with. Father, we thank You for what we have and help us not to complain about the things we do not have. Today Lord our hearts are overflowing with praise and thankfulness for all the wonderful blessings You have bestowed on us. We thank You Lord for filling our cups over and over again.*

*Heavenly Father we thank You for all the gifts You have bestowed upon so many to be able to play musical instruments. We thank You too Father for the melodious voices You have given to us to worship You. We ask Dear Father to help us to use all these gifts every day to lift up Your name in praise and thanksgiving because You are worthy Father to receive all of our praise, honor and glory. May we always have words of adoration and praise on our lips ready to make a joyful noise to You. Help us Righteous Father to continually praise You with all of our heart, soul, body and mind through the precious name of Your Son, Jesus. Amen.*

## July

# Jubilant Joyful Singing

### Day 23

*Shout for joy to the Lord all the earth, burst into jubilant song with music.*

Psalm 98:4

Our expression of thanks and praise to God should be one of jubilation and excitement because of all that He has done for us and will continue to do. Sometimes we are too lethargic in our worship of Him especially when things are not going the way we anticipate them to go. People of the world have a way of showing how they appreciate their heroes or idols, but we as followers of Christ do not show the same level of commitment and excitement. The psalmist tells us that we are to shout for joy to the Lord and to burst into jubilant songs with music, but yet we remain silent. God wants us to show to the world through our worship of Him that we are indeed happy people, who love and adore Him and who are not afraid to express our love and affection for Him at all times..

*Father God we want to thank You for Your incredible blessings over our lives. You have done so much for us to elevate us to a level higher than we ever dreamed about. We are just overwhelmed when we think of how much You love us and how little we love You in return. O God our Lord, we truly thank You for being such an awesome and wonderful Father to us and for supplying all our needs.*

*We are determined Lord to praise, adore and glorify Your name for ever and ever. Father, we will do so through all the abilities You have given to us to play musical instruments and to use our voices. We thank You for the gifts and talents with which You have blessed us and we ask You to help us never to stop using them to glorify and to honor Your name. Lord we owe it all to You and so we will ever praise and lift up Your most holy and awesome name in jubilant and joyful singing because You are worthy Father. We bless You Lord through the name of Your precious Son, Jesus. Amen.*

## July

# Rooted and Grounded in God

### Day 24

*Rooted and built up in him, strengthened in the faith as you were taught, and overflowing with thankfulness.*
Colossians 2:7

We who have a sound foundation in the Christian faith must demonstrate without fear or favor our allegiance to Almighty God. By devoting our time and energy in giving Him our praise and gratitude will signal to the world and especially to unbelievers that God is for real. To be rooted and well-grounded in the Lord, we need to study and apply His Word on a daily basis. Too often we fail in our efforts in studying the Word of God as frequently as we can, therefore giving the Devil the opportunity to tempt us to move away from God and to follow his tricks. The Word of God is our guide for living a fulfilled Christian life and the more we dig deeply into His Word the stronger our faith will become and the better it will be for us to resist the Devil.

*Dear Father in heaven, we thank You for giving us the grace we need for today. Father, we thank You for granting to us the power, strength and determination to face whatever hurdles or obstacles that may be in our way, and which we have to overcome. We know Lord that through Your grace and mercy, we will be able to outlast every challenge that we encounter as we try to live our lives in accordance with Your will.*

*Most gracious and loving Father, we thank You for Your Word and for the guidance and encouragement Your Word provides us to live godly and righteous lives pleasing to You. Help us Father to develop a fervent desire to study and apply Your Word to our lives and strengthen our faith in You. We know Father that the more deeply rooted and grounded we become in Your Word, is the better we will be able to resist the constant attacks of the devil to persuade us to move away from You. This we pray in Your name. Amen.*

# July

## Always Give Thanks

### Day 25

*We always thank God, the Father of our Lord Jesus Christ, when we pray for you.*

Colossians 1:3

The Psalmist tells us that in everything we must give God thanks. This means we are always to thank Him for the good times as well as the bad times that we will have in our lives. When we give thanks to God we should do so with an attitude of gratitude. It is He who has made us and the world in which we live, so our thanksgiving to Him must come from a loving and grateful heart. We should not be forced out of guilt to say thanks to God but it must become a part of what we do on a daily basis. God does not have days on which He specially doles out His blessings on us because He does so whether or not we ask Him to, so He expects of us our loyalty and sincerity.

*God of Grace and Father of all goodness, love and mercy, we thank You for every blessing You have given to us despite our many sins. You Lord have been a blessing to us through the good times and the not so good times we have experienced along the way in our lives and we want to thank You for being there for us. Lord we owe our very lives to You because You gave it to us and we ask You to help us never to take it for granted.*

*Father we thank You for all the gifts and talents You have given to us to bless Your name and we promise that we will always commit the time and make the effort to do so constantly. Loving Father we pray that You will enable us to come to You at all times with an attitude of gratitude because You have blessed us with so much. We thank You that Your love for us is boundless and that You always have our best interests at heart. May we always give thanks to You Father for any and everything with which You have blessed us. In the name of Jesus we pray. Amen.*

## July

# A Cupful of Thanks

### Day 26

*Then he took a cup, and when he had given thanks, he gave it to them, saying, "Drink from it, all of you.*

*Matthew 26:27*

Jesus has set us the greatest example of giving thanks to our Father God and He wants us too, to follow in His footsteps and be thankful each and every day for His blessings on us. We should always be ready to express our thanks to Almighty God for everything, for anything and for all things be it great or small, significant or insignificant. When we make known to God how appreciative we are of all His benefits towards us, we are certain He keeps on multiplying them even more. The story of the woman in the Bible who gave all that she had was commended by Jesus Himself for doing something that no one else did that day- giving of all that she had. This challenges us as God's followers to do likewise in not only giving of ourselves to Him but also our resources which are gifts from God and for which we must be thankful.

*Lord Jesus, we thank You for anything, everything and for all things. No matter what our challenges or problems might be Lord, help us to give You thanks for seeing us through. You have promised never to leave us nor forsake us or to give us more than we can cope with and for this we are thankful. Father, we thank You for being a tender, loving, compassionate and forgiving God and we thank You for believing in us. May we learn always to put You first and foremost in everything we do and help us to consistently show our gratitude to You for all Your many blessings.*

*Today Loving Father, we praise You and glorify Your name and we thank You that in the midst of our confusion and distress, You rescued us and delivered us from the evil one. Help us Dear Father to become more like Jesus in using all the opportunities we have to praise Your name and to give You thanks always. Thank You Father for giving to us Jesus and for the difference He has made in our lives. This we pray in the name of the Father, the Son and the Holy Spirit. Amen.*

# July
# Children Are Precious
## Day 27

*At that time Jesus said, "I praise you, Father, Lord of heaven and earth, because you have hidden these things from the wise and learned, and revealed them to little children.*
Matthew 11:25

Let us thank God for His Son Jesus who was obedient to His heavenly Father and showed His reverence and respect by praising Him for all the marvelous things He did and continues to do. We can learn so much from the life of Jesus and all the examples He has left us on how to be better people. Even though Jesus was and is the Son of God, He never took anything for granted with His Father. Over and over again, we see Jesus being constantly in prayer with His Heavenly Father because He knew that was the only way He could connect with His Father in heaven. We too need to become more like Jesus in constantly and persistently keeping in touch with Him through our consistent prayers. If God's Son Jesus spent so much of His time praying to His Father, how much more should we be doing so as well? We need to adopt a more childlike attitude in order to understand and appreciate the things of God.

*Father God we thank You for the life and witness of Your Son Jesus Christ. Thank You Lord for the life He lived on earth and the life He continues to live with You in the highest heaven. Thank You Father God that Jesus has been the same yesterday, today and forever and that He will never change. We know Lord if we follow Him, we shall never go astray or disappear from His holy presence. Lord we thank You that through the shed blood of Jesus all our sins have been washed away.*

*Father God, we pray that You will help us to develop a consistent prayer life that is in keeping with Your will and purpose for us. Thank You for the life of Your Son Jesus who has left us so many great examples of how we are to discipline ourselves in praying to You. We ask You to forgive us for the times when we abandoned our prayer life because of being too busy only to find ourselves straying further and further away from You. We thank You Father for having rescued us time and time again in bringing us back home to You. Lord, help us to develop a more childlike attitude so that we will not be afraid to truly worship and praise You as we ought to. This we pray in Your name. Amen.*

**July**

# God Hears Us When We Seek Him

## *Day 28*

*So they took away the stone. Then Jesus looked up and said, "Father, I thank you that you have heard me.*
John 11:41

Our Father God is always near us hearing everything we say and listening to our petitions. He knows our thoughts, actions and deeds and He knows everything about us. It is so important for us to keep in touch with God all the days of our lives as He is the only one who can really respond to our cries for help. Jesus acknowledged this when He said, "Father I thank You that You have heard me." We too can echo these words because we know that God has heard and responded to us over and over again. Sometimes we fail to act on our faith and so doubts often arise in our hearts as to whether or not God is really hearing us. We know that when we ask of God that we have to believe Him and trust Him and wait on Him to fulfill His promise. It is amazing how God works in mysterious ways and when we least expect it, He delivers on time.

*All-knowing, All-powerful, Almighty and Awesome Father, we thank You that in our distress when we called upon You and cried out to You, You heard our voices and You answered us. Lord if it had not been for You, we would not have been what we are today. We thank You Lord for bringing us out of darkness into Your marvelous light and for filling our hearts with happiness and peace. We rejoice in Your name today Father as we thank You for preserving our souls from all that is evil.*

*Father in heaven, we thank You for Your great faithfulness which is new every morning of our lives. We believe that You will fulfill all Your promises to us in Your Word and that You will never let us down. We thank You for all the blessed examples Your Son Jesus has left us on how to live a dedicated and committed prayer life. Grant us Father Your grace to remain faithful and steadfast in our faith and to always express our gratitude to You. This we ask in Your loving and precious name. Amen.*

# July

# Ever Always Thankful

## Day 29

*Jesus then took the loaves, gave thanks, and distributed to those who were seated as much as they wanted. He did the same with the fish.*

John 6:11

God works in mysterious ways His wonders to perform. Our God is a miracle working God and with whom nothing is impossible. Jesus has demonstrated time and time again in His life on earth how important it is to give thanks to God for all things. There was never a moment lost when Jesus did not find the time to give His Father in heaven thanks for something. He lived a life of praise and thanksgiving and never failed once in doing so. As Christians and as followers of Christ, we too are challenged to follow in His footsteps and make it our duty to be thankful to God at all times.

*Father we know that nothing is impossible when we put our trust in You. Thank You Lord that we do not have to be afraid of bad news because our hearts are steadfast, trusting in You. Lord we thank You for delivering our souls from death, our eyes from tears and our feet from falling. Thank You that we walk before You with hope in our hearts and life in our bodies. We thank You Father that we shall not die but live and declare Your works to all people. Father we thank You for all things knowing that You reign in the midst of everything You have created.*

*We beseech You Father to help us to commit our lives fully and totally to You knowing that You are our help in times of trouble and our Deliverer from the evil one. May we remain Father constantly connected to You in prayer and grant to us the strength and courage to resist the temptations that come upon us in subtle ways. Help us Lord to always be on our guard and to trust You to take care of any circumstance that may pose a challenge to us in our walk with You. Thank You Father for Your miraculous power demonstrated by Jesus and for giving Jesus to us as our Bread of life. This we pray Lord in Your name. Amen.*

## July

# All in Worship of God
## Day 30

*Whenever the living creatures give glory, honor and thanks to him who sits on the throne and who lives for ever and ever, the twenty-four elders fall down before him who sits on the throne and worship him who lives for ever and ever.*
Revelation 4:9-10

The day is coming when every creature God has created will once again give praise and thanks to Him and bow down and worship Him as we ought to. Our only hope in this life is God who is the beginning and end of our faith. Let us thank God that He sits on a throne that declares His supremacy over all the earth. Although there are those who do not believe in God, it does not change the fact that one day all those who believe that He does exist, will come face to face with Him to stand before His judgment seat. There we will all have to give an account of our stewardship while on earth and then He will usher those who have remained faithful to Him into His kingdom. We should be excited as John was to know that one day we all will bow down to our God to worship Him forever and ever.

*Everlasting God, Creator and Source of everything that was and now is, we give You thanks Lord for having created all things including us Your children. Father we know it is our duty to sing praises to You and to give You thanks for all the blessings You have showered down on us. At times Father, we have been negligent in really praising and thanking You as we ought to and we ask that You forgive us for our negligence. We promise You Father that we will always endeavor to spend time thanking You for Your goodness, kindness, love and mercy that You so freely and willingly lavish on us.*

*Today Lord we want to thank You for the joy we feel when we communicate with You in those quiet moments of our lives. Father, teach us to act on what we do know about You and Your love for us and to trust You in faith what we do not know about You. Lord help us to become excited about Your second coming and to prepare ourselves for that great and glorious day. We can only imagine Father what a day of rejoicing that will be when we hear our names being called to enter into that place You have gone to prepare for us. Lord hear our prayer and let our cry come unto You. Amen.*

# July

# Thanks for God's Reign

## Day 31

*"We give thanks to you, Lord God Almighty, the One who is and who was, because you have taken your great power and have begun to reign."*

Revelation 11:17

    It is God and God alone who should reign in our lives and He is the only one to whom we should give our allegiance. When we fail to praise and honor God we are doing Him a dis-service and instead elevating the devil. We, who believe in God, know the right of our Lord and Savior to rule over the whole world and this we need to celebrate. John gives us a taste of what is to come when Jesus returns to claim all those who have remained faithful to Him throughout their lives on earth. Unfortunately, not everyone will have this opportunity on His return because they chose not to acknowledge and accept Him as their Lord. We need to remain vigilant and steadfast in our faith even as we await the second coming of Jesus.

    *To You our Father God be praise, glory, dominion and power for ever and ever. We extol and magnify Your name O God because You are worthy of all our praise, all our gratitude and all of our thanksgiving. We realize Lord that without You we are nothing and we cannot do anything of value, but thanks to You that through Your Son, Jesus Christ, our Lord and Savior, we can do all things. May we this day offer to You our sacrifice of praise and thanksgiving even as we thank You for the serenity and peace that You give to our souls.*

    *Holy and Righteous Father, no one can ever understand Your unconditional love for us. You chose Father to take Your only Son and You offered Him as a living sacrifice for the remission of our sins. We were the ones who sinned against You Father and yet You took it upon Yourself to give us a second chance by offering Jesus to pay the price that we should have paid. We thank You Lord for having been so good to us and for showing us how to truly express our love for others. We ask You Father to continue to bless and protect us in the name of Your Son, Jesus we pray. Amen.*

# August

# Glory, Wisdom and Honor Belong to God

## Day 1

*"Amen! Praise and glory and wisdom and thanks and honor and power and strength be to our God for ever and ever. Amen!"*

Revelation 7:12

Every day gives us a new chance to praise, adore, magnify and lift up the name of our most high God. We can never thank Him too much because of all that He does for us constantly and unconditionally. Why is it so important for us to focus so much on giving God thanks? Well, when we think of all the wonderful and awesome things God has given to us as well as the many other blessings we receive from Him, then we have no choice but to render to Him our profound thanks and gratitude to Him to show Him that He is really appreciated for all that He does for us on a daily basis. Certainly without His care, provision and protection, our lives would never be the same.

*O Lord our God, we give You thanks for the good things we have known through Your bounty and mercy. We thank You Lord for seedtime and harvest and for all the richness of the world that gives us food and drink and means of being warm and being clothed. Lord we thank You for the opportunity to work and the time to rest and we thank You for the fellowship we share with others.*

*Help us this day Father to thank You for this our land of soft fresh breezes and for all the bountiful blessings You keep on heaping upon us. We realize Father that without Your care, protection and provision, our lives would never be where we find ourselves today. To You Father we attribute all honor, glory, power, praise and strength to Your name. We will always seek to worship and adore You Father because You deserve all of our gratitude. This we pray in Your name and for Your sake. Amen.*

# August

# Sweet Aroma of the Gospel

## Day 2

*But thanks be to God, who always leads us as captives in Christ's triumphal procession and uses us to spread the aroma of the knowledge of him everywhere.*

2 Corinthians 2:14

We are God's instruments to be used in spreading the good news of Jesus Christ to all around us. Let us not fail in our endeavors to go out to the lost and all those who are wandering like sheep without a shepherd and introduce Jesus, the Good Shepherd to them. There is no excuse for us not to be engaged in spreading the gospel to everyone who will listen, We are blessed that God has given us the resources to equip ourselves to study His Word and be able to impart it to others. Without us doing so, the Word of God will not be able to reach the masses who are so desperately in need of hearing the gospel. Let us as much as is humanly possible, arm ourselves with the Word of God and literally go out into the highways and byways to witness to all those who are yearning to hear the sweet aroma of God's Word beginning right where we live.

*O God our Creator, Redeemer and Friend, we give You thanks for the beauty and splendor of this day and for all of creation. Help us Father that we will ever seek to share the good news of salvation to all those with whom we come in contact. Lord we thank You for giving to us the boldness and the courage to tell to others all the excellent and marvelous things You have done for us and the many miracles You have performed in our lives*

*Father, we thank You for having called us to do Your will. We pray Father that You will so equip us to be able to spread Your gospel to the whole world beginning where we live. Too often Father we are reluctant to tell others of the good news about Jesus Christ and His ability to change and transform lives. May You challenge us Lord to become more determined to study Your Word so that we will be better prepared to share it with others. This we pray in Your holy and precious name. Amen.*

## August

# In Awe of God

### Day 3

*And the twenty four elders who were seated on their thrones before God, fell on their faces and worshipped God.*  Revelation 11:16

No matter what is our status, creed, position, nationality, race or color in this life, we must all give thanks and praise to Almighty God and worship Him in spirit and in truth. We believe that if our world is going to be a much better place in which to live, we all must fall on our faces as the elders did in this passage and worship the true and living God. There are just too many evil things going on all around us and so the more we focus on the negatives, the more difficult it is for us to see the good and positive things as well. Unfortunately, even those of us who name the name of Jesus are also caught up in the same things the people of the world are doing and so it makes our testimony ineffective and leaves doubts in the minds of those we are trying to witness to. We all should make the efforts to live as the Lord would want us to, so that our lives can shine for others to see.

O Loving Father God, Maker and Creator of this day, we pray that You would lift up our hearts that we may rejoice and be glad in You our Lord. Father we thank You for the shining sun and cloudless sky that we experience every day. We thank You for the flowering plants and fruit producing trees which we sometimes take for granted. Father we thank You for the exuberance of life and for all the laughter and beauty that make our lives so full and complete.

Lord we are grateful to You that there is no way in which we can fall outside of Your concern for us. We thank You Father that You are always aware of the dangers we face each and every day and we know that we can depend on You to protect and keep us safe. Lord help us to be shining lights in a world where darkness has permeated every corner of the earth and where many have turned away from You. Give us the grace Lord to remain steadfast in our faith even as we worship You in awe and adoration. Hear our prayer Lord and let our cry come unto You. Amen.

## August

# Praise From All Corners

### Day 4

*All the angels were standing around the throne and around the elders and the four living creatures. They fell down on their faces and worshipped God.*
                                                      Revelation 7:11

The Lord has made this and every other day so it is important for us to fall prostrate before Him and worship Him with our hymns and songs of praise and thanksgiving. This song of the angels, elders and the four living creatures show the reverence we should all have in God's holy presence. One day may be very soon all things in heaven and on earth shall at last join in the hymn of universal praise to God in Jesus Christ. His second coming is near at hand based on all the things happening in the world today and so we need to be preparing for that sweet day when Jesus returns to claim His very own. His return may seem long in coming but He will be coming back to fulfill all His promises. Let us continue praising Him from all corners of the earth.

*Most Gracious and Loving Father, we seek nothing else this day but to honor You and to give to You all our praise and thanksgiving for Your love and tender mercies of which we are most undeserving. Thank You Lord for assuring us of our infinite worth because we know that one day we will return to the earth from which we came and then we will be resurrected to begin a new life in Christ Jesus our Lord and Savior. Lord thank You that Jesus is the resurrection and the life and because He lives, we too shall live.*

*Father God, we ask for favor with You and with all those with whom we come in contact. Help us always Lord to obey Your commands and to be truthful and kind from deep within our hearts so that we can be at peace with both You and our fellowmen. Father we ask You to help us to prepare ourselves for the soon coming return of Your Son, Jesus our Lord and Savior. Time might seem to be so long Father for His return but we know that one day He is coming back again. As You draw us together Father from all the four corners of the world, may we all in one voice sing our praises to You in the name of Jesus our soon coming King. Amen.*

# August

# Grateful To Be Considered Faithful

## Day 5

*I thank Christ Jesus our Lord who has given me strength that He considered me faithful appointing me to His service.*

1 Timothy 1:12

Those whom God has called in His service must remain faithful to Him. There will be times when we feel like throwing in the towel but God is faithful in keeping His promises and so we should not give up but remain steadfast in our faith even to the end. Every opportunity we have of showing our appreciation to God through praise and thanksgiving we should consistently and persistently do so. Let us remember that many are called to follow Him but only a few are chosen to carry out His will. If we have been called by God to do a task, He will equip us to perform that task to the best of our ability. All we need to do is to make ourselves available for His service and He will honor His faithfulness to us.

Lord we thank You that it is not too late to accomplish everything You have placed in our hearts to do. Thank You for the window of opportunity we have each and every day to make a difference. Father, we thank You for preparing us to reach out in faith and take hold of that which You have entrusted to our care. This is our time and our moment Lord and we thank You for what You will enable us to accomplish in Your name.

Lord, help us to overcome our fears and inhibitions about sharing our faith with others. Father there is no greater gift than to tell others about Your love and the good news of salvation which they can receive through Jesus Christ. Give us we pray Father a perfect sense of Your timing and the right words to say to those we witness to. Lord, may people see Your love in us even as we express that love through our own lives. It is in Your name we pray Father. Amen.

## August

# God Created All Things Good

### Day 6

*For everything God created is good and nothing is to be rejected if it is received with thanksgiving.*
1 Timothy 4:4

Every good and perfect gift comes from God who gives to all liberally. We are never to take anything for granted but we should seek at all times to give thanks and praises to our God for everything and all things that He has created. Sometimes we fail to use the gifts God has given to us wisely, and often times we waste many opportunities to glorify God and lift up others with our gifts and talents. Let us not be like the servant who received the one coin to invest but instead of investing he hid it and it became unprofitable. God wants us to invest our gifts in serving others so that our returns will be manifold. Everything God has created, He has done so with the intention of being known and recognized as a good and perfect God.

Father God in heaven, we thank You for the plans You have for our lives. We thank You Lord for directing every step we take and even though we do not know where each step leads us, we can trust You with our lives. Thank You Father for working out every detail of our lives to our advantage and we thank You for the perfect timing in making all things well with us. Lord, we thank You that as long as we put our faith and trust in You everything will be all right.

Dear Father, we pray you would bless our work and use the gifts You have given to us to honor You and to bless others. Father we commit all that we do to You so that it may be used to glorify You. Give us the strength we pray Father, each day to accomplish what we set out to do and the ability and wisdom to do it to the best of our ability. Lord, we recognize and accept and appreciate that everything that You have made is good and You have given to us to use wisely. We ask You Lord to help us to take care of that which You have entrusted to us in the name of Jesus Christ, Your Son. Amen.

# August

# None Excluded

## Day 7

*I urge then first of all that requests, prayers, intercession and thanksgiving be made for everyone.*
1 Timothy 2:1

We should count it all joy to intercede on behalf of others because we are called to be our brother's keeper. God wants us to be caring, loving and compassionate people even as He is and this means that we must always look out for the good of others. In today's fast paced world, we become too preoccupied with our own challenges and issues and often times forget that there are those who are worse off than we are. As Christians we ought to be concerned about and sensitive to the needs of others as well as our own. In our prayers, we should lift up others before the throne of grace seeking God's blessings and forgiveness for all.

*Most Holy and Righteous Father, thou who art high and exalted above the heavens, we thank You for allowing all our dreams and aspirations to be fulfilled. Lord we thank You for not allowing people, or disappointments or adversities from preventing us achieving our goals in life. Thank You Father that You have a solution for every problem we will ever encounter along the way and we thank You for sending the right people in our lives. Today Lord we want to thank You for helping us to fulfill that which You have called us to in Christ Jesus.*

*Heavenly Father, we pray that You will grant us success in all that we do and continue to guide us on the right path. Forgive us for the times when we only thought about our own needs and wants instead of thinking about others. We ask You to help us Father to lift up others in prayers and to take their needs to You as well. In Your mercy we ask You to look favorable upon us and grant us Your peace in the wonderful and precious name of Your Son, Jesus our Lord and Savior. Amen.*

# August

# What's Your Message?

## Day 8

*Let the message of Christ dwell among you richly as you teach and admonish one another with all wisdom through psalms, hymns, and songs from the Spirit, singing to God with gratitude in your hearts.*
Colossians 3:16

    As brothers and sisters in Christ, we should bear up one another at all times and not only focus on ourselves. Remember that no man is an island and no man stands alone. We need each other for love, support and to build relationship. There are so many people in life who are hurting and they need to be comforted. God has blessed us tremendously with the ability to offer encouragement and support to all those who need it, Many people are afraid to seek help because of their pride so we need to be sensitive how we respond to their needs. We should never assume that because someone may not express his or her feelings that everything is alright. We really never know what people are going through until they share their stories and that is why we need to bear up one another always in our prayers. Let our message to others be one of love and encouragement.

    Father in heaven, we know that it is a good thing to give thanks to You, to sing praises to Your name and to declare Your steadfast love for us in the morning and Your faithfulness by night. Lord please open thou our lips so that our mouths can sing Your praises. Dear Lord, help us to be of assistance to others by encouraging them and giving a helping hand when needed. We know Lord that You desire of us to pray for others, to love others and to go the extra mile. Lord we thank You for always creating opportunities for us to be a blessing to others.

    Father we are aware of many people who are suffering and who are going through difficult and challenging situations in their lives and in their families. May You help them Father to work out these difficulties and challenges with Your help and we pray that we might find ways to help ease their burdens. Father we know how sensitive people can be so teach us how we should approach them so as not to cause them to feel embarrassed in anyway whatsoever. May our message to them Father be one of compassion, love and mercy and help us that everything we do to be of help to others, to do so in the name of Jesus. Amen.

# August

# Living the Peace of Christ

## Day 9

*Let the peace of Christ rule in your hearts, since as members of one body you were called to peace. And be thankful.*

Colossians 3:15

The one thing the world yearns for is to have lasting peace. That peace can only come through Jesus when we allow Him to reign in our hearts. Jesus came to the world as the Prince of Peace and until He returns, there can be no lasting peace on earth. Despite all the efforts mankind is making towards achieving universal world peace that will not be until Christ comes again and establish His new kingdom. In the meantime, we should all strive to be at peace with ourselves and with others. Jesus Himself said, "My peace I leave with you, my peace I give to you. Not as the world gives but as I give." May we always seek to live in the peace of Christ.

*Almighty and everlasting God, we thank You for sending Your Son Jesus Christ into the world to bring peace which passes all understanding. Father we know that the peace we seek in the world is elusive because the world cannot offer us the peace that You give. You have said in Your word Lord that Your peace You give to us, Your peace You leave with us and it is not the peace that the world gives. Thank You Lord that Your peace is from everlasting to everlasting.*

*Lord help us this day to stand in complete honesty before You to acknowledge that we have all sinned and fallen short. We have not loved others as we ought to Father and as such we cannot find true peace within us. We ask You Lord to give us the peace which passes all understanding and which only You can give. Thank You Father that one day Jesus will return and fill our world with peace that we are longing for. This we pray in Your name. Amen.*

# August

# Watch and Pray Thankfully

## Day 10

*Devote yourselves to prayer being watchful and thankful.*

*Colossians 4:2*

    The key to obtaining God's goodness and mercy is through a faithful and committed prayer life. Praying daily should be the hallmark of every Christian's life and we should not allow anything or anyone from preventing us from so doing. When we devote ourselves daily to prayer, the devil will not be able to have a foothold on our lives and try to persuade us to move away from the One we serve. Praying daily keeps us in tune with our Father and helps us to become stronger and wiser in our faith. With God's continued guidance and protection, we can withstand the fiery darts of the devil or anything he may throw at us.

    *Father God, Sustainer, Provider, Creator and Friend, we give You thanks for the wonderful gift of life with all its joys and opportunities as well as its challenges and failures. From the very depth of our hearts Lord, we thank You that Your love for us never fails and even in our faithlessness and disobedience, You continue Your kindness towards us. Lord we thank You for Your strength which sustains us when we are weak; for Your patience which bears with us in sin and for Your guidance and comfort which helps us in our distress. We pray this day Father that You will help us to be a blessing to others even as You have been a blessing to us.*

    *Father we thank You for the peace You give to all those who seek You and call upon Your name. We ask You Father to give us the zeal and burning desire to live a devoted and purposeful daily prayer life. Help us Father to keep in tune with You each and every day so that we can remain connected to You always. Do not allow the devil to enter in and steal us away from You but please hold on to us tightly and do not let us go. Give us the discipline Father to be steadfast and resolute in our prayer life. This we pray in the name of Jesus. Amen.*

# August

# Faithful Perseverance

## Day 11

*First, I thank my God through Jesus Christ for all of you, because your faith is being reported all over the world.*
Romans 1:8

Faithfulness to God does pay huge dividend. Through our steadfast faith and trust in God, others are blessed and encouraged to live a life acceptable to God. When the world is lamenting and crying about what is going on, as Christians we remain firmly grounded in our faith and trusting the Lord to take us through all situations. It is our faith that we have to rely on in these troubled and troublesome days when evil seems to be good and good evil. It is very depressing to see how many Christians are turning a blind eye to corruption in high places and celebrating wrong doing. We who are followers of Christ must stand against all that is evil and live out our faith for the world to see.

*O Holy Father, we praise You for Your love, forgiveness and grace in Your Son Jesus Christ; for the abiding presence of Your Holy Spirit and for the fellowship we have with You and with others. Lord we thank You that if we remain faithful to You, You will continue to bless and prosper us in everything we do. Thank You Lord for the assurance You give to us of eternal life through Your precious Son Jesus Christ. Lord we thank You that we do not have to be afraid of anything or anyone because You have promised never to leave us nor forsake us.*

*Heavenly Father we pray that You will help us never to become deceivers who try to live double standard lives. We cannot say Father that we love You but cannot stand up for the truth and what is right and pleasing in Your sight. We know Father that the world is looking on us and the lives we live and the honesty and integrity with which we represent You. We confess Father that many times we have sacrificed exercising our faith in You because we are afraid what others will say for taking a stand against injustice. We ask You to forgive us Father in the name of Your wonderful Son, Jesus our Savior and Lord. Amen*

## August

# Our Sinful Nature

### Day 12

*Thanks be to God, who delivers me through Jesus Christ our Lord! So then, I myself in my mind am a slave to God's law, but in my sinful nature a slave to the law of sin.*
Romans 7:5

It is God and God alone who can deliver us from any adversity through His Son Jesus Christ. Like Paul we all have a sinful nature and therefore can become slaves to the law of sin. Thank God that we can find forgiveness and deliverance through the blood of Jesus. Nothing can wash away our sins but the shed blood of Jesus who paid the price on a cross so that all those who believe in Him will not perish but have everlasting life. Without the blood of Jesus, we cannot be delivered from our sinful nature and so we all need to be cleansed of our sins so that we can spend eternity with Him.

Father God we thank You that we can be delivered from the bondage of sin through the precious blood of Your Son Jesus Christ. We know Lord that we try but our sinful nature keeps us from truly worshipping You as we ought to. We thank You for the provision You have made for us to be forgiven and to live a new life in Christ. Lord, thank You for having been so good to us and for Your pardon and remission of our sin.

We thank You Father for delivering us from all that would prevent us from truly surrendering our lives to You. So often Lord, we have allowed our pride and the things of this world to prevent us from worshipping You as we should and instead we have allowed the devil to occupy that space. Forgive us Father for falling short and help us to mend our ways by renouncing those things that are interfering with our relationship with You and give You our wholehearted attention. We surrender our all to You Father in the name of Jesus we pray. Amen.

# August

# Instruments of God's Righteousness

## Day 13

*Do not offer any part of yourself to sin as an instrument of wickedness, but rather offer yourselves to God as those who have been brought from death to life; and offer every part of yourself to him as an instrument of righteousness.*

Romans 6:13

God wants us to offer ourselves as instruments of peace, right living and a holy sacrifice to Him. We should always try to do what is right and pleasing to Him and not resort to doing those things that are against His will for our lives. We must remember that our lives are not our own as we belong to God and so whatever we do, we must do so according to His will and purpose. Let us not allow anything to prevent us from worshipping our Father as we should or from walking in His footsteps. May we always seek to offer ourselves to God as His instrument of right living.

*Lord God, Loving and Everlasting Father, we thank You for giving us the opportunity to offer ourselves as living sacrifices to You which is holy and acceptable in Your sight. We know Lord that we are sinners saved only by Your grace and delivered from the bondage of the Law through the efficacious blood of Your Son Jesus Christ. We thank You Father for delivering us from death to life so that we can live with You forever and ever.*

*Lord help us to keep away from the evils of this world and stay focused on You. It is so easy for us Father to stray far from You when we become exposed to the things of this world. Help us Lord to shun evil and to offer up ourselves to You as holy and living sacrifices to be used by You to do whatever You may desire us to do. We thank You Father for always working on us and for molding and shaping our lives as You see fit in the name of Your Son, Jesus our Lord and Savior. Amen.*

## August

# Fully Accepted By God

*Day 14*

*Whoever regards one day as special does so to the Lord. Whoever eats meat does so to the Lord, for they give thanks to God; and whoever abstains does so to the Lord and gives thanks to God.*

Romans 14:6

The Lord accepts us for whom and whatever we are. He gives us choices and does not place a limit on us as long as what we do is pleasing to Him and we do so with a grateful heart. Paul in this passage of Scripture is pointing out something that we need to take heed of. At no time should we try to impose our beliefs on others or judge them by our standards. We must always welcome others who may share a different opinion from ours and respect their own personal beliefs. We should recognize that God is our ultimate judge so it is not for us to be judgmental of others.

*Forgiving, Forgetting, Forgivable Father God, we thank You that You do not place any restrictions on our lives but rather You have given us the ability to think and to act in accordance with Your will and purpose. Whatever we may do, think or say as long as we do so to glorify and magnify Your name, You will accept our praise and our gratitude to You. Lord we thank You for determining our future and all we have to do is to just follow Your leading.*

*Father, help us never to become too judgmental of others based upon what they eat, or how and when they worship You or what they may abstain from eating or doing. Lord, You made us to serve and worship You and it is You who controls our very being. Forgive us for the times when we have belittled others because of their faith or religious affiliation or their form of worship, We are sorry Lord for our actions and we seek Your forgiveness in the name of Jesus we pray. Amen.*

# August

# Following Our Own Desires

## Day 15

*For although they knew God, they neither glorified him as God nor gave thanks to him, but their thinking became futile and their foolish hearts were darkened.*

Romans 1:21

It is so easy for us to fall into sin and to turn away from God when we follow the evil desires of our hearts and fail to seek God's favor. We should always glorify and magnify the name of the Lord as true followers of Him. We cannot say that we are followers of Christ and yet not give Him all the praise and glory due to His name. Consider how much time we spend on doing other things that are so temporary but yet fail in giving to God what is rightfully His. We know enough about our Father God that thanks and praise are due to Him yet we reluctantly offer these to Him. Out of the abundance of our hearts, we should and must acknowledge the only true and wise God who is indeed the Creator of all things.

*Magnificent, Marvelous, Merciful and Mighty Lord and Father, we thank You for being such an awesome, adoring and accessible God who is always available to supply all our needs. Father we know that we do not always do the things that are pleasing in Your sight and we thank You for not punishing us as we so rightly deserve. We pray Lord that You will help us not to become too complacent or to take anything for granted, but enable us each day to give You thanks for all Your blessings and mercies which are new every morning.*

*Forgive us Lord for the many times we have failed to acknowledge You as our Lord and Savior and to thank You for all that You do for us. Forgive us Father for turning away from You and embracing the things of this evil world. We truly repent Father for all the wrongs we have done and for not honoring You the way we should. Give us another chance Lord to remedy our foolish ways and to glorify Your name and none other. This we ask in the loving and precious name of Your Son, Jesus. Amen.*

## August

# Sound Teaching

*Day 16*

*But thanks be to God that, though you used to be slaves to sin, you have come to obey from your heart the pattern of teaching that has now claimed your allegiance.*

Romans 6:17

To know God is to know the truth and to know the truth is to know His Son, Jesus Christ who is the way, the truth and the life. Let us give God thanks for delivering us from the slavery of sin through His Son. Paul alludes to the fact in this verse that we have all been slaves to sin but through the grace of God we are no longer slaves to sin but slaves to obedience or slaves to righteousness. Through the shed blood of Jesus Christ, we have been redeemed and set free to live according to the will of God. When we become a slave to anything, it robs us of our relationship with God because we are not focusing on Him but that thing which now occupies our mind. Our allegiance should always be to God first and foremost and everything else must be secondary.

*Living and Loving Heavenly Father, thank You for freeing us from the bondage and slavery of sin and for making us obedient to Your word which has brought about transformation in our lives. Lord thank You for Your Word which is life and which is sharper and more powerful than any two-edged sword piercing our very innermost being. Father we pray that You will enable us to abide in Your Word so that we might not sin against You.*

*Thank You Lord that You sent Your only Son Jesus Christ into the world to redeem lost humanity from their sin. Because of this great sacrifice You made Lord for us, we have a chance of receiving forgiveness and the hope of being with You one day in Paradise. Lord You are our only hope and we put our faith and trust in You. We thank You Father that though we keep on sinning, we have the opportunity of being redeemed if we but confess our sins to You our Heavenly Father. Grant us this day Your forgiveness Lord in the name of the Father, the Son and the Holy Spirit. Amen.*

## August

# Appointed To God's Service

*Day 17*

*I thank Christ Jesus our Lord, who has given me strength that He considered me faithful, appointing me to His service.*

*1 Timothy 1:12*

When we remain faithful to God in all that we do, He will prepare us and use us to carry out His will and purpose. We should always make ourselves available for service to the Lord as it is the Lord who gives us the strength and the will to carry on. We thank the Lord for His constant blessings and His outpouring mercies upon us despite our waywardness. All that we do for the Lord on this earth He will reward us one day. Let us not get tired in doing good for others as this is the will of God for us to love others even as we love ourselves.

Purposeful, Patient and Plenteous in Mercy Father God, we come before You this day with a grateful and thankful heart and words of adoration and praise for all the wonderful and amazing blessings with which You have blessed us. Lord we thank You for choosing us to be involved in Your service to humanity and for the way in which You are using us to reach out to others. Our hearts are glad and our spirit rejoices in You our Lord and our God.

Father, help us to always make ourselves available in serving You and others. Thank You for the calling You have placed on our lives to love others and to show care and concern for their welfare. O Lord, there is so much to be done and sometimes we feel so inadequate and unprepared. We thank You for giving us the strength and courage to keep keeping on and for enabling us to be of help to others. We ask You Father to strengthen our faith even as we do that which You have called us to do in the name of Jesus, Your Son we pray. Amen.

## August

# Gladly Receive with Thanksgiving

## Day 18

*For everything God created is good, and nothing is to be rejected if it is received with thanksgiving.*
                                                                1 Timothy 4:4

Let us give thanks to God for everything He has created. Sometimes we do not appreciate enough what He has blessed us with and how fortunate we are to have a God who is so loving, kind and compassionate. We must give Him thanks every day and not to take what He does for us for granted. Too often we become ungrateful when we do not receive what we want and we fail to be thankful for everything and for all things, The Bible reminds us that in everything we are to give thanks and that means everything whether it is good or bad. This is hard to accept but just as the Lord is with us in the good times and the bad times, so we must learn to cope when the hard times come upon us as well as the good times.

Father we thank You for the beauty and splendor of the earth; for the hills, plains and valleys; for snow covered mountains; for the streams, rivers, seas and oceans; for all plants and animals that live on land and in the sea and most of all we thank You for Your Son, Jesus Christ, our Savior and Lord. Thank You Lord that You created everything good and perfect and we pray that You will help us to cherish and appreciate all of Your creation.

Father we thank You that today we can find comfort in knowing that You created us in Your own image and that we are Your children. Forgive us Lord for the times when we have been ungrateful and have failed to thank You for all Your blessings upon us. We thank You Father for being with us through the good and the bad times and for carrying us through every impossible situation we have experienced. You have truly been a wonderful and awesome Father to us for which we are eternally thankful. For all Your mercies Lord, we give You thanks in the name of Jesus. Amen.

## August

# Live By Love

## Day 19

*Let the message of Christ dwell among you richly as you teach and admonish one another with all wisdom through psalms, hymns, and songs from the Spirit, singing to God with gratitude in your hearts.*

Colossians 3:16

Whatever we do for the Lord, we must do so with a sense of gratitude and thankfulness for He is the one who makes all things possible even when we see the impossible. It is His desire that we love and support one another at all times. The message of Jesus is for us to win the world with our love for one another and telling others about Jesus and His love for all of humanity. When the world see and hear us talking about Jesus and His love for lost humanity and how He gave His life on a cross to save us from sin, many will turn away from their sin and follow Him. Jesus does make a big difference in our lives and that is why we should always encourage others to seek Him while He may be found and call upon Him while He is near to us.

*Invisible, Incomprehensible, Infinite and Infallible Lord, You who in Your wisdom has seen fit to make us Your disciples, we pray Lord that as You prepare us through Your holy word to proclaim the good news of salvation to both believers and non-believers, that Your Holy Spirit the Comforter would take charge and control of our lives and use us to honor and to worship You. We know Father that in the scheme of things there are many to be won for Your kingdom and so through Your grace and mercy, You will enable us to reach out to others and tell them of Your love and forgiveness.*

*Lord we thank You for the message of salvation You have given to us to share to the world. Help us Father to be sincere and true as we present the gospel of Jesus Christ to the lost and the unsaved. Help us Dear Father to make our lights so shine that others will glorify You and surrender their lives to You. We know Father that the world is watching us and so we ask You to make us worthy of the high calling You have placed on our lives. All this we pray in Your wonderful and awesome name. Amen.*

## August

# Ever Thankful and Watchful in Prayer

### Day 20

*Devote yourselves to prayer; being watchful and thankful.*

*Colossians 4:2*

Every Christian's life must be infused by the indwelling of the Holy Spirit in order to live a consistent, committed and sincere prayer life which is pleasing to God. In today's busy and fast paced world when we become caught up in so many different things, we have to be very careful that we do not neglect to pray. Sometimes when the trials, tribulations and temptations of life assail us, the first thing we choose to do is to lose focus on the Lord and focus more on our issues. Like Peter as long as he kept His eyes on Jesus he could walk on the water, but the moment his eyes were focused elsewhere he found himself sinking. If we want to sink, just take our eyes off Jesus, but if we remain focused on Jesus, we will be able to overcome the hurdles in our way.

Father God we know that our only channel of communicating with You is through prayer. Thank You Lord for the examples Jesus has left us to follow in living a disciplined and devoted prayer life. We cannot do the things that we have to do Father without being in constant contact with You so please help us to connect with You as often as we can even when our thoughts are drawn to other things. Lord we thank You that You have made it possible for us to be able to do all things through Your Son, Jesus Christ.

Loving Father, guide our thoughts and minds as we seek to focus more and more on You. Too often Father we become easily distracted by the things of the world and we lose our focus on You. Help us Father to devote more and more of our time in faithfully and fervently praying to You as often and as intentionally as we can. We know Father that Your Word tells us that the effectual fervent prayer of a righteous man avails much and therefore we should remain consistent in our prayer life. Lord, may we always seek to follow You in the name of the Father, Son and Holy Spirit. Amen.

## August

# You Are Known By Your Deeds

### Day 21

*First, I thank my God through Jesus Christ for all of you, because your faith is being reported all over the world.*
Romans 1:8

When as Christians we stand up and exercise our faith in the Lord Jesus Christ, the world will take note and God will strengthen and bless us abundantly for taking a stand for Him. Too often we allow the world to dictate what we do with and how we live our lives instead of allowing God to. Our faith in the Lord Jesus Christ should stand us in good stead to proclaim the good news of the gospel as we live out our lives as the Lord would have us to. We should not allow nothing or anyone to prevent us from doing what the Lord has called us to do. His calling on our lives must be first and foremost and we must be willing to follow as well as to go where He sends us. It will not always be easy but with His help we can do all things.

*Most Holy, Righteous and Awesome Lord God, thank You for being the epitome of our lives and our very being. We know Lord that when we exercise our faith and remain strong, bold and brave in following You even in the face of challenges and difficulties, those around will wonder as to how that can be. Father we thank You for Your constant faithfulness and never ending love for us despite our shortcomings and sinful nature.*

*We certainly cannot thank You enough Lord for the ways in which You have nurtured, protected and blessed us and for giving us a new lease on life. We want to thank You Father for strengthening our faith in You and for all the things we have been able to do in Your name. Nothing Lord will be able to separate us from Your love if we remain in You and You in us. Thank You so much Lord for accepting us even as we are and for using us to do Your will. This we pray in the name of Jesus. Amen*

## August

# Rescued Once And For All

### Day 22

*Thanks be to God, who delivers me through Jesus Christ our Lord! So then, I myself in my mind am a slave to God's law, but in my sinful nature a slave to the law of sin.*  
Romans 7:25

It is the law of sin that enslaves us and puts a stranglehold on our lives. Our only liberation from this monster is through the precious blood of Jesus Christ that was shed on Calvary's cross. Without the shedding of Jesus' blood, we would still be offering sacrifices to God to appease Him for our sins. We thank God that He saw the need to send His only Son Jesus once and for all into the world to pay the ultimate price for our sins on Calvary's cross. Without the shedding of Christ's blood there would be no remission of our sins and we would continue to live in our sinful condition. Let us thank God each and every day for delivering us from the bondage of sin and for rescuing us once and for all.

*Lord thank You for the love which drew salvation's plan. Thank You for the love which brought it down to man. Thank You for the gulf You spanned at Calvary to rescue us from the bondage of sin. O God, You did not have to do what You did for us at Calvary when You offered Your only Son to die in our place because of our sin. We owe our very lives to You Lord and we thank You for this great sacrifice You made for us so that we might have abundant and everlasting life.*

*Father we give our lives to You so that You can use us to do Your will. We will not run away from You Lord, but will totally surrender our lives to You in obedience to Your calling on our lives. We regret deeply Father for sinning so much that You had to sacrifice Your only Son, Jesus to redeem us from our sin. We promise Lord that we will serve, honor and respect You and do all we can to remain faithful to You and to Your Word. Heavenly Father we thank You for setting us free from the bondage of sin and the law that enslaved us. Forgive us we pray Lord in the name of Your Son, Jesus our Savior. Amen.*

# August

# All To Jesus We Surrender

*Day 23*

*Do not offer any part of yourself to sin as an instrument of wickedness, but rather offer yourselves to God as those who have been brought from death to life; and offer every part of yourself to him as an instrument of righteousness.*
Romans 6:13

St. Paul the Apostle encourages us to offer our bodies as living sacrifices that are holy and acceptable to Almighty God. This we should not take lightly, as our God is a holy and righteous God and He desires of us to be holy also. At no time we should offer any part of ourselves as an instrument of wickedness but instead we should offer ourselves as people of faith and those who have been brought from death to life through the resurrection of the Lord Jesus Christ. God wants all those who follow Him to offer every part of us as instruments of righteousness. All that we do must be in keeping with the will of God.

*Father God in heaven, help us to offer up ourselves to You as a living and holy sacrifice which is the right thing for us to do. Lord we thank You for the opportunity You have given to us to live a life in total obedience to Your Holy Word. We praise You Lord and give You thanks for having brought us from death and giving us new life through Your Son Jesus Christ. We could not ask You for more Lord and we thank You today for Your amazing love that You so graciously lavish on us.*

*Gracious and loving Father, if it had not been for Your love for us and the sacrifice You made for us through Jesus Your only Son, our lives would be miserable and unproductive. We thank You Lord, that each and every day we can offer up ourselves to You in obedience and as instruments of righteousness. We know Father what You desire of us is to live our lives to honor and to praise You and to offer unto You our gratitude and thanksgiving. Thank You Father for bringing us out of darkness into Your marvelous light. This we pray in the name of Jesus. Amen.*

## August

# Give Thanks To God For Everything

### Day 24

*Whoever regards one day as special does so to the Lord. Whoever eats meat does so to the Lord, for they give thanks to God; and whoever abstains does so to the Lord and gives thanks to God.*

Romans 14:6

Everything that we do or say should at all times and in all places bring glory, honor and praise to our King of kings and Lord of lords. We should not become the judges of others as only God can judge us for the good or bad that we do. Too often we tend to judge others by our own standards and expect them to comply with our beliefs. The Apostle Paul here is saying that whatever one does he does so unto the Lord and not to man. It is unfortunate that there are some people because of their religious beliefs think that they have the right to condemn others for when they worship, or what they eat or do not eat or how they choose to live their lives. Let God be the judge as He is the Creator and Maker of us all and He has the final say.

*Merciful and Gracious Father, this is the day that You have made, help us to rejoice and be glad in it. Thank You for waking us up this morning to a bright and beautiful day and for all Your blessings. Remind us O God as we go through this day that it is You who give to us the strength to do all that we have to do. Help us Dear Lord never to judge others on how or when they worship or what they eat or how they choose to live their lives, because You are the ultimate Judge of heaven and earth and one day You are coming back to do so.*

*We thank You Father that we can depend on You to fulfill what You have promised and even though at times, we become so impatient, we know that You always deliver on time. Grant us Father Your wisdom, knowledge and understanding so that we will be able to discern between right and wrong and good and evil. Help us Dear Lord never to judge others by our standards but to leave it up to You who one day will judge us according to what we did or did not do for You. It is in Your name we pray. Amen.*

## August

# Be Wise And Not Foolish

## Day 25

*For although they knew God, they neither glorified him as God nor gave thanks to him, but their thinking became futile and their foolish hearts were darkened.*

Romans 1:21

God does recognize whether or not we are genuine in our worship of Him. Our actions and what we say speak volumes about our relationship with God. Many times we think that we are doing the right thing in honoring God but in truth and in fact we might just be honoring ourselves. When the focus is on us and not on God, then we are living a double standard life. We cannot say that we love and respect God on the one hand but yet on the other hand we are doing things that are displeasing to Him. As Christians we have to be genuine and faithful in all aspects of our lives because that is the way we are being judged by the world.

*We thank You Father in heaven for this moment in time when our hearts can be united with You in prayer and when we can forget everything else and just focus on Your holy presence. Father we thank You for giving to us life, good health, talents and the many opportunities to utilize all of these in our praise and worship of You. Father God may we ever faithfully and consistently seek to glorify, adore and lift up Your precious name.*

*Merciful Father, so often we have betrayed You by the lives we portray to the world. We say that we love You but we do things that are to the contrary. Truly we cannot say we love You Father but yet have hatred and bitterness in our hearts towards others. If we really know You Father, then every day we will glorify and honor Your name giving You thanks for all the blessings You have bestowed upon us. Help us loving Father to turn away from our wicked ways and turn to You who alone can cleanse us from all our unrighteousness. We ask You Father to grant us Your wisdom and take away from us all our foolish and stupid ways. This we pray in Your Son's name. Amen.*

# August

# No Longer Slaves But Free

### Day 26

*But thanks be to God that, though you used to be slaves to sin, you have come to obey from your heart the pattern of teaching that has now claimed your allegiance.*
Romans 6:17

Let us thank God that through the shed blood of His only Son Jesus Christ, we are no longer slaves to the ravages of sin. Only God could have delivered us from sin and set us free. This He did by sending His Son, Jesus to the cross to be crucified. We thank God for this great sacrifice He made on our behalf and as a result, all those who believe on the name of Jesus can be saved from their sin. We who follow and serve the Lord should not fail in telling others who do not believe of what God did to redeem lost humanity from sin. Christ paid the debt He did not owe so that whosoever believes on Him should not perish but will have everlasting life.

*Our Father God, we thank You for all that has come into our lives through the readings of Your holy word, our worship with fellow believers in Christ, the service that we offer to others and our tithes and offerings we give in our quest to expand Your kingdom here on earth. We give You thanks Father for all those whom have ministered to our needs and have helped us along life's journey. To Your most holy and precious name Lord, we ascribe all glory and honor and dominion and power.*

*O God our Father, we owe our allegiance to You and to none other than Your Son, Jesus Christ our Lord. Thank You Father for giving to us so much and for blessing us the way You do. Father we are certainly not always deserving of Your love for us because of all our failures and shortcomings. We thank You for having loved us the way You do and for always providing our daily needs. Father we surrender our lives to You this day and ask You to use us for Your glory. This we pray in Your wonderful and holy name. Amen.*

# August

# The Sweetest Name We Know

### Day 27

*Always giving thanks to God the Father for everything, in the name of our Lord Jesus Christ.*
Ephesians 5:20

We are constantly encouraged by God's word to give thanks to Him at all times. Sometimes we forget that even when we are experiencing challenging and difficult times, we need to still give thanks to God for He is the only one who enables us to overcome our difficulties and challenges. When we offer up our thanks to God we do so in the name of and through His Son, Jesus Christ. God did not spare His only Son, but gave Him as a ransom to pay for our sins and the sins of the whole world. The more we think about God is the more we appreciate what He has done for us and what He will continue to do. None of us can understand the mind of God but His Son Jesus because the Bible declares that Jesus and His Father God are one.

*O Lord our God, we acknowledge that You love us with an everlasting love and for this we are very thankful. We know Father that when we are faced with the trials and tribulations of life, it is our tendency to blame You rather than thanking You for giving us the strength to endure it all. You have promised never to leave us nor to forsake us or to give us more than we can bear. Forgive us Lord for not thanking You enough for all that You have done for us and more.*

*Father we acknowledge that we have not always given to You what is Yours but instead we have paid Caesar what is his. Forgive us Father for the many times we have failed to give You thanks and to really express our gratitude to You for all the wonderful and awesome blessings You have lavished on us. We pray Father that You will show us how to become more like You in all our ways and that we will constantly express our love and appreciation for all Your benefits towards us. We ask You Father to bless us in the name of Your Son. Amen.*

# August

# Lifting Up Others in Prayer

## Day 28

*For this reason, ever since I heard about your faith in the Lord Jesus and your love for all God's people, I have not stopped giving thanks for you, remembering you in my prayers.*

Ephesians 1:15-16

Often times we feel that what we do for others is not always appreciated and as true as that may be, our encouragement is for us to give rather than to receive. Our ultimate reward will come from the Master Himself who has promised to reward all those who remain faithful to Him. We give thanks for all those who have not compromised their faith but have remained loyal and true to their Creator God. As God's people, He wants us to love everyone in the same way in which He has loved us. Our world will only be a better place for all people when there is love shared among us. God is love and His love extends to all generations so everyone is included.

*Teach us this day loving Father to look at the things we see that You have created and to look at them without bias or prejudice and to give You thanks for all of creation. Too often Father we take so many things for granted and we fail in our efforts to give You all the praise and glory that You so well deserve. Lord grant that this day we will not fall into any temptation and if we do please deliver us from all that is evil. Father we thank You that in the midst of everything that we might be going through, we can still praise and honor Your name.*

*Forgive we pray Father for the times we have failed You and have not lived up to our expectations. Help us Father to demonstrate more love and generosity to all those who are less fortunate than we are or even those who we do not even know. You have taught us how to love Father by loving us first and for sending Your Son Jesus into the world to be our Savior and Lord. Thank You Father for Your unconditional love for us Your people and help us to pass that love on to others as well. Lord God, our world is really devoid of love and so we ask You to enable us to spread this love to all those around us in the name of Jesus, our Savior. Amen.*

# August

# Controlling Our Tongues

## Day 29

*Nor should there be obscenity, foolish talk or coarse joking, which are out of place, but rather thanksgiving.*
Ephesians 5:4

The children of God must be careful with their choice of words for God expects the best from us. We must be in the world but not of the world so others must know who we are as Christians and whose we are, children of the most High God. To indulge in the use of filthy and lewd language is not of those who call themselves Christians. This is how people of the world behave and so we must guard ourselves against idle talk and foolish actions. In everything that we do we must be above board and walk in a way that represents the Lord Jesus Christ. The Bible tells us that by their fruits you will know them so we need to bear good fruits in our lives so that others will be challenged to follow in our footsteps.

Loving Father we pray that this day You will give us the wisdom and understanding to refrain from idle jesting and to guard our tongues from saying anything that would dishonor Your name. Lord we thank You that in the name of Jesus Christ we can have victory over every ounce of evil and temptation that may come upon us. We thank You Lord that we can renounce Satan and all his angels through the precious blood of Jesus even as we take a stand to resist the evil one.

Father we thank You for being the Supreme Ruler of the universe and for holding all things together. In our sin sick world Father, help us to walk circumspectly in all that we do so that the light of Christ will shine through us to others. Help us Father, to refrain from using loose and vain language which could cause others to lose faith in us and turn away from You. Lord, please help us that what we say, do or think will be acceptable to You. This we pray in the name of Jesus. Amen.

# August

# Supporting One Another in Prayer

## Day 30

*As you help us by your prayers, then many will give thanks on our behalf for the gracious favor granted us in answer to the prayers of many.*

2 Corinthians 1:11

We are never to neglect praying for one another as this is how we build up each other in the faith. Prayer is the foundation on which our faith is built and it is our means of staying in tune with our Father in heaven. Even unbelievers depend upon us Christians to pray in times of calamity or when they are going through untold hardships. We should never cease from praying as our prayers have power and can change lives and situations. Our God hears our petitions and supplications and He does answer our prayers in His time. The Apostle Paul encourages believers to pray continually and this means that there is no letting up or to relax. We are living at a time in our history when the need for more praying has never been greater and so let us all join hands and hearts as we lift up one another and others to Almighty God in our prayers.

*Gracious and merciful Father, we thank You for all the necessities of life that You have so readily and willingly given to us. So often Father we take for granted the little things around us that make life more meaningful and bearable. We thank You Lord for the air that we breathe, for the windows that let in the air and keep out the cold and the rain. We thank You for the gas and electricity that we use for cooking and for doing so many other things. Father, we know it would be very difficult to exist if we did not have all the things that You have made available at our disposal and so we just thank You for anything, everything and all things today and always.*

*Heavenly Father we thank You for the medium of prayer that is so important to us to keep in tune with You. Help us Lord to be consistent and faithful in not only praying for our own needs but also for the needs of others. We give You thanks Father for all those who over the years have lifted us up in prayers and because of their intervention, we have become who we are. Help us Father that in the same way we have been prayed for, that we also will pray for other believers as well as non-believers. Thank You Lord that You always answer our prayers no matter how long it takes. We give You thanks Lord in the name of Your Son, Jesus Christ. Amen.*

# August

# What Is Your Concern?

## Day 31

*Thanks be to God, who put into the heart of Titus the same concern I have for you.*
2 Corinthians 8:16

It is a good thing for us to remember those who are going through challenging and difficult times in their lives and to constantly lift them up in our prayers. We all should be concerned about the individual and collective needs of others and to lift them up in our prayers. The Lord is able to change situations that may seem impossible to us but with God He can turn things around. The Bible tells us not to become weary in well doing but to be persistent in what we do for others believing that God will respond to our helping others in ways that we cannot truly understand. Our God is a good God and He never fails to deliver on His promises as long as we remain faithful to Him.

*Gracious and loving Father, we thank You for the opportunity You have given to us to pray for those who are experiencing trials and temptations and doubts about their faith. We pray Father that in the precious name of Your Son Jesus Christ, that You would reach out to the many who find themselves doubting Your existence. Lord we thank You for revealing so much to us through Your word and we pray that You will continue to enable us to be of help to others.*

*Father we ask You to give us the wisdom, knowledge and understanding to do the things that are right and pleasing in Your sight. Thank You that You are a just and forgiving Father and we can always come to You whenever we want to. Give us we pray Father a burning desire for the souls of others and may we remember to pray for those who are really finding life challenging and difficult. Lord we give You thanks for those who have doubts yet believe. Strengthen their faith we pray Father in the precious name of Your Son, Jesus. Amen.*

# September

# Being Kind Enriches Our Lives

## Day 1

*You will be enriched in every way so that you can be generous on every occasion, and through us your generosity will result in thanksgiving to God.*

2 Corinthians 9:11

    Jesus expresses His love for those who are generous and cheerful givers. It is indeed much better to give than to receive as it is in our giving that we truly receive God's blessings in abundance. God has given to us all that He has and so we in return must give back to Him and to others. Giving is a better option than receiving since it is in giving that we really receive and the blessings come pouring down upon us. We are thankful to God that we are all enriched in every way when we give and we should give until it hurts. Our praise and thanksgiving must always be given to Almighty God because He keeps on doing so much for us.

    *Father God, how can we truly thank You enough for all the myriads of blessings You have bestowed on us. We realize Lord that only when we give generously and unconditionally that we receive Your blessings over and above that which we deserve. Father we thank You for showing us how to take the negative things of life and turn them into positives. Lord we thank You that today You have blessed us with more than what we need to live a happy and productive life.*

    *Lord God, You have been faithful to us in Your giving and Your myriad of blessings upon us and You want us to be as generous to others even as You have been to us. We know that when we give, our lives are enriched and others are blessed through our generous. We thank You Father that it is indeed more beneficial to give than to receive because it is in giving that we truly receive in abundance. Thank You dear Father for giving to us Your only Son which is the greatest gift You could have given to us. We ask You to bless us in the name of Your Son, Jesus, our Savior. Amen.*

# September

# Generosity Is Contagious

## Day 2

*We always thank God for all of you and continually mention you in our prayers.*

1 Thessalonians 1:2

Too often we only focus on ourselves and not others. God wants us to be concerned about one another and always lifting them up in our prayers. Every day we are challenged more and more to place others before ourselves and by so doing, we learn to bear one another burdens making the load easier to carry. As followers of Jesus Christ, we are to be constantly in prayer to bring all our petitions and supplications for ourselves and for others. Through our prayers we can lift up the needs of all those who desire us to do so to Almighty God on their behalf.

*Father in heaven, we thank You that when we do not know what to do, we can always turn to You in prayer. Lord we thank You that we do not have to spend any empty or fruitless moments in our lives. Father You have given to us Your word and so help us that we will daily feed upon Your word and apply it to our hearts. Father we thank You for all that You do for us and for giving to us the medium of prayer through which we can reach up and out to You.*

Father God, You are our King of kings and Lord of lords and we just want to lift up Your Holy name because of who You are. We give You praise and honor and glory Lord for Your splendor and majesty and for the way You come into our lives and provide us with Your peace. Loving Father, may our generosity of love and consistency in prayer be a hallmark for us as Christians and we pray that You will give us the ability to keep on praying and lifting up others in Your name. Lord, hear our prayer and let our cry come unto You. Amen.

## September

# God At Work In Us

### Day 3

*And we also thank God continually because, when you received the word of God, which you heard from us, you accepted it not as a human word, but as it actually is, the word of God, which is indeed at work in you who believe.*

1 Thessalonians 2:13

As Christians we need to remember that God's word is at work within us at all times and it is expedient that we who are believers accept everything His word tells us to do. In this verse we observe that the Thessalonian Christians had responded with faith to the word of God when he preached to them. Notice they accepted what he said as God's Word and not the word of men and that is what is expected of us today also. The Apostle Paul understood very well that the Word of God had touched their lives and was bearing much spiritual fruit. In the same way today when the Word of God is preached, lives are touched and transformed and so like Paul, we must continue to proclaim the good news to those who need to hear it.

*Our Father God, we are so grateful and thankful to You that You have recorded in Your Holy Word so many illustrations of the truths You want us to know. Help us Lord to accept Your word and apply it daily to our lives. Lord we thank You that You see in us something that You can develop and we praise You for believing in us. We give You thanks today for all the wonderful truths contained in the Bible about You.*

*We thank You Father that Your Word can touch and transform lives and so help us to be committed to the task of telling others about You and Your love for them. Lord help us to be consistent in all that we do for You because You have always been consistent in all Your ways. Father we pray that as Your Word goes forth into every corner of the globe, that many will come to know You and none other. Father God we thank You that You are always at work in us and for this we give to You all the praise and glory in the name of Jesus. Amen.*

# September

# More Than Enough

## Day 4

*How can we thank God enough for you in return for all the joy we have in the presence of our God because of you?*
1 Thessalonians 3:9

When we assist others especially those who have committed their lives in promulgating the gospel, it brings a sense of joy not only to those who receive but also to those who give. We cannot thank God enough for all His wonderful benefits towards us. Every day we receive God's blessings and because of Him we all can enjoy the best life has to offer. Joy comes from knowing that God is in charge of our lives and that His loving kindness and tender mercies are always available, God never with hold anything from us and He wants us in return to pass on the blessings He has bestowed upon us to others.

*O God of wisdom and goodness, please give us hearts that are grateful and thankful for all the many blessings You have bestowed on us. Help us never to be afraid or reluctant in sharing these blessings with others. Lord we thank You that You have promised to supply all our needs and as such You want us to be generous in giving to others. Father we give to You all that we are and have and ask You to use us and what we have to benefit those who are less fortunate than we are.*

*Lord we pray that You will touch our hearts to be of help to others every time we have the opportunity so to do. Thank You for the joy You give to us Father for doing good to others so that they can feel loved and joyful too. Lord we have been blessed so much by You and we want to be a blessing to others as well. Father we thank You for Your Word that encourages us to give rather than to receive and may You help us to be good stewards of what You have given to us. We thank You Father today for the opportunity You gave to us to be a blessing to others and we pray that You will continue to help us to do so in the name of Jesus, our Lord and Savior. Amen.*

## September

# Lead By Example

## Day 5

*After he said this, he took some bread and gave thanks to God in front of them all. Then he broke it and began to eat.*

Acts 27:35

The Bible exhorts us to give thanks for everything, anything and for all things. Even when trials and troubles come our way, we need to give God thanks for carrying us through. Jesus has left us His examples of giving thanks in every situation. All of His life on earth He would find time to give thanks to His Heavenly Father as often as possible and He expects us to do the very same. When we give thanks to God we are expressing our appreciation to Him for all His goodness towards us. We need to set the examples to our children especially and for others in general in making it a habit to give thanks to Almighty God at all times and in every place where we might find ourselves. By so doing, they will learn of the significance and importance of giving thanks always.

*Lord we thank You for filling the earth with Your goodness and for everything You have provided to meet our daily needs we give You thanks. Father we pray that You will help us to be ever grateful and thankful to You for all things and at all times. We know Lord that we have often times forget to honor and adore Your name and for this we seek Your pardon and forgiveness.*

*We thank You Lord Jesus for setting us the example of giving thanks to our heavenly Father as often as we can. Help us Dear Lord to set aside times when we just come into Your holy presence to express our thanks and gratitude to You for all that You do for us day in and day out. Lord we confess that we do not thank You enough and for this we seek Your forgiveness and mercy as we ask You to make us more committed in our prayer life. This we ask in Your awesome and glorious name. Amen.*

# September

# Proclaiming God's Pre-eminence

## *Day 6*

*Everywhere and in every way, most excellent Felix, we acknowledge this with profound gratitude.*

Acts 24:3

It is indeed a very good thing to give God our thanks and praise in our worship of Him. Without His presence in our lives, everything we do would be meaningless. The Apostle Paul encourages us to acknowledge with profound gratitude the goodness of God everywhere we may go and in every way possible. Our commitment and obligation is to God and not to man. Even though we must be obedient to our leaders and show our respect for them, our gratitude to God should be first and foremost. God deserves all our praise especially as we see the world around us He has made and the things He has done in our lives. Though many try to deny His existence, those of us who believe that He exists, will one day come face to face with the risen, crucified Lord and for that too we must be thankful.

*Heavenly Father, we thank You that Your word is truth and even as Your word speaks to our hearts and our needs, help us Lord to become so immersed in Your teaching that we may become a light to others. Lord even though life may be challenging and tempestuous at times, we will ever proclaim Your name and Your greatness and goodness to the world. Lord we thank You for Your steady, secure and unfailing love for us and for delivering us from the evil one.*

*O Merciful and Loving Father, we ask You to help us to be bold and strong as we seek to witness in Your name. Remove from us Father all forms of timidity or fear when proclaiming Your word to those in high places. We know Father that there are many who are living in sin and need to hear Your living and transforming Word. Prepare us Loving Father to do Your will and all that You have placed upon us to do for You. We give You thanks Father for all Your blessings in the name of Jesus. Amen.*

## September

# Thanking God Always

### Day 7

*I always thank my God for you because of his grace given you in Christ Jesus.*

*1 Corinthians 1:4*

We should always give God thanks for not only what He does for us, but to thank Him as well for others. Day after day we receive blessings from the Lord that He gives to us so generously and faithfully and we in return should give Him praise and honor because He is so worthy of it all. Each day as we spend time with the Lord in quiet meditation, let us remember to thank Him for how great He is and for never failing to show His love for us. Our God indeed is a good and righteous God, all wise, unchanging and sovereign and for all these attributes we need to praise Him and to lift up His name on high.

Most gracious, loving and infectious God, we thank You for Your life-changing words that reveal the true persons we are. Lord we truly thank You for accepting us as we are and for giving us the grace, power and strength to make real and lasting changes in our lives. Since we accepted You Father our lives have never been the same again and for this we want to thank You with our whole minds, hearts and souls. Father we thank You that You are indeed the way, the truth and the life and with You we are safe.

Loving Lord Jesus, You have done so much for us for which we have not always expressed our gratitude and praise. Help us Lord Jesus to come to You even now to tell You how much we love You and appreciate all that You do for us. May we make our praise and thanksgiving be a part of our daily routine and help us Dear Jesus to be consistent and persistent in our efforts. We thank You Lord Jesus that when we offer up our praises to You, we are drawn closer to You and we feel Your holy presence very close to us. We ask You to continue to bless us in Your name. Amen.

## September

# Victory Through Christ

### Day 8

*But thanks be to God! He gives us the victory through our Lord Jesus Christ.*

1 Corinthians 15:57

The battle is not ours but the Lord's. Let us let go and let God take charge and control and entrust our all to Him. The Lord will not fail us nor will He shorten His hands towards us. Great is His faithfulness every day and we can depend on Him to be faithful even to the end of our journey here on this earth. Our victory over sin and the grave does not come from man but through the Lord Jesus Christ who paid the price for our sin on the cross so that we can be redeemed. Our whole lives should be about praising the King of kings and Lord of lords and live in such a way that all that we do bring honor and glory, dominion and power to His great and awesome name.

*Lord we want to thank You for the signs You have provided for us through Your Word which if we follow and obey Your teachings, will lead us in sharing life with You forever. Father, we thank You that Your Word enables us to be wise for salvation through faith in Your Son Jesus Christ and we thank You Father for this privilege You have extended to us. Thank You dear Lord for accepting us the way we are and thank You that we can cast all our burdens on You today and always.*

*Righteous and ever loving Father, we thank You for giving us the victory over sin and death through Your Son Jesus Christ who conquered death and rose triumphantly from the grave and ascended into heaven to be with You. Lord Jesus thank You that You are our only hope of salvation and we need to follow in Your footsteps so that one day we too can be with You in heaven. Our Father, we thank You for giving us victory in the name of Jesus, Your Son. Amen.*

# September
# Returning Thanks in Humility
## Day 9

*One of them, when he saw he was healed, came back, praising God in a loud voice.* <sup>16</sup> *He threw himself at Jesus' feet and thanked him—and he was a Samaritan.*

Luke 17:13-16

God is no respecter of persons and as long as we show our gratitude to Him, irrespective of who we are, He will heal us from our infirmities. When we think of how many people are being marginalized and discriminated against, it hurts to think or to believe that there might just be some of those who profess to be followers of Christ. Jesus would not be pleased with us if we were to treat others with disrespect and with any form of hatred or animosity for He is love. Many people today because of their color, race or religion are treated inhumanely and often times ostracized. This is not of God because He made all of us in His very own image and so we need to be more tolerant and loving in our dealings with those who may be different from us.

Dear Heavenly Father we want to thank You for Your words that bring life and healing to our sin sick soul. Father thank You that Your words provide comfort and give us strength when we are weak and desperately in need of You. Help us Lord to hide Your words in our hearts so that we will not sin against You or depart from Your holy and righteous ways. Lord we want to thank You for the abundant life You promise to us if we only believe and trust in You.

Help us Dear Father to be mindful of the needs of others and to treat others with love and respect. There have been times Father when we have viewed others as being less than we are and as such have treated them with impunity. Forgive us Father for the ways we have acted and behaved towards those who do not look like us nor share our beliefs. You want us Father to be loving, kind and compassionate to all those who are in need and who come to us asking. Instead of turning them away Father, help us to show our love and concern for them and to help them in any way possible. Loving Lord, help us to come to You in humility thanking You for all Your wonderful blessings in the name of Jesus, our Savior. Amen.

## September

# Redeeming The Times

## Day 10

*Coming up to them at that very moment, she gave thanks to God and spoke about the child to all who were looking forward to the redemption of Jerusalem.*
Luke 2:38

It is God and God alone who can redeem us through belief in His Son Jesus Christ. What a wonderful experience it must have been for Anna at that moment in time to have lived to witness the coming of the Lord Jesus into the world. There is no greater feeling one can have but to be in the presence of Jesus Christ. He alone can transform our lives and make us and mold us into the kinds of people He wants us to be. We should all try and let go of the worldly things that occupy our time and turn to Jesus who can liberate us from our sin and set us free. Jesus Christ, God's Son will be pleased when His people seek Him and call upon Him and He will respond to their calls.

*Almighty and everlasting Father God, thank You for always being near, always caring and for always listening to our prayers. We thank You Lord for helping us to look to You in every situation and for bridging the gap which exists between us at times. Lord, we thank You that we can depend on You at all times for taking the very best care of us. We thank You for sending Your Son Jesus into the world to make a difference in our lives and for redeeming us from our sins.*

*Today Lord Jesus we rejoice at Your coming into the world to save lost humanity. We thank You for all those who witnessed Your birth and for the tremendous transformation it brought to their lives. We are encouraged Father to know just how much You love us and the extent to which You went in expressing that love for us. We owe You Father a debt of gratitude for all that You have done for us and continue to do. Help us always Father to give unto Your name our praise and thanksgiving. We thank You Faithful Father for redeeming the world through the death of Your Son and for the opportunity we have of becoming heirs in Your kingdom. For all these blessings Lord, we give You thanks in Jesus' name. Amen.*

# September

# Growing In Faith

## Day 11

*We ought always to thank God for you, brothers and sisters and rightly so, because your faith is growing more and more, and the love all of you have for one another is increasing.*

2 Thessalonians 1:3

As God's people who are called and commissioned to do His will, let us not forget to remember and pray for all those who are of the household of faith in Christ Jesus our Lord. There is the tendency for us to neglect those who work so hard to spread the good news of salvation because we are too busy doing the things we see as being important to the detriment of not praying for or remembering those who are really laboring in the vineyard. When we lift up one another, our faith in God is strengthened and our love for each other increases. Let us always endeavor to pray for our brothers and sisters in Christ especially those who are being persecuted for their faith and for the spreading of the gospel.

Immortal, Invisible and Immovable Loving Father, we thank You for being at the very heart and center of our lives. You who are great, mighty and powerful and work in such mysterious ways, we thank You for remembering such insignificant persons as we are. Lord we will never understand nor comprehend the depth of Your love for us and for this we give You all our praise and gratitude. Lord we thank You that in the midst of our struggles and confusion, You break forth and give us a glimmer of hope.

Heavenly Father, we are thankful for all those whom You have called and set apart to do Your will. We thank You for all the men and women throughout the history of the world who have made themselves available to be used by You for the spreading of Your Word to every corner of the globe. Help us Father to continually pray for them even as they labor in Your vineyard. Give them the courage and the strength we pray Father to carry on the work You have entrusted to their care and may they never be in want. Merciful Father we thank You for strengthening our faith and for challenging us to do great things for You in the name of Jesus, we pray. Amen.

## September

# Remembering Others Consistently

### Day 12

*I thank my God every time I remember you.*

Philippians 1:3

It is a good and wonderful thing to always keep brothers and sisters in Christ in our prayers. We are strengthened when we lift up one another at all times and we should not fail in doing so without ceasing. God wants His followers to be unified in their efforts in supporting one another in all aspects of the various ministries in which they are involved. We can hold up each other in our prayers and our financial support especially for those who may be less fortunate than we are. Whenever strangers come amongst us, we must treat them with love and be generous in our giving to them. The Bible teaches us to be kind and compassionate and to always put the needs of others before our very own. Too often we neglect to do what we have been called to do by God our Father and as a result we are not as effective as we should be in our ministry.

*Living, Loving Lord, we thank You for pulling us out of the pit time and time again. Help us Father never to forget what You have done for us and may we always praise You and to share with others Your faithfulness. Thank You for being a God who is constantly watching over us and protecting us from all harm and danger. Lord we really do not know what we would do without You and for all that You have done for us, we give You our thanks and praise.*

*Father we thank You for all those who remember us in their prayers and we ask You to help us to remember others as well in our prayers with consistency. Father give us the burning desire to be of help to others especially those who are so desperately in need. You have called us out of darkness into Your marvelous light and we know that You want us to make our lives shine for You. We thank You Father for all those whom You have called to do Your will and we ask that You will always provide for them and may they never be in need. This we pray in Your name. Amen.*

## September

# Having A Clear Conscience
## Day 13

*I thank God, whom I serve, as my ancestors did, with a clear conscience, as night and day I constantly remember you in my prayers.*

2 Timothy 1:3

Our lifeline to God is through the medium of prayer. We should always make prayer a very important part of our daily lives. We give God thanks for all those who have influenced our lives and have left us a legacy to follow. We owe it to our families, friends, teachers, pastors, Sunday school teachers as well as all those who guided us along the Christian pathway. Because of their guidance, encouragement and sound teachings, we have become who we are today and for that we are so grateful. Let us all play our part in helping to mold the lives of the next generations to come so that they will not depart from the Word of God but will according to all that He has commanded us to do.

Immortal, invisible, only wise God, we thank You for helping us to overcome the things that would cause us to be separated from You. Help us Father to always remind ourselves how much we have to lean on You and not on our own understanding. In everything Father and for all things, we know we must give to You our praise and gratitude because You have been to us our source of help and sustenance. O Lord, we want to thank You today especially for the way in which You have worked out things for our good.

Father God we give You thanks for all those who have helped to guide and to encourage us in our Christian walk with You. Lord, without our families, friends, teachers, pastors and Sunday school teachers who have guided us throughout our lives in our Christian walk with You, we probably would not have made it this far. We give You thanks for them Father and we appreciate all that they have done for us to remain focused on You. Give us a clear conscience Father as we seek to lift up our petitions to You in the name of Jesus, we pray. Amen.

# September

# A Joyful Attitude

## Day 14

*In all my prayers for all of you, I always pray with joy.*
Philippians 1:4

The joy of the Lord is our strength and the more we pray to Him is the more joyful our lives become. Our joy comes from the Lord when we know Him and follow in His footsteps. It is not always easy to remain joyful due to circumstances that we may encounter in our walk with God, but we must remember that He is in control of our lives and He will never allow anything or anyone to steal our joy. Like the Apostle Paul, let us too remember that when we pray for others, we will do so with hearts full of joy. We must have joy within us so that we can share this joy with others that they also may experience the joy of the Lord.

*Living, Loving and Amazing Father, we thank You that if we consistently and persistently come to You in prayer, joy will always abound in our hearts. Lord we thank You that You are the only one who can bring true and everlasting joy into our lives and for this we are ever grateful. We pray Father that You will help us to remain passionate, focused and directed even as we come to You as we are.*

*Father, today we want to thank You for Your joy which strengthens and sustains us through the difficult circumstances in life that we may experience. We thank You Father that true joy comes from knowing You and having an intimate relationship with You. The joy that the world offers Father is temporary but we thank You that the joy You offer to us does not only strengthen us but it is everlasting. To You Father God we attribute all praise and glory in the precious name of Jesus. Amen.*

## September

# Our Assignment
## Day 15

*Hezekiah assigned the priests and Levites to divisions—each of them according to their duties as priests or Levites—to offer burnt offerings and fellowship offerings, to minister, to give thanks and to sing praises at the gates of the Lord's dwelling.*

2 Chronicles 31:2

God accepts our worship of Him if it is meaningful and purposeful. We must acknowledge all that God does for us by demonstrating our gratitude to Him. All of God's people must become involved in helping to build His kingdom here on earth in preparation for advancing to His heavenly kingdom. All the things we need to do to ensure our salvation must be done here and now as we will not be able to do so when we die. God has given us many opportunities to live as He has purposed us to and if we neglect what He wants us to do, it will be to our detriment. What assignment has God given to us to do for him and how are we carrying it out?

Heavenly Father, we thank You for Your word which brings life and healing to our souls. Thank You that Your word comforts and strengthens us when we need it the most. Lord we thank You that if we hide Your word in our hearts, we will not sin against You and we will live in abundance and favor. Help us Lord to memorize Your word so that we will be able to use it when we are confronted with the devil's temptations. Enable us Dear Father to carry out the task You have assigned each and everyone of us to do on this earth for You.

Gracious Lord we thank You that You accept our worship of You if it is meaningful and purposeful. Sometimes Father we become lazy and out of touch as to how we should come before You with praise and thanksgiving in our hearts. We do not always Father demonstrate an attitude of gratitude to You but rather we come to You with a nonchalant attitude which impacts our relationship with You. Forgive us Father for having fallen short of what You truly expect from us and help us to try to make amends for our wayward ways. This we pray in the name of Jesus, Our Lord. Amen.

## September

# Dedicating Our Lives To God

## Day 16

*Then Hezekiah said, "You have now dedicated yourselves to the Lord. Come and bring sacrifices and thank offerings to the temple of the Lord." So the assembly brought sacrifices and thank offerings and all whose hearts were willing brought burnt offerings.*

2 Chronicles 29:13

If we come before our heavenly Father with the right attitude and offer to Him our thanks of praise, He will accept our praise and offerings and bless us abundantly. We thank God that we do not have to offer sacrifices with animals to seek forgiveness since Jesus offered Himself as our living sacrifice, We should offer up to God however our sacrifices of praise and thanksgiving as often as we can with willing and contrite hearts. God is so deserving of our praise and adoration because He is just an awesome and loving God who cares so much for His children. Every time we enter into the house of the Lord, we should first rededicate ourselves to Him and then offer up our sacrifices of thanksgiving and praise because He is so worthy to receive our honor, glory and adoration.

Lord we thank You for arming us with the truth and teaching us to use the sword of the Spirit effectively. Father we thank You that we can come into Your holy presence with our offerings of praise and thanksgiving. Thank You Father that nothing is too small or too insignificant that You will not accept as long as we do so with humility and a contrite heart. We know our God that You are indeed deserving of all the accolades we can offer up to You.

Father God, we thank You for the ultimate sacrifice You made for us by sending Your Son Jesus to first of all live among us in human form and then to offer Him as a living sacrifice to die on a cross for our sin. Lord, in Your mercy on us, You allowed Jesus to pay the price we owed and died the death we should have died all because of Your unconditional love for us Your wayward children. Father we thank You so much for loving us even when we sin and have fallen short. Please forgive us Father of our sin and cleanse us from all our unrighteousness. This we ask in the name of Jesus, our Savior. Amen.

## September

# Deliverance From Our Enemies

## Day 17

*Cry out, "Save us, God our Savior; gather us and deliver us from the nations, that we may give thanks to your holy name, and glory in your praise."*

1 Chronicles 16:35

When we have tried everything else and fail, it is usually at that time that we cry out to God to save us and to deliver us from our distress. We need to turn that around and cry out to Him first because in all things He is pre-eminent. From the beginning of time God has been and will continue to be our Deliverer not only in the good times but in the bad times as well and that is our reason for trusting Him with every facet of our lives. We should always seek to give to God our praise and thanksgiving not only for all the wonderful blessings He has blessed us with, but because He is our God and He alone is worthy of our praise. He's the One who delivers us from all our enemies.

Heavenly Father we thank You that in our distress when we cried out to You for help, You heard us and delivered us from all our fears. Thank You Lord for strengthening us with all power according to Your glorious might so that we will have great patience and endurance even as we face up to all that this life throws at us. We know Father that we do not give You the thanks and praise that You so very well deserve, but we want You to know Father that we truly and sincerely thank You from the bottom of our hearts for all the wonderful things You do for us day in and day out.

Father, teach us that we will always turn to You for help in all situations and not to rely on others. You alone Father know us intimately and what our needs are and You have told us to ask of You and we shall receive. Many times Father we have sought the advice of others before coming to You and only when we fail to get what we are seeking, we then turn to You. Lord forgive us and may we learn to give to You our praise and thanksgiving not only for all the wonderful and awesome blessings with which You have blessed us but more so because You are deserving and worthy of our praise. It is in Your name we pray Father. Amen.

## September

# Special Assignment

*Day 18*

*He appointed some of the Levites to minister before the ark of the Lord, to extol, thank, and praise the Lord, the God of Israel.*

1 Chronicles 16:4

The God of Israel is the same God we serve and worship and as Christians our desire should always be to praise and glorify His precious name. God has given to all of us different gifts to be used to glorify and to magnify His name. What we do with our gifts is entirely up to us but know that one day we will have to give an account about our stewardship. We have heard many stories of how people throughout the ages have used their gifts to bring honor and glory to God's name, while many wasted their opportunities to invest wisely and reap the rewards. If we are good stewards of what the Lord has blessed us with, He will keep on multiplying what He has given to us because we would have proven ourselves worthy of His blessings. Let us ask the Lord for wisdom and understanding even as we perform the task He has given us to do.

*Indestructible, Infallible, Indescribable, Incredible and Invisible Father God of heaven and earth, we lift our voices to You in adoration and praise as we thank You for demonstrating to the world Your might and power in everything that You do. Lord we cannot comprehend or understand the magnificent and impossible things that You do to prove to the world just how awesome You are. Father when we look at ourselves and realize that You created us in Your very image, we just fall on our knees and pray a prayer of thanks to You. Thank You Lord that today we can count every blessing You have bestowed upon us.*

*Father God, we thank You for all the many gifts with which You have blessed us and we ask You to help us to be good stewards in the way we use these gifts to honor You. Father we acknowledge that whatever we do with our gifts is entirely up to us but we know that one day we will have to appear before You to give an account of our stewardship. Help us Dear Father never to waste the many opportunities You have given to us to make a difference in the lives of others by using our gifts and talents to witness to them. Lord we ask You for wisdom and understanding to guide us as we do the work for which You have called us. May we always Lord seek to bring honor and glory to Your name as often as we can. This we ask You in the name of Jesus, our Lord and Savior. Amen.*

## September

# Pray In His Presence

## Day 19

*David praised the Lord in the presence of the whole assembly, saying, "Praise be to you, Lord, the God of our father Israel, from everlasting to everlasting."*

1 Chronicles 29:10

It is indeed a good and honorable thing for us to sing praises to our God when we gather together to worship Him. We should never be afraid to express our deepest gratitude to God for all His bountiful blessings. From everlasting to everlasting, we will praise God's holy name forever and ever throughout the earth. His goodness and mercy to us who call upon Him will always be made available if we remain faithful to Him. When we assemble ourselves together as Children of God in His house of worship, our only focus should be to lift up His name and to express our love and adoration for Him. The more we draw closer to God and to our brothers and sisters in Christ, the closer will God draw near to us and be ever present with us.

Our Father God we thank You that You are the only one who knows what is in our heart and how we are thinking. We thank You for cleansing us and for healing us so that we can live with a pure and contrite heart even as we focus all our thoughts on You. Lord Jesus we thank You for the opportunity You have given to us to share with others what You have done for us and through us. Father we thank You that ever since You came into our hearts, our lives have never been the same again.

Loving Lord Jesus, help us that when brothers and sisters assemble together to worship You that our only focus should be to lift up Your most high and precious name and to attribute to You all praise and glory. Father in Heaven, we realize that the more we seek to draw closer to You is the closer You will draw to us and keep us in Your holy presence at all times. Thank You Father that Your goodness and mercy will always be available to us if we remain faithful to You to the very end of our lives on this earth and into eternity. Hear our prayer Lord and let our cry come unto You. Amen.

# September

# The Gifts of God

## Day 20

*"But who am I, and who are my people, that we should be able to give as generously as this? Everything comes from you, and we have given you only what comes from your hand."*

1 Chronicles 29:14

God is the giver of every good and perfect gift and it is our duty to give back to Him the best of what we have. Too often we forget that all of our possessions belong to God that He has entrusted to us to use wisely while we are here on earth. We should never be afraid or reluctant to return to Him that which He has blessed us with. We should give to Him our tithes and offerings and all that we have to use to glorify and edify Him and to be of help to those in need. God in His wisdom and understanding has seen fit to bless us the way He has done and in return He wants us to be a blessing to others. Let us then not become weary in well doing because this is what the Lord wants us to do in order to bring honor and glory to His name forever and ever.

*Lord we thank You for Your words that bring life and healing and meaning to our aching souls. Father we thank You that Your words comfort us and give us strength when we need it most. We want to thank You Father for giving to us everything that we need to exist and to live a good and happy life. Help us Lord that whatever we do for You on this earth will be done to the best of our abilities because You always give to us the best. We thank You Father that You are the giver of every good and perfect gift and it is our duty to give back to You the best of what we have,*

*Lord, forgive us for the many times we have acted as if all we have is ours when everything we possess comes from You. Help us Dear Father never to be afraid of giving back to You what You require of us. You Father have given to us abundantly and yet You have just asked us to return a little portion of what You have blessed us with which we find difficult at times to do. Forgive us Lord for not living up to our expectations and for letting You down so often. Grant us Lord the will to do what is right and pleasing in Your sight. This we pray in the name of Jesus. Amen.*

# September
# Sharing God's Word With The World

## Day 21

*That day David first appointed Asaph and his associates to give praise to the Lord in this manner. Give praise to the Lord, proclaim his name; make known among the nations what he has done.*      1 Chronicles 16:7

Too often we spend so much time focusing on the negative and unpalatable things rather than turning our attention to all the wonderful things happening around us and give God the praise and glory. Amidst all the crises we might be going through in this life, God is still in control of our lives and our destiny. Even in the throes of calamities and natural disasters, God uses these to draw our attention to Him as the only one who can bring order to disorder and chaos. Like David, we must continuously and consistently give praise to the Lord and proclaim and make known to the world what the Lord has done for us His people. The more we glorify and thank God for His goodness and faithfulness towards us, the more others will learn to appreciate and honor the God whom we serve.

*Gracious and loving heavenly Father, we thank You for giving to us Your gift of salvation and for Your indescribable gift of eternal life and the power to do Your will today. Lord help us that this day we will be used as instruments by You to proclaim the good news of salvation to whomever we come in contact. Father for Your goodness and mercy which You have so willingly lavished on us, we give You our thanks and we pray Lord that You will always help us to express our gratitude to You at all times.*

*Lord Jesus, we are living in a world where the negative things tend to dominate our time and we forget about the good things that are happening in the world and around us. Lord, we know that despite all the challenges and difficulties we might be going through in this life, You are still in control of our lives and our future. Father help us to appreciate that the more we glorify and lift up Your name for all Your goodness and faithfulness towards us, is the more those who do not know You will want to get to know You better. Lord we ask You to bless us through Your Son, Jesus. Amen.*

# September

# Worship That Is Acceptable

## Day 22

*Therefore, since we are receiving a kingdom that cannot be shaken, let us be thankful, and so worship God acceptably with reverence and awe.* — Hebrews 12:28

God's kingdom is unshakeable and unmovable and so we do not have to be afraid as we stand on a sure and secured foundation. There should be no limit to how we show our gratitude and thanks to our heavenly Father for all the wonderful things He does for us. When we come into the holy presence of the Almighty, we must do so in reverence and awe because He is God. Even as the heavens declare the glory of God, so should we His chosen children sing praise and bow down in worship to our King of kings and Lord of lords. There are many kingdoms on earth, but God's kingdom that cannot be shaken is the true and everlasting kingdom.

Immortal and Invisible only wise God, we thank You that You rule supreme in heaven and on earth. Thank You Father that Your kingdom is an everlasting kingdom which will never be shaken. Help us dear Lord to come before You with singing and thanksgiving and always with a grateful heart. Father we thank You that even though heaven and earth will pass away that Your kingdom will be forever and ever and we look forward in being with You one day in Your kingdom.

Father we realize that there are many kingdoms on this earth but there is none equal to Your kingdom because Your kingdom is from everlasting to everlasting. We pray Father that You will help us to stay steadfast and immovable in our faith so that we will have the glorious opportunity of being with You in heaven where Your throne is. Father we can only imagine what a day of rejoicing that will be when all those who have remained faithful to You will be ushered into Your Holy of holies. We give You all our praise and thanksgiving in the wonderful name of Jesus. Amen.

## September

# He Is Lord Of All

### Day 23

*Mattaniah son of Mika, the son of Zabdi, the son of Asaph, the director who led in thanksgiving and prayer; Bakbukiah, second among his associates; and Abda son of Shammua, the son of Galal, the son of Jeduthun.*
Nehemiah 11:17

God accepts all our praise and thanksgiving no matter from whomever it comes. He is God and it is He who has made us all and so we should express our gratitude to Him wherever and whenever. In the same way people of gone by days expressed their thanks and appreciation to God, so we too need to express our gratitude to Him through our prayers. God has been so gracious, kind and tenderhearted to us in every situation and so it behooves us to show our hearts of gratitude to Him at all times. We will be blessed and God honored every time we lift up His mighty name and give Him our praise for there is absolutely none like Jehovah.

Thou art worthy O Lord our God to receive all our honor, praise and thanksgiving at all times and in all places because Lord You are indeed everywhere. Father we thank You for being such a wonderful, awesome and majestic God. You are supreme in all that You do and no one can equal Your power and might. Thank You Lord that no matter what language we speak You understand us and we thank You for being such an understanding and loving Father to us.

We thank You heavenly Father for accepting our praise and thanksgiving no matter who we are. Whether we are sinners or saints Lord, You still love us without any conditions. Lord You have blessed all of us with gifts and talents and You send down Your rain on the just and the unjust alike. We know Father God as Your children, we must put You first and foremost in our lives and always and continually lift up our voices in praise and adoration to You. Continue to bless us Father and cause Your face to shine upon us always. In the name of Jesus we pray. Amen.

# September

# Be On Your Guard Always

## Day 24

*I had the leaders of Judah go up on top of the wall. I also assigned two large choirs to give thanks. One was to proceed on top of the wall to the right, toward the Dung Gate.*

Nehemiah 12:31

We all have a special role in advancing the kingdom of God here on earth and it is wise for us to discover what that role is and to do it accordingly. As soldiers of the cross, we need to equip ourselves at all times to fight all the spiritual battles that will confront us daily. The Bible is our weapon of defense against the fiery darts of the devil and like the prophet Nehemiah we need to be prepared to defend the cause of Jesus Christ. When we as God's people come in His name and lift up our voices to Him in praise and thanksgiving, nothing will be able to stand against us and the devil has to take his flight. Let us all stand firm in the name of the Lord and declare His holy name to the nations of the world and to always be on our guard.

*Father in heaven, we thank You for the diverse gifts You have given to us to use to glorify and to honor Your name. Help us Lord never to measure what we can do for You by the standards of others, but to use those gifts You have given to us the best we can to praise and to glorify Your name. We thank You Father for being our true and reliable companion and for not leaving us alone to stumble or fall. We thank You Lord for assigning angels to watch over us and to protect us in everything we do and wherever we may go.*

*Lord as Your soldiers here on earth, help us to be resolute in carrying out our duties in protecting all that You have entrusted to our care. Father may we make a conscious effort in thanking You daily for all Your benefits towards us. We thank You for not withholding anything from us but for constantly blessing us and protecting us from the many dangers around. May we Father praise and sanctify Your name knowing that You are our God and we need to magnify and glorify Your name forever and ever. Help us Dear Heavenly Father to always be on our guard in the name of Jesus. Amen.*

# September

## Taking Your Place

### Day 25

*The two choirs that gave thanks then took their places in the house of God; so did I, together with half the officials.*
Nehemiah 12:40

In this life not everyone will give thanks to God or praise His holy name. However, God loves both those who recognize Him as their Lord as well as those who disown Him. He is no respecter of persons. We should not allow those who do not believe in God to persuade us to renounce Him as many believers have done. Instead we should stand firm in our faith and declare who God is and the transforming influence He has had on our lives. The Bible tells us that by our fruits we will be known, so let our lives and fruit bearing be worthy of the Lord so that others can see Him within us. We all need to stand in His Holy presence and proclaim to the world whom God really is and what He means to us.

*God of might and power and love, we thank You that even though we may not love You as we ought to, You still love us with a passion. We thank You Father that You are indeed the same yesterday, today and forever and that You will ever provide our daily needs. Help us to come into Your presence with a song of praise and thanksgiving, knowing that You are deserving of it all. Lord Jesus we thank You for all the plans You have in store for us to prosper.*

*We recognize loving Father that not everyone will love or honor You or even believe that You exist. Lord though there are those who fail to give You thanks and praise for what You have done for them, we will ever remain grateful to You Father for Your bountiful blessings You have given to us. Help us dear Father always to show our praise and thanksgiving to You especially when we enter into Your house of worship with fellow believers. You Father God made the heavens and the earth and everything in it and for all these we are eternally thankful. May we Father take our place in Your Holy presence and tell the world about You in the wonderful and precious name of Jesus, we pray. Amen*

# September
## Praise God No Matter What
### Day 26

*And the Levites—Jeshua, Kadmiel, Bani, Hashabneiah, Sherebiah, Hodiah, Shebaniah and Pethahiah—said: "Stand up and praise the Lord your God, who is from everlasting to everlasting. Blessed be your glorious name, and may it be exalted above all blessing and praise."*

Nehemiah 9:5

No matter what is happening in our lives or wherever we may be, it is our duty to stand up and praise the name of the Lord to demonstrate to the world that He is God and that there is no one else like Him. Who can understand the mind of God, the Maker and Creator of the earth? None of us in our finite minds can and so that is why we are to demonstrate how much we love and appreciate Him for His greatness and mighty power. The song tells us that there is no God like Jehovah because all the other gods are false and inanimate but our God is for real. It is our duty then to exalt and magnify His holy name and to give Him all the praise, glory and thanksgiving due to Him.

*Heavenly Father, we thank You for cleansing us from all unrighteousness and for having made us new creatures through Your Son Jesus Christ. Lord thank You for washing away all our old ways of thinking and behaving and for enabling us to live new, productive and meaningful lives. We thank You Father that through Jesus, we can come to You boldly to the throne of grace to worship and adore Your holy and blessed name. Father we thank You that the more we praise and lift up Your name the more Your blessings come pouring down on us.*

*Loving and living Father God, help us always to stand up and praise Your name because You are from everlasting to everlasting. May we Father learn how to bless, glorify and exalt Your most blessed and holy name at all times and in diverse places. You are indeed Father God worthy of our praise, thanksgiving and adoration and that we should do as often as we can. It is our duty Lord to exalt and magnify Your name in the beauty of holiness even as we bow down before You to worship You. Our Father, we know that no matter what may be happening around us or going on in our lives, we are to praise and magnify Your name in all places and at all times. This we pray in the name of Jesus. Amen.*

# September
# The Impact of Giving Thanks
## Day 27

*Taking the five loaves and the two fish and looking up to heaven, He gave thanks and broke the loaves. Then He gave them to His disciples to distribute to the people. He also divided the two fish among them all.*

*Mark 6:41*

    Is it not amazing how Jesus was always at the right place at the right time and how He always takes care of our needs? We are to trust Him with our lives as He knows what's best for us. There is so much we can learn from the life of Jesus who while He was on earth lived a sinless and perfect life. He was always giving thanks to His heavenly Father and was continually in touch with Him through prayer. We as followers of Christ must follow in His footsteps by emulating the examples He has left us to follow. We do not have to read any other book for guidance but the Bible as it contains all we need to know on how Christ lived His life on earth and how we in return should live ours as well.

    O Loving and Merciful Father, we thank You today for the way in which Your Son Jesus takes care of all our needs and those of others. Please remind us Lord that we are to show our gratitude to You at all times even as Jesus did. Lord, we thank You for having invested so much in us and thank You for not giving up on us even when we sin so much. Father we thank You for being a God of love and compassion and we thank You especially for giving us choices. We acknowledge Father the impact giving thanks to You has on our lives and we ask that You accept our profound thanks and gratitude to You for all that You have done for us.

    Lord Jesus, thank You for all You have done for us including giving Your very life as a sacrifice to save us from our sins. Lord Jesus, You lived a perfect life while You were on earth and we ask You to help us to follow as much as possible in Your footsteps and to challenge ourselves in walking a life worthy of our calling. We thank You Lord Jesus that You have promised to be with us Your children even to the end of our lives here on earth and in the life to come. We are so happy Jesus for loving us the way You do and for always being there for us. We give You all our praise and thanksgiving Jesus and ask You to accept us just as we are. This we pray in Your name and for Your sake. Amen.

## September

# God's Gift of Grace and Faith

## Day 28

*For it is by grace you have been saved, through faith— and this is not from yourselves, it is the gift of God— not by works, so that no one can boast.*

Ephesians 2:8-9

No matter how hard we may work and how involved we are, this cannot save us. We are saved through God's grace alone and nothing else. The plan and process of salvation is a gift from God and it is accessed through grace in our Lord Jesus Christ. It has been grace through faith we have been saved and not because we are good or deserving; rather it is because God is good and gracious to us all. We must understand that faith is not a good work in itself that God rewards. Faith is simply casting our unworthy selves on the mercy of a kind and forgiving gracious God.

*Oh Father in Heaven, we thank You that it is through Your marvelous grace and grace alone that we are saved through faith and not by any good deeds that we have done whatsoever. Lord we thank You that we did not have to do anything to deserve Your grace or to earn it. You gave it to us freely just by believing through faith that Jesus is Your Son and He died to save us from our sins. We thank You Lord that our salvation is secured because of the shed blood of Jesus, our Savior and Lord.*

*Lord Jesus we thank You for the gift of new life You have given to us once we accept You and believe in You. Lord Jesus, You know that we could not save ourselves through the good works that we do and so You have made this possible through Your grace which is freely given to all those who will accept it. Help us dear Jesus to remain well grounded and rooted in our faith so that we will not stray far away from You. Father without Your marvelous and amazing grace, we just could not make it on our own and so we want to thank You for making all of this possible through Your Son, Jesus our Savior. Amen.*

# September

# In Christ Alone

## Day 29

*Salvation is found in no one else, for there is no other name under heaven given to mankind by which we must be saved.*

Acts 4:12

Many people seek to find joy and happiness in material things and the of worship idols. However, the only one who can satisfy our needs and give us a real purpose for living is none other than our Father God. Ever since the creation of the world, mankind has been on a desperate search for meaning to life; for love and health; peace and prosperity; youth and beauty and for happiness. All these are good but they are all temporary. The only source of life, light, love, peace and happiness can only be found in the one name under heaven given among men whereby we can be saved-the Lord Jesus Christ. All of us therefore must acknowledge our need of salvation that can only come through belief in God's Son, Jesus Christ.

*Most gracious and loving Father, we truly thank You that salvation is found in no one else but Your Son Jesus Christ. We thank You Lord that only His name has the power to save such wretches like us. Lord we just praise You for bringing us back from the brink of disaster and for having spared our lives to be the persons we are today. Lord Jesus You are indeed the only one who can make a difference in our lives and we give You thanks for all that You have done for us.*

*Lord Jesus our Savior and soon coming King, we realize that we cannot be saved through our good works but by believing on You and we will be saved. Lord Jesus we acknowledge our need for salvation that can only come through no other name but Your precious name. Lord Jesus we pray that You will help us to humble ourselves, confess our sins and seek Your forgiveness so that we can live with You for the rest of our lives. We thank You Lord that salvation is found in non other than Your Son, Jesus and in His name we want to thank You for giving Him to us. Amen.*

## September

# Prophetic Testimony

### Day 30

*All the prophets testify about him that everyone who believes in him receives forgiveness of sins through his name.*

Acts 10:43

The only mediator we have between ourselves and the Lord, is His Son Jesus Christ who alone can forgive us of our sins. It is good to know that everyone who believes on the Lord Jesus Christ receives forgiveness of sins through His name. Yet there are so many unfortunately who do not believe and run the risk of being lost forever. Our command is to testify to the world about Jesus Christ and the transformation He can bring about in the lives of those who would only believe in Him. We should not stop proclaiming the good news of salvation to all those around us until they accept the Lord Jesus Christ as their Lord and Savior. How pleased our heavenly Father is when one sinner turns away from sin and accepts His Son as their Savior.

*Merciful and loving Lord, we thank You that only You alone can forgive us of our sins and no other. Thank You that through the name of Jesus Your Son, we are covered and we are forgiven and set free. We pray Father that in the same way You forgive us of our sins, we too will forgive those whom have sinned against us. Lord we thank You that once we believe and confess our sins, You forgive us and cleanse us from all our unrighteousness.*

*Lord Jesus we thank You that all people can be saved if they confess their sins, repent and seek Your forgiveness. Forgive us Lord Jesus for allowing our pride and ignorance to get in the way of seeking Your forgiveness and for trusting in You and accepting You as our Lord and Savior. We pray for all those Lord Jesus who once knew You but now they have gone their own way and have forgotten their first love. Lord Jesus bring them back into the fold and restore them to a right relationship with You. This we ask in Your wonderful and precious name. Amen.*

# October

# Peaceful Slumber

## Day 1

*I will both lie down in peace, and sleep; for you alone, O LORD, make me dwell in safety.*

Psalm 4:8

With God in control of our lives, there is certainly no need to be afraid as He promises to take care of us. Sometimes we find it difficult to be at peace with ourselves and with others because our minds are troubled and anxious about life and its challenges. We can learn from the psalmist how to lie down in peace and sleep because of his trust in God and His protection and providential care. Our protection and safety are as a result of the power and presence of the Lord only and we should learn to rely on Him to take us through the difficult and challenging periods of our lives. When the Lord is with us we do not have to fear because His banner over us is love and because He loves us He will keep us from all harm and danger.

*Heavenly Father, we thank You for ever being near to us and for always listening to our prayers and our call for help and for always showing that You care for us. Help us Dear Lord to look to You always in every situation and to never allow a gap to become between us. Lord thank You for providing a place of safety for us so that when we feel overwhelmed and threatened by life's challenges, we can take refuge in this abiding place. We want to thank You Lord for being in control of our lives and for always protecting and guiding us.*

*Lord Jesus we thank You that with You in control of our lives, there is no reason why we should worry or be afraid because You have promised not only to protect us but to provide all our needs. Lord You know that at times we become anxious about life and our anxieties make us even more fearful, We pray and ask You Lord Jesus to strengthen our faith in You and to trust You to take care of us in every situation and circumstances of life. Hear our prayer Father and let our cry come unto You. Amen.*

# October

# Reaping Abundantly

## Day 2

*Let us not grow weary doing good, for in due season we shall reap if we do not lose heart.*
Galatians 6:9

As believers in Christ, we need to sow seeds of love and kindness so that we can receive the blessings that come from Almighty God. Here in this verse, the apostle Paul encourages us to not become weary in doing good for others for when we do good we will reap abundantly. We as Christians need to take responsibility for what God has asked us to do because eternal life comes from planting God's Spirit by faith in Jesus Christ, and not by works of the flesh, we must keep on doing good. We should not get tired of doing good for each other as one day the harvest is coming and we will indeed reap His blessings in abundance.

*Father God, we thank You that as long as You lead us and we follow You, we have absolutely nothing of which to be afraid. Lord it is our resolve to follow You today and every day of our lives as long as we live. Thank You our God for strengthening our faith in You so much that we are willing to take up Your cross and follow You. Lord, we want to thank You for having invested so much in us to the extent of offering up Your only Son to die on a cross to save us from our sin.*

*Father God, help us not to grow weary in doing good for others because that is what You have commanded us to do. We pray Father that we will become responsible in how we use our resources to bless others. You have given us more than enough Father so that we can be a blessing to those who are so desperately in need. Lord Your word has declared it is better to give than to receive because it is in giving that we receive from You more abundantly. We ask You Lord to continue to bless us in the name of Jesus. Amen.*

# October

# True Repentance

## Day 3

*I have not come to call the righteous, but sinners to repentance.*

Luke 5:32

  God is a merciful, forgiving and compassionate Father, so let us not be afraid to confess our sins to Him. Jesus made it abundantly clear that He did not come to call or to seek out those who are righteous but all sinners to repentance. We are all sinners saved by God's grace through faith in Jesus Christ and He has called us out of darkness into His marvelous light. Without Jesus Christ in our lives, we are lost and destined for hell, but thank God for sending Jesus into the world to be our Savior and Lord. True repentance means that we have accepted that we are sinners, we make confession of our sins and our lives become transformed and vowing to walk with Jesus for the rest of our lives.

  *Gracious Father, we thank You so much that You did not send Jesus into the world to save the righteous but to save sinners such as we are. Thank You Lord that there is nothing that we can personally do to save ourselves, but through belief in Your Son and repentance of our sin, we am saved. Father we thank You for pulling us out of so many horrible pits and placing us on solid ground. Help us that we will never forget to praise You and to share with others all the wonderful things You have done for us.*

  *Lord Jesus we know that we are sinners saved by grace through faith in You and not because of any good works we have done. Lord Jesus we thank You that You came not to call those who think they are righteous but sinners just like us. We praise You Lord Jesus for having called us out of our darkness of sin into Your marvelous and transforming light. We realize Lord Jesus that without You we are lost and hell-bound, but thanks to You for the sacrifice You made for us by giving Your very life on a cross to save us from our sins. It is in Your wonderful name we pray. Amen.*

# October

# Forgive and Forget

## Day 4

*Be kind and compassionate to one another, forgiving each other, just as in Christ God for gave you.*

Ephesians 4:32

Jesus has taught us how to love and to be kindly affectionate one to the other, showing love and compassion and forgiving those who have wronged us. Jesus is our greatest example of one who was and is kind, compassionate, merciful and forgiving. We too must put into practice as followers of Christ these characteristics as well so that the world will know we are really genuine in all that we do and the lives we are living out each and every day. There are times when we forget what our mission on this earth is which is to love God first and then loving others even as we love ourselves. Let us all make a concerted effort as children of God to be truly kind, compassionate, forgiving and forgetting even as the Lord Jesus Christ has done for us.

*O Lord our God, we give You thanks for all Your kindness and compassion You have lavished on us so generously. Thank You Lord for the many opportunities You have given to us to demonstrate our love and compassion for others. Help us Father never to take anything for granted but to constantly express our gratitude to You for Your never ending blessings on us. Lord we want to thank You for the reassurance You have given to us time after time that You will never leave us nor forsake us.*

*Lord Jesus we thank You for forgiving us of all the wrongs we have done to You and to others. We confess Lord that we have not always been kind and compassionate to others and sometimes we find it so difficult to forgive others and forget what they have done us. As Your followers Lord Jesus, help us to walk in Your footsteps doing the things You did while You were on earth and loving and forgiving others even as You have forgiven us. Loving Jesus, we know that the only way we can impact the lives of others is to be Christ like in all that we do. We ask You Lord Jesus to bless us even as we pray in Your name. Amen.*

## October

# Our New Image

## Day 5

*Therefore, if anyone is in Christ, he is a new creation; the old has gone, the new has come!*

2 Corinthians 5:17

We take on a new lease on life when we allow Jesus to come into our hearts and take up residence. We praise the Lord that anyone can come to Him at any time and turn his life over to Him and become a new creation. Once we surrender our lives to the Lord Jesus Christ, the old self is gone and we become new creatures in Christ. It is not the Father's will that any of His children should perish but that all of us would have eternal life by believing in His Son, Jesus Christ. What a privilege and opportunity we all have to become children of God and yet so many have been rejecting Him. Let us continue to pray for those who are still contemplating giving their lives to Jesus.

Great God and Creator of the universe, we thank You for having created us in Your own image and for calling us Your children. Lord we thank You that through belief in Your Son Jesus, our old sinful nature is wiped away and we become new persons in Jesus Christ. We acknowledge Lord that we do not know what will happen to us either today or tomorrow, but You do and for this we are eternally thankful. Lord we thank You for supplying all our needs always.

Heavenly Father, we thank You that once we believe in You and accept Jesus Christ as our Savior, we become new creatures with our old selves being transformed into something beautiful. Lord Jesus, we give You thanks for the transformation that takes place in our lives when we truly surrender our lives to You. Thank You Lord Jesus for taking these sinful and wretched lives of ours and turning them around and making us new creatures in Your kingdom. We praise You Father in the name of Your Son. Amen.

# October

# God Our Stronghold

## Day 6

*The LORD is my light and my salvation—whom shall I fear? The LORD is the stronghold of my life—of whom shall I be afraid?*

*Psalm 27:1*

Those of us who are believers in the Lord, do not have to be afraid because God is our light and salvation and the stronghold of our lives. With God we are well protected and nothing can break through His defense because it is strong and well fortified. The psalmist tells us in Psalm 46:1 that God is our refuge and strength and a very present help in times of trouble, so we have no reason to be afraid since He is always there to protect us. What an assurance we have to know that the God whom we serve is the God who has secured our salvation through Jesus Christ and therefore nothing will be able to separate Him from us.

*Loving and compassionate Father, we thank You that when we suffer, You strengthen us with Your Word and with Your Spirit so that we can endure with Your joy the suffering we may have to bear for a season. We take comfort in the fact Lord that You have promised never to give us more than we can possibly cope with and for this we are thankful. Lord we pray that You will help us to hold on to You because You are the stronghold of our lives.*

*Lord Jesus, we thank You that You are indeed our light and salvation and in You we find refuge from the storms of life. Lord Jesus we cannot thank You enough for Your protection and provision and for the ways in which You guide us through troublesome and raging waters. Merciful and forgiving Lord, we just cannot go through this life without You being by our sides because You are indeed the stronghold of our very being. Thank You Jesus for not letting go of us and for making us feel so secured. It is in Your name we pray. Amen.*

# October

# Guarding What We Have Entrusted

## Day 7

*That is why I am suffering as I am. Yet I am not ashamed, because I know whom I have believed, and I am convinced that he is able to guard what I have entrusted to him for that day.*

2 Timothy 1:12

The pain and suffering we may experience in this life is nothing compared to that of our Lord Jesus Christ that He endured on a cruel, bitter cross. We too must be prepared to bear our suffering with His grace as He has promised that His grace is sufficient for all the discomforts and pain of life that we may be going through. As Christians, we should never be ashamed to suffer for the sake of the Lord Jesus Christ because we know whom we believe and we are convinced that He is able to guard what we have entrusted to Him until He returns. Life will not always be easy but we serve a God who has promised to be with us even to the end of our lives on this earth and that is why we must trust Him with our total being.

*O Lord our Father, we thank you for the suffering Jesus went through in order to redeem us from sin. We know Lord that we would never be able to cope with the pain and agony Jesus experienced on the cross, and so we want to thank You for Your intervention on our behalf. Lord, we owe our lives to You and we pray that You will give us the strength and courage to keep on praising You for all that You have done for us. Lord Jesus, we thank You especially for guarding and protecting us from those who would cause us harm and for the hedge You have built around us to protect us.*

*Heavenly Father we know that the pain and suffering we may have to endure in this life, is nothing in comparison to that which Jesus bore on a cross for our sins. Give us Your grace loving Father to endure our sufferings that You have declared is sufficient for us to bear the discomforts and pains of this life that we may experience. Make us bold and strong Lord to suffer for You too because You have assured us that You will guard what we have entrusted to You even until Jesus returns. Father, this we pray in Your name and for Your sake. Amen.*

# October

# God's Slow Anger and Rich Love

## Day 8

*The LORD is gracious and compassionate, slow to anger and rich in love.*

Psalm 145:8

The Lord whom we serve and worship, is indeed a gracious, kind and compassionate God who never takes His eyes from off His children. Let us thank Him always for His mercy and compassion that He never fails to bestow upon us no matter how much we sin. In the same way the Lord has shown to us His compassion and His love, He would have us to be kind and compassionate as well to one another. Sometimes we are too quick to respond to others harshly or in a manner that is not of God and so the Lord would want us to be slow to anger and rich in love towards others even as He is towards us.

*Gracious and Compassionate Father God, we thank You for constantly having compassion on us by supplying all our needs and more. You are truly a loving and wonderful God who is deserving of all our praise and gratitude. Give us this day Lord a greater sense of gratitude to You for all Your mercies and goodness that You have shown to us over and over again. At no moment of the day Lord have we lacked Your care or have had to stand alone and for these blessings we are grateful.*

*Loving Father, we thank You for Your mercy and compassion which You never fail to bless us with no matter how ungrateful we have been. Lord, give us Your grace that we too can be loving, kind and compassionate to others. Help us Dear Lord to try not to become angry or upset with those who may offend us, but rather may we take the high road in forgiving them and loving them even as You would do for us. It is in Your name we pray Father. Amen.*

# October

# Submission The Godly Way

### Day 9

*Submit yourselves, then, to God. Resist the devil, and he will flee from you. Come near to God and he will come near to you. Wash your hands, you sinners, and purify your hearts, you double-minded.*

James 4:7-8

Those of us who would be followers of Christ must first of all submit our lives to Him and act and behave in accordance with His will and purpose for us. To be able to resist the devil, we need to immerse ourselves in the Word of God that is our weapon to defeat him. Every day we need to spend time in studying and meditating on God's Word and applying it to all areas of our lives. The devil is very persistent in pursuing believers in Christ and so we must equip ourselves to fight him off in the name of Jesus with our sword, the Bible that contains God's holy Word. As Christians we cannot afford to be double-minded, but we must always remain faithful to our Father God and come to Him with clean hands and purity of hearts.

Heavenly Father, we thank You that if we come near to You, You will come near to us. Forgive us for the many times we have drifted far away from You especially when we want to have our own way. Lord we thank You for having sent Your Son Jesus to be a light in a dark world and to illuminate our own lives so that we can be used by You to be of service to others. Purify our hearts O God and cleanse us from all that is evil so that we will be free to praise and honor Your precious name.

Lord we thank You for ordering our footsteps and for preparing the path You want us to travel. Help us Father to remain firm and resolute in our faith in order to resist the devil so that he can fly away from us. Help us Father to study, meditate on and apply Your Word to all aspects of our lives so that we can become well grounded and firmly cemented in You. Father, may we come to You with clean lips and pure hearts so that we will not sin against You. This we ask in Your mighty and powerful name. Amen.

# October

## Seek Wisdom

### Day 10

*He who trusts in himself is a fool, but he who walks in wisdom is kept safe.*

*Proverbs 28:26*

The Bible exalts us not to lean on our own understanding but instead to depend on God's wisdom. It is foolish to think that we can put trust in ourselves alone and not in God, because we will fail and only God can help us in every situation. It is not easy to consistently make good choices and put wisdom before our own personal desires, But when we ask God to help us in doing so, our lives will turn out better than they ever could have, had we chosen our own desires over God's will. Let us bring all our issues and challenges to God and then listen to what He has to say to us and not our own foolish desires and see the difference it makes in our lives.

*Heavenly Father we thank You for providing purpose and direction for our lives and for pouring out into our hearts and minds the wisdom we need to fulfill that purpose. Help us Dear Lord to never lean unto our own understanding but in everything we do, say or think, to truly acknowledge You as the only wise and living God. Lord we thank You that when the way seems dark before us, You give us the grace to trust You.*

*Merciful Lord Jesus, forgive us for not being consistent in the choices we make. Often times Father we have put our own personal desires before seeking You and only when things do not work out the way we would want them to, that is when we turn to You. Lord forgive us for our many sins and help us to bring all our desires and issues to You and listen to what You have to say to us through Your Holy Spirit, our Comforter. We give You thanks and praise in the name of Jesus. Amen.*

# October

# Unbelievable Awesome

## Day 11

*However, as it is written: "No eye has seen, nor ear has heard, no mind has conceived what God has prepared for those who love him."*

1 Corinthians 2:9

We can only imagine what God has in store for those of us who sincerely love and worship Him. The half has not been told as to what blessings the Lord has stored up for all those who put their faith and trust in Him. The Word of the Lord declares that no eye has seen nor ear has heard or our minds have conceived what the Lord has prepared for all His children who love and worship Him. This is indeed very good news and we should all try to prove ourselves worthy of this awesome provision God has made for us.

*Most holy and righteous Father, we thank You that Your calling on our lives to do Your will has brought meaning and a sense of purpose to our existence. Thank You Father for the wisdom, patience and spiritual insight You have given to us as we seek to serve and to follow You. Thank You Lord for giving to us the integrity, skills and right attitude that please You as we serve in the various ministries in which we are involved. Father we thank You for all the many blessings You have stored up for us and help us Father to prove ourselves worthy of these blessings.*

*Loving Father, You have said in Your Word that eyes have not seen nor ears heard or minds conceive what You have prepared and have in store for us. Your love and kindness Father are beyond human comprehension and we will never truly understand why You love us the way You do despite our sinful nature. We sincerely thank You Father for enrolling us into Your kingdom and for giving to us the best of what You have. Lord You are an awesome and phenomenal God and for all Your bountiful blessings, we say thanks to You in the wonderful and precious name of Jesus. Amen.*

## October

# Jesus The Bread of Life

### Day 12

*Then Jesus declared, "I am the bread of life. He who comes to me will never go hungry, and he who believes in me will never be thirsty."*

John 6:35

There are many today who are seeking and searching for someone who can make a difference in their lives. That someone is none other than the Lord Jesus Christ who is indeed the bread of life and the only one who can transform lives. Jesus Himself said that He is not only the Bread of life, but He is the Way, the Truth and Life and whoever comes to Him, they will be saved. Jesus gave His very life for the sins of the whole world so that those who believe in Him will not perish but will have eternal and everlasting life. He is the only one who can quench our spiritual thirst with the water of life that He gives to us. Let us encourage others to trust Him today and for the rest of their lives.

*Heavenly Father, we thank You that Your Son Jesus is the bread of life and only He alone can quench our thirst. Help us Lord to believe in Jesus so that we will never thirst again. We thank You Lord that Jesus is the fountain of life and from Him will flow springs of living water which can satisfy our spiritual dryness. Lord we want to thank You for guaranteeing us rooms in the kingdom You are preparing for all those who love and serve You.*

*Mighty God, we thank You that anyone who comes to You will never go hungry because You are the Bread of life and from You come springs of living water. Thank You Dear Jesus that You are the Way, the Truth and the Life and without You in our lives everything is meaningless. We thank You Lord Jesus for giving to us abundant life that is from everlasting to everlasting. Thank You Father God for giving Jesus to us, and thank You for the difference He has made in our lives. For all these and other blessings we give You thanks in the name of Jesus. Amen.*

# October

# Speaking The Truth Always

## Day 13

*Truthful lips endure forever, but a lying tongue lasts only a moment.*

Proverbs 12:19

God requires us to come into His holy presence with clean lips and a pure heart so that He can acknowledge us as His children. Words of truth are consistent and can withstand all tests, while lies are soon found out and exposed. People who speak the truth will have an established reputation among others and what they say can be trusted and believed. On the other hand, those who habitually indulge in lies cannot be trusted and they have a bad reputation for lying. Our Father God expects us to speak the truth at all times and to be humble enough to accept when we have done wrong and seek His forgiveness.

*O God our Father, we thank You for being closest to us when we are farthest away from You and for Your holy presence in time of distress and despair. Lord we thank You that You require us to be truthful in everything we do or say and to live lives that are holy and acceptable in Your sight. You know Father how easy it is for us to travel down the wrong road that leads to destruction and so we thank You for giving us the courage and the strength to resist the devil.*

*Lord Jesus we are all prone to telling lies especially when we find ourselves in some kind of trouble. Father instead of us admitting when we are at fault, we will try to lie our way out of the situation in which we find ourselves. Remind us Loving Father that lying lips are an abomination to You and every lie we tell will soon be found out. Forgive us we pray Lord for the sin of lying and help us to cultivate being truthful at all times. Lord we ask You to help us to speak the truth always no matter what it may cost us. In the name of Jesus we pray. Amen.*

## October

# Our God is a Shield

## Day 14

*For the LORD gives wisdom, and from his mouth come knowledge and understanding. He holds victory in store for the upright, he is a shield to those whose walk is blameless.*

Proverbs 2:6-7

Our God is a Rewarder of good gifts to those who walk in the path of righteousness and who try to live a good and upright life. We must acknowledge that it is the Lord who gives us wisdom, knowledge and understanding and that we cannot achieve these on our own. He is our shield and protector and He gives us victory if we live upright in our Christian walk with Him. The Lord will never let us down because He has our best interests at heart and He has promised never to leave us or forsake us. All of us who call upon the name of the Lord should walk in a way that we remain blameless which will bring glory and honor and praise to His name.

Father in heaven, we thank You for the wisdom You have bestowed upon us. Help us Lord to wait upon You and to put into practice the things You show us in Your Word. Lord we thank You that You reward us with good gifts when we remain obedient to Your commands. Thank You for being our shield and buckler and for gifting us with knowledge, wisdom and understanding.

Thank You heavenly Father for Your Word that reminds us that it is You who bless us with Your knowledge and understanding and we are to use these gifts to honor You in everything that we do. Help us Father to read Your Word, memorize it, meditate upon it, pray it, believe it and above all live it throughout all the days of our lives. Thank You Father for being a shield to all those who walk blameless before You. We give You thanks Father for all these blessings in the name of Your Son, Jesus. Amen.

## October

# What Do We Lack

*Day 15*

*Jesus looked at him and loved him. "One thing you lack," he said, "Go and sell everything you have and give to the poor, and you will receive treasure in heaven. Then come, follow me."*

*Mark 10:21*

It is unfortunate that we do not always respond when the Lord makes demands on our lives. To follow Him means we must be willing to make sacrifices. This young man had the best chance of his lifetime and yet he threw it away because his heart was not in the right place. When we allow riches and the things of this world to have a stranglehold on our lives and put these before God, we lose out on receiving His eternal life. The Bible asks the question as to what profit would a man have to gain the whole world and lose his soul? It is not worth it just to live for the temporary things of this world and to miss out on God's promise of eternal life with Him forever. Let us not store up our treasures on earth that will vanish away but instead let us store up our treasures in heaven which will last forever.

*Gracious Father, we thank You that You can do anything through us if we will simply yield ourselves and all that You have blessed us with to You. Lord, help us to make ourselves more available to You to do what You desire of us. Father we praise You and give You thanks for challenging us to leave all and to follow You. May we dedicate our time, talents and treasures to You so that You can use us to do Your will.*

*Lord Jesus thank You for challenging all of us to seek first Your kingdom and everything else will be given to us. We pray Father that we will never allow our fame or fortune to prevent us from wholeheartedly serving You and putting You first before everything else. Thank You Dear Jesus for making a big difference in our lives and for giving Your very life so that we all may be able to live with You in paradise forever. We thank You and praise You Lord in the precious name of Jesus we pray. Amen.*

## October

# Elusive Peace

### Day 16

*Peace I leave with you; my peace I give you. I do not give to you as the world gives. Do not let your heart be troubled and do not be afraid.*

John 14:27

One thing the world is devoid of and that is lasting peace. True and lasting peace can only come from our Father above who promises to give us the kind of peace that passes all human understanding. For years the world has been seeking for peace but there continues to be wars and rumors of wars throughout the ages. Jesus has promised to give us the peace that the world cannot give. His peace is everlasting while the world can only offer peace that is temporary, elusive and conditional. We are living in a troubled and troublesome world where people are always searching for true and meaningful peace in their lives and in their relationships. However, this peace can only be found in Jesus Christ who is not only our Prince of Peace but the only one who can bring tranquility to our troubled souls.

*Eternal Father, we thank You that You are the only One who can give us everlasting peace. Thank You Lord that with You in control of our lives we do not have to worry or be afraid for You have promised never to leave us nor forsake us. Lord thank You for being our refuge and our strength and a very present help when we are faced with challenges of one kind or another.*

*Heavenly Father the one thing for which we long so much in this world is that of peace, yet this peace is so elusive because true peace can only come from You. Lord the kind of peace the world offers is temporary and conditional, but You offer to us the peace which passes all human understanding and which is forever and ever. Thank You gracious Father that we do not have to worry or our hearts become troubled because You are in control of our lives. Lord hear this our prayer and let our cry come unto You even as we pray in the name of Jesus. Amen.*

## October

# Faith Comes From God's Word

*Day 17*

*Consequently, faith comes from hearing the message, and the message is heard through the word of Christ.*
                                                    Romans 10:17

The more time we spend studying the Word of God is the more our faith becomes stronger and deeper our belief in our Maker and Creator. The message of Jesus Christ must be told to all people everywhere so that on hearing the good news of salvation, people will be moved to accept the Lord Jesus Christ through faith as their Savior and Lord. Jesus' message is about love, joy, peace, longsuffering, gentleness, goodness, faithfulness, meekness and self-control. As Christians we need to obediently proclaim the gospel of Jesus in such a way that others will receive His Word and become transformed by the renewing of their minds.

Lord we thank You for strengthening our faith through the study of Your Holy Word. Thank You Father for the hope You give to us to know that if we have but a little faith and believe in You we can do great things for You. Please help us Lord that in everything we do to have a positive attitude and to live with a mind-set of patience and courage as You work Your will in our lives. Father, we want to thank You for the life changing experiences we have had through faith in Jesus Christ.

Heavenly Father, we thank You for manifesting Your love towards us by sending Your Son, our Lord and Savior, Jesus Christ to die for us to set us free from our sins. Teach us Father as to how we can proclaim this good news to others so that they will come to know You through faith in Your Son, Jesus, our Lord. Father, help us never to fail in spreading the good news of salvation to all with whom we come in contact so that they can know more about You and all the wonderful things You have done for us and what You will do for all those who accept You. This we ask in Your wonderful and special name. Amen.

# October

# Fulfilled Promise

### Day 18

*I am with you and will watch over you wherever you go, and I will bring you back to this land. I will not leave you until I have done what I have promised you."*

Genesis 28:15

We must spend time thanking God for all the promises He has made to watch over us and to keep us safe. No matter how far we have wandered away from God, He always seeks to bring us back to Him. Once the Lord begins a work within us, He will never leave us until He has accomplished all that He has promised. Believers in Christ are His chosen people and so He takes special care of all those who are faithful and committed in following Him. God's love surpasses any other love and so we do not have to worry about anything, because we serve a God who not only keeps His promises but fulfills them.

Loving Father, we thank You for the joy and peace You bring to our lives every day and for Your promise of watching over us wherever we may go and whatever we may do. Lord we thank You for instilling in us a love for You and for giving us the opportunity each day to thank You for all the wonderful blessings You keep pouring down on us. Thank You Father for caring so much for us even when we wander far away from You.

Mighty God, we thank You for being with us and for watching over us wherever we may go. We thank You Father for bringing us back into the fold when we go astray and for rescuing us time and time again. We give You praise and glory Lord for not leaving us nor forsaking us but for staying with us even to the end as You have promised. You have been so good to us Father and we want to thank You for remaining faithful to us no matter how unworthy we have been and for fulfilling all of Your promises. This we pray in Your name and for Your sake. Amen.

## October

# Everything Will Be Blessed

*Day 19*

*He will love you and bless you and increase your numbers. He will bless the fruit of your womb, the crops of your land—your grain, new wine and oil—the calves of your herds and the lambs of your flocks in the land that he swore to your forefathers to give you.*

Deuteronomy 7:13

Our God never fails in delivering His promises. From the beginning of time until now He continues to be faithful to His Word and promises. The Lord has promised to love and to bless us and to increase all that He has given to us. He has promised to bless everything we possess and so we must trust Him at all times. When we fail to keep our promises, He will never fail to keep His. The Lord has demonstrated over and over again His deep and unconditional love for us His children even when we take Him for granted. Let us bless and praise His holy name at all times and in all places even as we give Him thanks for His many blessings.

Gracious Father, we thank You for the work of Your hands and for all the beauty and splendor we see in all that You have created. Lord we thank You for being a wonderful and awesome God who never fails in honoring Your promises. We thank You Lord that You have promised to bless everything You have given to us and we really want to thank You for replenishing the earth with Your goodness.

We thank You Lord for Your amazing love that always seeks to meet our needs. We pray in faith Father recognizing that You are able to do all things and that all Your promises of Your Word are true and we thank You for never failing to deliver on these promises. Father we thank You for having revealed to us time and time again Your unconditional love for us which You have expressed through Your Son, Jesus Christ, our Lord and soon coming King. Thank You Father for treating us so special knowing how much we have sinned and wandered far away from You. We give You thanks Father for blessing everything in the name of Your Son, Jesus, we pray. Amen.

# October

## We Are His Forever

### Day 20

*But God will redeem my life from the grave; he will surely take me to himself.*

*Psalm 49:15*

Our ultimate goal in life as Christians is to be with our Lord and Savior Jesus Christ when He returns to claim His chosen ones who remained faithful to Him. Even as Jesus overcame the grave so will God redeem us from the grave and raise us up to eternal life in Him. God has paid the ransom for our sin through the sacrifice of His only dear Son Jesus on the cross of Calvary. When we die, God shall take us out of the tomb and take us up to heaven where He has prepared a place for us. This must be our goal to be with the Lord one day where there will be no dying or crying or suffering but everlasting joy with the Lord forever.

*Lord we thank You that Your great love for us conquers the fears that we have. We thank You Father that we do not have to fear dying, or being rejected or being abandoned by You because You have promised to redeem our lives from the grave and to take us with You to paradise. We am grateful and thankful to You Lord for giving us the courage to take a stand for You and for the confidence You give to us to defend our faith. May we learn Father how to honor and praise Your name for all Your goodness towards us.*

*Heavenly Father we thank You for taking all condemnation, guilt and fear from us and for giving us the assurance that You have redeemed our lives from the grave and that one day You will take us unto Yourself. Help us Father to walk in true spiritual freedom in this world and in the one to come. Thank You Lord Jesus for paying the ransom for our sins by giving Your very life for us and for making us Your very own for ever. All these and other mercies we ask in Your name. Amen.*

# October

# When God Holds My Hand

## Day 21

*For I am the LORD, your God, who takes hold of your right hand and says to you, Do not fear; I will help you.*

Isaiah 41:13

When God is in control of our lives we have no reason to fear because He is always there to guide and protect us from all harm and danger. Our God is a good God and one who is always concerned about His children and He ensures that we are well protected and kept safe from all harm and danger. Without His continued care and protection we would be prone to getting into harm's way and all kind of dangerous situations. He is God and He knows what is happening in our lives and that is why He goes before us and fights for us and helps us to fight the battles that confronts us and assures us not to be afraid because the battle is His.

O God our loving Father, we thank You for being our refuge in every time and circumstance of need. We thank You Father for being there for us to guide us through the dark and doubtful periods of our lives. We thank You most precious Father for the path You have carved out for us to follow and pray that You will help us not to depart from the straight and narrow way. Lord we thank You that it is only in You that we can trust and no one else.

Lord we thank You for being willing to fight for us and that You will always help us to be victorious. Father we realize that without Your constant care and protection, we would be vulnerable to all kinds of dangerous and life threatening situations. Thank You for reassuring us Lord that our lives are in Your hands and that You will always protect us from all harm and danger. Lord we praise You for always holding our hands and protecting us in the name of Jesus. Amen.

# October

# Forgiveness Is Reciprocal

## Day 22

*For if you forgive men when they sin against you, your heavenly Father will also forgive you.*

Matthew 6:14

Forgiveness is reciprocal. When we forgive others, God also forgives us of our sins. Forgiveness is knowing that we have done wrong, accepting that we have done wrong, confessing that we have done wrong and seeking God's pardon for all the wrongs we have done, The Bible tells us that we have all sinned and fallen short but if we confess our sins to God He will forgive us and cleanse us from all our unrighteousness. We forgive others when we let go of the hurt and resentment and give up any claim to be compensated for the pain or loss we have suffered or experienced. To forgive others is not the easiest thing to do but in the eyes of God it is the right thing to do.

*Heavenly Father we are very grateful for Your forgiveness. Thank You that it is the name of Jesus that covers our sin when we believe in Him. Lord even as we have received pardon for our sins from You, kindly empower us to also forgive others who might have done us wrong. We thank You that through the shed blood of Your Son Jesus, we are forgiven and set free from the bondage and shackle of sin. Lord we thank You for giving us the power to forgive others as well as forgiving ourselves.*

*Lord Jesus You know it is not easy for us to forgive those who have caused us much hurt and injury but it is what You desire of us to do. Lord Your Word declares that we all have sinned and have fallen short and we need to confess our sins and to seek Your forgiveness so that we can be set free again. Forgive us Lord for all the wrongs we may have done to others knowingly or unknowingly and help us to constantly confess our sins to You so that we can be in a right relationship with You always. All this we ask in Your wonderful name. Amen.*

## October

# Walking In His Footsteps

### Day 23

*This is to my Father's glory, that you bear much fruit, showing yourselves to be my disciples.*

John 15:8

We can only become productive and fruitful followers of Christ when we put our faith and trust in our Father God. As children of God, we will be known by the fruits we bear through the lives we live and how we conduct ourselves from day to day. It is not only good enough for us to know the Word of God, but to live out what His Word says in a practical way. We can only glorify God when we are truly committed in being obedient to His Word and following His blessed examples. The only book many people will read is the book according to the life each and every one of us lives so it behooves us to lead exemplary lives.

O Lord our God, we thank You for Your words that speak to our hearts and need. Lord Your word is our daily nourishment and we thank You for the Bread of Life You provide every single day. How can we ever truly thank You enough for all the wonderful and awesome things You have done for us? Lord we want our lives to bear much fruit for You and we dedicate our lives to serving You as best as we can. Thank You for all the resources You have given to use to make this happen.

Lord we know that we can only become fruitful and productive followers of Your Son, Jesus Christ when we put all of our faith and trust in You. Father You want us to bear much fruits for You and we can only do so through the lives we live from day to day and how we put Your Word into practice. We thank You Lord Jesus for being our example and for the perfect life You lived while on earth. May You help us Lord to continue to bear good fruits for You. This we pray in the name of Jesus. Amen.

# October

## Return To The Lord

### Day 24

*If you return to the LORD, then your brothers and your children will be shown compassion by their captors and will come back to this land, for the Lord your God is gracious and compassionate. He will not turn his face from you if you return to him.* — 2 Chronicles 30:9

The God whom we serve is a loving, kind, gracious and compassionate God who is full of mercy and forgiveness. Let us thank Him for never neglecting us and as long as we are prepared to turn away from our evil and wicked ways, He is willing to accept us back even as we are. The problem with many of us is that due to our sinful nature and our constant sinning, we find it very difficult and challenging to leave our bad habits and turn to the Lord and seek His pardon and forgiveness. God will never turn his face or His back on us even as we do to Him. He loves us too much to treat us otherwise and so we must return to Him and seek His forgiveness and He will show us His mercy and compassion.

*Lord Jesus, we bow in humility before You and thank You for the power to obey and follow Your word. Father many times we have strayed far from You but thank You for seeking us out and bringing us back to You. We know Lord at times we have been very stubborn and want to have our own way, but we want to thank You for being patient with us and forgiving us of our silliness. Father we just want to thank You for being a gracious and compassionate God and one who loves us unconditionally.*

*Lord Your Word declares that if we return to You, You will not turn Your face away from us but You will show us compassion. We thank You Father for all the promises You have made to us Your children and for keeping those promises always. Sometimes Lord we find it difficult to turn away from our sins and turn to You because we feel that we are too far gone. Thank You Lord that You are a kind, merciful, gracious and compassionate Father and You love us so much that You will do anything to rescue us from our waywardness. Please help us Father to turn away from our stubborn ways and return back to You even as we do so in the name of Your Son, Jesus. Amen.*

# October

# The Spirit of Son-ship

## Day 25

*For you did not receive a spirit that makes you a slave again to fear, but you received the Spirit of son-ship. And by him we cry, " Abba, Father."*
Romans 8:15

God is our Father who cares for us and loves us unconditionally and that's why there is no need for us to be afraid of Him. We are indeed heirs of the Most High God and as heirs to His throne, we have the privilege and opportunity to call our God, "Abba Father." God did not spare His own Son, Jesus but gave Him up to the world so that all those who believe on Him will become sons of God. Because of Jesus, we are no longer slaves to fear, because through the cross, He took away all our fears and replace them with the assurance that we who believe in Him have received the Spirit of son-ship. We must thank God for the access we have to His Son, Jesus Christ and the changes He has brought about in our lives.

Lord we thank You for Your patience as we seek to learn important lessons from our past. Help us dear Lord to never be afraid of trusting You, knowing that You did not give us a spirit that makes us slaves to fear but of a sound mind. Father we thank You that we can rely on You no matter what the situation might be. Lord we thank You for being the ever-present, ever-loving and everlasting God and Father in our lives.

We appreciate and thank You Father for caring so much for us and for loving us unconditionally. Because of this great love for us Father, we know that we do not have to be afraid for as long as we trust You, You will continue to take care of us. Loving Father, we thank You that despite our many sins, we can call You "Abba Father" without having to ask You to. You are indeed our wonderful and awesome Father God and we want to thank You so much for making us so special to You. All these mercies we ask in none other name than Your Son, Jesus our Savior. Amen.

## October

# Childlike Humility

*Day 26*

*Therefore, whoever humbles himself like this child is the greatest in the kingdom of heaven.*

*Matthew 18:4*

    Childlikeness is a virtue that all of us as Christians should embrace and live out in our daily lives. Humility is such an important aspect of all those who have accepted the Lord Jesus Christ as their Savior and Lord. Jesus was humble throughout His life on earth and He has taught us that we too should humble ourselves before Him. Staying humble means that we know exactly our place and to feel that sense of humility. At no time should we allow our ego to get in the way of practicing and living lives that are truly humble. Jesus uses the example of being like children in their humble ways to teach us the lesson of what true greatness is all about and that is about being humble.

    *Father in heaven, we are so thankful to You that through humility we can become great in Your kingdom. Lord we thank You that despite all the situations and circumstances which might deny Your eternal Kingship, that You rule supreme over the world and that You are in full control of everything. Help us this day Father to rejoice and be glad that Your kingdom is not of this world but it is a heavenly kingdom where one day we will reside with You.*

    *Lord Jesus, we pray that You will teach us how to be humble even as You were humble while You lived on earth. Lord Jesus, it is not always easy to be humble but if we want to enter into Your kingdom, then we will have to live according to Your Word and the examples You have left us to follow. We thank You Lord Jesus that unless we become like little children who are still innocent and sincere, then it is going to be difficult for us to enter Your kingdom. Give us we pray Father that childlike humility which only You can give in the name of Jesus, Amen.*

# October

# Doing What's Right

## Day 27

*Do what is right and good in the LORD'S sight, so that it may go well with you and you may go in and take over the good land that the LORD promised on oath to your forefathers.*

Deuteronomy 6:18

God's people are expected to do what is right, good and honest in His sight so that it will be well with us as we seek to please Him. Whatever promises the Lord has made, He will fulfill all in due time so when we feel like giving up, just remember that God never forgets and that He is always in control. We all need to trust Him and to wait and see the mighty and powerful things God will do when His people call upon Him and remain obedient to His Word. Sometimes it seems a very long time since we prayed to God and ask for something to the point of forgetting, until God showed up at the time when we needed Him to answer our prayers.

Heavenly Father, we thank You for creating us for good for goodness is good for us especially as we seek to live our lives according to Your word. Lord we thank You that there are rewards for living a good, just, holy and upright life which is acceptable unto You. We thank You Lord for keeping watch over us day and night and for protecting us from the traps and snares of the devil. Help us this day Father to give You all the praise and all the glory even as we wait on Your promises.

Gracious Father, we thank You for always being there for us and for never changing. We thank You that You are the unchanging and unforgettable God who keeps Your promises always and delivers when You desire to do so. We thank You Lord that if we do what is right and good in Your sight, it will always go well with us. Thank You Father that You are the God of miracles and that You show up when we least expect You to. We give You thanks and praises for all Your benefits towards us in the name of Jesus we pray. Amen.

# October

## God's Special Creation
### Day 28

*For this reason a man will leave his father and mother and be united to his wife, and the two will become one flesh.*
Ephesians 5:31

    The Word of God has made it explicitly and abundantly clear, the unity and oneness that must exist between a man and a woman who have been married. This is indeed very serious business but so many take it too casually even some Christian couples. In the beginning God created Adam and then Eve because He saw that the man Adam was lonely and he needed a companion, so He made Eve as a helpmate for Adam. The relationship between a husband and his wife should be something beautiful and the one thing that binds them together is love. Where love is lacking in the marriage there is going to be issues of one sort or another. In the midst of the relationship between a husband and his wife is God. He should always be the central figure in this union because He not only created the individuals but He also gave to us the institution of marriage. And the institution of marriage is that which God commanded to be between a man and a woman so that the human race can continue to replenish the earth with children.

    *Loving Father, we thank You for the gift of a wonderful spouse with whom we have become one flesh. Words are not adequate enough for us to thank You for providing such a beautiful, charming, loving and delightful companion who loves You dearly and one who walks in the path of righteousness. Lord You are truly an amazing God and we thank You for blessing us with a wonderful family.*

    *Heavenly Father sometimes we tend to take our spouses for granted and relationships can become strained which impacts the entire family. Help us Dear Lord always to be sensitive to the feelings and needs of our spouses and to try and be the best husband or best wife we can be. Help us Father never to forget the vows we took to love and care for each other, in sickness and in health, until death do us part. Unfortunately Father many marriages have gone on the rocks because there was not the willingness to try and make them work. Bless we pray Father all couples who have been joined together in holy matrimony and also their offspring in the name of Jesus, we ask. Amen*

# October

## Rewards Galore

### Day 29

*"I tell you the truth," Jesus said to them, "no one who has left home or wife or brothers or parents or children for the sake of the kingdom of God will fail to receive many times as much in this age and, in the age to come, eternal life."*

Luke 18:29-30

Total commitment in doing God's will pays big dividends. As Christians we cannot be half or partially committed, it must be one hundred per cent all the way. If we are going to be true followers of Jesus Christ then we must be prepared to give up certain things in order to become fully committed to Him. When we give up anything to follow Christ, He says all of us will be duly rewarded. Some of us might be called to leave our homes and countries to go to other countries to spread the Word of God as many have done and are doing. Jesus promises that those who make this sacrifice for Him, will be blessed many times in this world and the one to come.

*Dear Lord, we thank You for the assurance that You have given to bless us if we renounce everything else for Your kingdom. It is not always an easy decision to make Lord but it is the right decision and we thank You that we can count on Your promises. Creator God, help us to see where we are called to shepherd Your creation today and we thank You for the tools You will make available to us to carry out Your will and purpose.*

*Father God, we thank You for the call You have placed on our lives to become witnesses in a world that is becoming more and more hostile to those who proclaim the good news about Your Son, Jesus Christ. Give us the strength and courage Father to stand up and face the challenges we may encounter because we know that we are not alone but You are with us in every situation. We thank You Father for the blessings and rewards that await us not only in the present but in the world to come. All these and other mercies we ask in the name of the Father, Son and Holy Spirit. Amen.*

# October

# Healing Comes From God

## Day 30

*Heal me, O LORD, and I will be healed; save me and I will be saved, for you are the one I praise.*
Jeremiah 17:14

God our great physician listens to our cry for help and for healing and responds in His time. The Lord can heal us from whatever illnesses or health challenges we might be experiencing if we ask Him to. He does not always answer us the way we would want Him to but He surely does what is in our best interest. We should not become discouraged or disillusioned with God if our requests and prayers are not answered in a timely manner but keep on trusting Him to do His good will in our lives. The Bible encourages us to give thanks in everything but we do not always do so especially when we are going through rough times in our lives. We must remember and accept that He is God of the good times and the bad times and we are to thank Him for both.

*Lord, we thank You for providing for all our needs and not just our wants. We thank You that when we are sick or just under the weather and we cry out to You for help, You hear us and You fulfill the desires of our hearts. Father we thank You that Your resources are limitless and that You have an abundance of blessings stored up for us. Lord, we thank You and praise You for Your goodness and the faithfulness of Your provision and for being with us in the good times and the bad times.*

*Father God, we thank You for listening to our many cries for help and for healing and for responding in Your time. Sometimes Father we became anxious and upset when our requests are not answered as we would want them to. We acknowledge that Your thoughts are not our thoughts neither Your ways our ways because You are God and You work according to Your will and purpose for our lives. Help us Father to give You thanks for everything including the bad things that may happen to us because You are the God of both the good times and the bad times. It is in Your name we ask this Father. Amen.*

## October

# God's Way Is Best

### Day 31

*No temptation has seized you except what is common to man. And God is faithful; he will not let you be tempted beyond what you can bear. But when you are tempted he will provide a way out so that you can stand up under it.*

1 Corinthians 10:13

Every day we are faced with temptations of one sort or another. Let us hold on to God who alone can keep us from falling prey to temptations and He will never give us more than we are able to endure. God is always faithful and He keeps His promises, so whatever He says He is going to do, He will honor because that is who He is. Had it not been for the goodness of God, we could never overcome the many temptations that confront us every day. With His help and guidance, we are able to withstand the fiery darts of the devil and all that he may throw at us. Remember His Word promises that He will not let us be tempted beyond what we can bear and when we are, He will provide a way out so that we can stand up under it. His way is the best to follow.

*Father we thank You that You are the only one who knows all that is in our hearts. You know Lord all the temptations we have been through and still going through and those who have caused us to sin against You in thought, word and deed. Yet we thank You Lord for not giving to us more than we can possibly cope with and for providing a way for us to be able to stand up and face the challenges and trials that we experience daily.*

*Righteous Father, we give You thanks for Your faithfulness in keeping Your promises and for doing what You say You will do. Every day Father we are tempted in one way or another and we want to thank You for not allowing us to be tempted beyond what we can possibly bear. We applaud You Father for providing a way out for us so that we can stand up under the temptations we face each and every day of our lives. We thank You Father that to follow You is the best way forward and we give You thanks in the name of Jesus. Amen.*

## November

# God's Only Son

### Day 1

*She will give birth to a son, and you are to give him the name Jesus, because he will save his people from their sins.*

*Matthew 1:21*

God in His divine mercy and love for mankind gave to the world His greatest gift of all-His only Son, Jesus Christ, our Lord and Savior. The story of Jesus' birth is one that we will never stop celebrating. Our loving and forgiving Father saw the need for sending His only Son into the world, born of human flesh to become our Savior and Lord. This indeed is a true story as recorded in the Holy Bible and although there are those who deny the existence of God and therefore by extension deny the historicity of Jesus' birth and life on earth, we who are followers of Christ believe every Word as recorded in the Bible. One day we will know the reality of God's creation and the existence of His Son, Jesus Christ when He returns to claim His very own.

*Almighty and most merciful Father, You who loved the world so much that You sent Your one and only Son, Jesus, to redeem us from sin, we pause to give You thanks Lord for this wonderful and awesome gift to humanity. The more and more we think about Your love Lord for us, is the more we want to praise and shout hallelujah to Your precious and holy name. O Lord our God, please accept our attitude of gratitude to You for this awesome gift to the world.*

*Most holy Father God, we thank You that in the fullness of time, You sent us Your Son Jesus to be our Savior, Redeemer and Lord and the one who would deliver us from our sins. We cannot express Father our appreciation to You enough for this great gift of Your Son, Jesus whom You sent into the world at a time when there was no hope for lost humanity. We open our hearts Father to Jesus so that He can make a difference in our lives. This we pray in Your name and for Your sake. Amen.*

# November

# Receiving God's Favor

## Day 2

*For surely, O LORD you bless the righteous; you surround them with your favour as with a shield.*

Psalm 5:12

The blessings of the Lord are always given to those who live a holy and upright life. It is good to know that the righteous are blessed by Almighty God and always live under His care and protection. All those who accept God's care, protection and perfection and have given their lives to Him, are the righteous and are indeed blessed by God. Righteousness means taking God's commandments seriously and obeying them and doing what He says we are to do even as Jesus Christ Himself did.

*Father God, You are worthy to receive all our praise and thanksgiving for Your bountiful and manifold gifts to us. Thank You O God that if we live holy and righteous lives, You will bless and prosper us abundantly and surround us with Your favor. Lord we know that we are not worthy enough to come into Your holy presence in our sinful state, but we thank You that through Your Son Jesus, You have given us the privilege to come before Your throne of grace just as we are.*

*Father in heaven, we thank You for the multitude of Your promises which assure us that You will strengthen us in every situation and because of Your power, we are winners. We thank You Father that You bless the righteous and that You surround them with Your favors. Help us Dear Father to continue to keep Your commandments and remain obedient followers of You even as we live according to Your Word. It is in Your name we pray. Amen.*

# November

# Seek God And Live

## Day 3

*This is what the LORD says to the house of Israel: "Seek me and live."*

Amos 5:4

When we seek the Lord we will find Him and He will reveal Himself to us through His Son, Jesus Christ. In Isaiah 55:6, we are encouraged to seek the Lord while He may be found, and call upon Him while He is near. It is important that we seek after the Lord to follow Him and not the things of the world. The Lord tells us that we are to first seek Him and then everything else will be added to those who seek Him. Those who seek after God will not only find Him but they will receive many blessings from Him. When we seek after the things of God they will last but when we seek after the things of this world, they are only temporary and will soon disappear.

*Lord we thank You that You have promised to deliver us from every evil work and preserve us for Your heavenly kingdom. We know Lord that we do not wrestle against flesh and blood, but against principalities, powers, rulers of darkness and the hosts of wickedness in the heavenly places. Lord, we thank You that You have put all these enemies under our feet, and there is nothing covered that will not be revealed, and hidden that will not be known. Father, help us to seek You so that we may live.*

*Heavenly Father help us to seek You and live because without You we are just as dead. We thank You Lord that Your Word promises that if we seek You, we will find You and You will draw near to us. Dear Father, we pray that You will guard us against seeking after the things of this world which are temporary, but enable us to seek after Your kingdom which is from everlasting to everlasting. Surely we know Lord that goodness and mercy will follow us all the days of our lives if we seek after You.. Hear our prayer Lord, and let our cry come unto You. Amen.*

# November

# Sweet Sleep

## Day 4

*When you lie down you will not be afraid: when you lie down, your sleep will be sweet.*
                                            Proverbs 3:24

    It is a wonderful feeling to know that we do not have to be afraid when we go to sleep as our Lord is always there watching over us. Living wisely causes us to sleep soundly, because we know that the Lord watches over us at night as well as during the day. The psalmist David said in Psalm 4:8 that in peace we will lie down and sleep for the Lord makes us dwell in safety. These are encouraging words indeed to know that the Lord constantly keeps watch over us and protects us from all harm and danger. When we honor the Lord and have a clear conscience, we are not going to be kept awake fearing for the consequences of our actions.

    *Father in heaven, we thank You that our deliverance comes from You and no one can pluck us from Your hand. Father God, we thank You that You are always beside us even when we lay down to sleep and there is nothing that we need to be afraid of or worry about. Lord we thank You that we do not have to be anxious for nothing, but in everything by prayer, supplication and with thanksgiving, we can make all our requests known to you and Your peace which surpasses all understanding, will guard our hearts and minds through Your Son, Jesus Christ.*

    *Loving Lord, we give You thanks for the assurance that You have given to us not to be afraid because You always form a hedge of protection around us. When we honor You Lord with a clear conscience, we do not have to remain awake fearing what may happen to us while we sleep. Help us wonderful Father always to trust You and to know that with You in control of our lives, nothing will overcome us. We give You Praise Father in the mighty name of Jesus. Amen.*

# November

# No To The World

## Day 5

*For the grace of God that brings salvation has appeared to all men. It teaches us to say "No" to ungodliness and worldly passions, and live self-controlled, upright and godly lives in this present age.*

*Titus 2:11-12*

God's amazing grace given to all who seek it will enable us to live the kind of lives that are acceptable unto Him in the world of which we live. God's salvation is available to anyone and everyone who will submit their lives to Him and take a stand against worldly lust and passions and instead living self-controlled, upright and godly lives in this world. God's grace is given to all those who will accept it freely and His grace alone is sufficient to keep us from falling prey to the evil one and secured in Him.

*Thank You Dear Lord that we do not have to be afraid of bad news because our hearts are steadfast trusting in You. Father we thank You that through Your grace we are able to resist anything that brings dishonor to Your name and which guides us into living upright and godly lives which are pleasing and acceptable to You. We give You thanks Father that we can walk with hope in our hearts and life in our bodies because of Your steadfast love for us.*

*Gracious Father we thank You that salvation is available to all those who are ready and willing to submit their lives to You and to take a stand against worldly lust and passions and instead living lives that are self-controlled, upright and godly. We thank You Lord that Your grace is sufficient to keep us from falling prey to the devil and evil in this world. Help us Father to walk circumspectly before You all the days of our lives on this earth. Give us the strength and courage to say no to the things of this world as we pray and ask You for all these benefits in the name of Jesus. Amen.*

# November

# God's People Are Called

## Day 6

*I will plant her for myself in the land; I will show my love to the one I called "Not my loved one." I will say to those called "Not my people", "You are my people" and they will say, "You are my God."*

Hosea 2:23

No matter what the situation might be in our lives, our Father God still loves and cares for us because we belong to Him. God's chosen people were the Israelites who kept on forsaking Him and often times turning away from Him. Time after time, God used different people to speak to His chosen people including Hosea the prophet to warn them of His love for them and for them to return back to Him. We too have walked away from God and have sought to have our own way, but God in His mercy and love for us and not wanting us to perish, offered His only Son, Jesus Christ to bring us back to Him.

O God our loving heavenly Father, we thank You that no matter how far we may wander from Your holy presence, You will never leave us nor forsake us. Lord thank You that we are Yours and You are our God. Early in the morning Lord we will arise and give You all our praise and thanks which You so well deserve. Help us dear Father this day never to be afraid of calling out to You to have mercy on us and to thank You for all Your bountiful blessings You have so willingly given to us.

Thou art worthy mighty God to receive all our praise, glory and honor for all the wonderful blessings with which You have blessed us. Even though Father we have wandered far away from You and have sought to have our own ways, You have never abandoned us but instead You have loved us with an everlasting love. We thank You Lord for forgiving us of our sins and restoring a right relationship with You. All these and other mercies Lord we pray in Your name. Amen.

# November

# In Weakness There Is Strength

### Day 7

*He gives strength to the weary and increases the power of the weak.*

Isaiah 40:29

It is in our weakness that God makes us strong and gives us the power to overcome any obstacles in our way. We have all experienced times of weariness and weakness in our lives and it is in those times that we look to the Lord more than ever to give us renewed energy and strength to fight on. Our heavenly Father declares that the battle is not ours but His and He goes before us every step of the way to ensure that we will be victorious. So whenever we may be feeling down and out, let us remember to trust God and He will see us through all our circumstances.

*Almighty God our heavenly Father in whom we live and move and have our being, we thank You that in our frailty and weakness You make us strong and You increase our power. Lord help us this day in showing our gratitude to You, to serve You with a loyal and steadfast heart; to give and not to count the cost; to fight and not to heed the wounds; to toil and not to seek for rest; to labor and not to ask for any reward except that of knowing that we do Your will through Your Son, Jesus Christ.*

*Most gracious and loving Father, we thank You for all the promises of Your Word and for the invitations You extend to us to follow and to serve You always. We thank You Lord that in our weakness You make us strong and when we are weary You empower us to keep keeping on. Thank You Father for inviting us to draw near to You and for Your promise that You will respond by drawing near to us also. It is in Your most holy and awesome name we pray. Amen.*

# November

# Love Without Exception

## Day 8

*For God so loved the world that he gave his one and only Son, that whoever believes in him shall not perish but have eternal life.*

John 3:16

Let us thank God for giving to us His greatest of all His gifts-His Son, Jesus Christ. God's love for us transcends time and eternity and as long as we remain true and faithful to Him, He will always love us. The world in which we live would be a much better place if there was more love being shown and shared among believers and non-believers alike. Imagine God did not spare His only Son from suffering on a cross, but because of His unconditional love for all people, He was willing to make the ultimate sacrifice of His Son to save us from our sins and to give us new life in Christ. We too have no option but to love others even as we have been commanded to by God Himself to do.

O Holy Father, Almighty, Everlasting God, we thank You for sending Your only Son, Jesus Christ into the world to deliver us from our trespasses and sins. Thank You Lord that You sent Jesus into the world not to be served but to serve and to become a ransom for all those who believe. Father in heaven, we thank You that it is through the shed blood of Your Son Jesus that we have been born again and made children of Your kingdom.

Father God we cannot thank You enough for the great love You have demonstrated for us through the death of Your Son, Jesus on a cross. Lord, we owe You our lives as You gave a life in order to rescue us from our sins and to give us a second chance to inherit eternal life. Help us dear Father to love others in the same way You have loved us and continues to love us so that this world may be a better place for all to live. Lord, we ask these and all other blessings in Your loving and precious name. Amen.

# November

# Blessings Galore

## Day 9

*For I will pour water on the thirsty land, and streams on the dry ground; I will pour out my Spirit on your offspring, and my blessing on your descendants.*
Isaiah 44:3

God's promises are ever certain, ever sure and He fulfills them in His time. It is God our Father who replenishes the earth with His goodness and gives us the various seasons. When we are in desperate need during the dry times, we reach out to God to send us rain and He does to quench the thirsty and parched land. God gives us living water through Christ to quench our spiritual thirst and longing for Him. Not only is God willing to forgive us His sinful children, but He wants to pour out the power of His Spirit upon us so that new spiritual life will spring up within us. Acts 2:17 tells us that God says He will pour out His Spirit on all people in the last days and our sons and daughters will prophesy, young men will see visions and the old will dream dreams. We pray that God will soon do a mighty thing among His people especially in these troublesome and trying times.

*Holy and righteous Father, You who are the giver of all good and perfect gifts, and so we praise and thank You for all that is joyful and peaceful in this earthly life of ours. Lord we thank You for the love You constantly express for us through Your manifold blessings bestowed upon us again and again. Dear Father, please help us not to take Your blessings for granted, but rather to declare our gratitude and thankfulness to You at all times and in all places.*

*Father God we thank You that Your Word is true and that what You promise will come to pass. We thank You Father that You have promised to pour out Your Holy Spirit on all people in the last days and there will be transformation in the lives of both young and old. Lord, we believe that the time is near for the return of Your Son, so help us to get ready for we do not know exactly the time or the hour when Christ will appear. We honor and magnify Your name Righteous Father for all the many blessings with which You have blessed us. In the name of Your Son, Jesus Christ, we pray. Amen.*

# November

# Truly Connected

## Day 10

*"I am the vine; you are the branches. If a man remains in me and I in him, he will bear much fruit; apart from me you can do nothing."*

John 15:5

A tree has many parts that are interdependent for survival and so it is with us too. We are dependent on Jesus who is the true vine and we are the branches. For the branches to bear fruits they must remain connected to the trunk from which they get their nutrients. In the same way for us to bear much fruit for Christ we must remain connected to Him or else we cannot be productive. Christ is our vine and we are the branches and from time to time He has to prune us so that we can become more fruitful in doing His work. It is Jesus and He alone who brings forth fruit because those who are separated from Him can bear no fruit.

O God, You who are the Father of our spirit, the lover of our souls and the Lord of our lives, we offer to You our praise and worship. Lord, You who are the vine and we the branches, we thank You for the life-saving power that flows from You to us thus enabling us to become fruitful and productive persons. Lord we want to thank You for Your gift of eternal life through Your Son, Jesus Christ our Lord and Savior.

Heavenly Father, we thank You that Your Son, Jesus Christ is our vine and we are the branches and without Him, we cannot do anything. Help us Dear Lord to remain connected to Jesus so that we can live useful and productive lives fit for Your kingdom. Forgive us Father for the times when we have remained dormant and unproductive and failed in winning souls for Your kingdom. Give us Father the thirst and zeal for Your Word and enable us to become more fruitful in our endeavors for Your sake. This we ask of You Lord in the mighty and powerful name of Jesus. Amen.

# November

# Remembering The Needy

## Day 11

*But the needy will not always be forgotten, nor the hope of the afflicted ever perish.*

*Psalm 9:18*

Those who put their faith and trust in God will not be forgotten and their hope will always prosper. As children of God, we are poor and needy for His grace and He has provided a throne of grace for those who love Him to come to for help in time of need and He will supply all their wants out of the fullness of grace in Christ Jesus. God's promise is to always remember those who are in need and to give hope to those who might be going through afflictions of one kind or another. To God be praised for His continued blessings and provisions on His people.

*O Father Almighty, we thank You for having raised Your Son, Jesus from the dead and give to Him Your glory so that our faith and hope might be in You and You alone. Lord we thank You that You will never forget us nor cause our hope in You to perish in anyway. Thank You dear Father for being the only constant in our lives and help us to always put our faith and trust in You as You are the only one who can keep us from falling.*

*Lord God, Your Word declares that those who are poor are blessed and that the kingdom of heaven will be theirs. Thank You heavenly Father that the poor are not forgotten by You and nothing they hope for will perish. You are indeed a wonderful and awesome Father and we give You thanks for all the abundance of blessings You have in store for us. Father, we owe our very lives to You and we ask You to continue to bless us and cause Your face to shine upon us always. This we pray in the name of Jesus. Amen.*

# November

# God Makes All Things Possible

## Day 12

*"Have faith in God," Jesus answered. "I tell you the truth, if anyone says to this mountain, "Go throw yourself into the sea" and does not doubt in his heart but believes that what he says will happen, it will be done for him.*

Mark 11:22-23

    A little faith in God will enable us to do great and mighty things for Him. Let us be bold and attempt big things in His name. No matter how huge and insurmountable the problems and challenges we might be facing, if we put our faith in the God who is able to do all things, He will enable us to overcome anything and everything that lies within our path. Jesus encourages us to have faith in God who gives us the strength to be able to do all things. The story of Daniel and his three friends, Shadrach, Meshach and Abednego as recorded in the Old Testament, demonstrates how strong their faith was in God who they trusted to deliver them from the impossible situations in which they found themselves. Confronted by lions and a burning furnace, they vowed never to worship any false gods but rather they would trust and depend on their God to deliver them and He did. We too need to exercise our faith in God and leave every situation we face into His hands.

    O Savior of the world, we thank You that if we put to the test the little faith we have, You will use us to do unimaginable things for You. Remove from our hearts Father all the doubts we might have, and help us to step out in faith to do Your will. Lord we thank You that we can always depend on You to fulfill Your promises so that there is absolutely no need for us to be afraid of failing.

    Strengthen our faith in You Mighty God so that we will be able to stand up against any adversity that may come upon us. Father, make us bold and strong to resist the idols of this world which are ever present around us. May our faith be as strong as Daniel and his friends who defied the king's order to bow down and worship idols but rather trusted in You to deliver them. Give us we pray Father Your mustard seed faith so that we will be able to do great things in Your name. Hear our prayer we beseech You Father and let our cry come unto You. Amen.

# November

# Trusting In God Always

## Day 13

*He will swallow up death forever. The Sovereign LORD will wipe away all tears from all faces.*
Isaiah 25:8

As God's people, we all have to face adversity in this life, but God will make a way for us to be comforted. Many of us have experienced the passing of loved ones that has left us sad and with a deep sense of loss and regret. We sometimes find it very difficult to overcome our deep-rooted feelings of grief and we often ask questions as to why this had to happen. God in His mercy and love always work out everything together for good and we certainly cannot question Him. He knows how we feel and the emotions we have and that is why He has promised to wipe away all tears from our eyes and give us His peace.

Lord God Almighty, we know that it is not Your will for us to perish but to have everlasting life. Thank You Father that even though we must physically die, it is not the end as You have promised us new life when You return again to receive those whom have remained faithful and have kept Your commandments. Help us loving Lord to seek You at all times and when we find You, to worship and bow down before Your throne of grace with an attitude of gratitude.

Heavenly Father, You are acquainted with all our sorrows and grief especially when we lose loved ones. We thank You for the comfort You bring us through the Holy Spirit our Comforter. May we look to You Father during periods of loss and loneliness and when our hearts are heavy because those whom we love have been taken away from us. We thank You Father for the assurance that You will wipe away all tears from our eyes and that one day there will be no more weeping or crying. This we ask Lord in Your wonderful name. Amen.

# November

# Love Our Enemies

## Day 14

*But I tell you: Love your enemies and pray for those who persecute you, that you may be sons of your Father in heaven. He causes his sun to rise on the evil and the good, and send rain on the righteous and the unrighteous.*
Matthew 5:44-45

It is not always easy for us to love those who have done us wrong, but as Christians it is the right thing to do according to the will of God. Jesus has given us a new command to love those who may persecute us and say all manner of evil against us for His name's sake. When we heap coals of love, mercy and compassion on those who seek to do us wrong, they will certainly be amazed of our actions. As followers of Christ we must set the right examples even as Christ has done. On the cross, Jesus asked forgiveness for those who had sought for His crucifixion because He said that they did not know what they were doing. No one understood the depths of God's love for us His children when He gave up His very Son to die for the sins of the world. We too are called upon to love and forgive those who have offended us even as Christ did for us.

Jesus our Lord, no one else suffered as You did and yet You not only forgave those who inflicted so much pain and agony on You but You also loved them so unconditionally. Father we Your humble servants have no choice but to love those who have also done us wrong and have tried to damage our reputation. We thank You dear Jesus that You have made it possible for us to be able to love and to forgive others even as You have loved us and forgiven us.

Father we admit that we have not always been kind to others and neither have we loved them as we should. We pray Father that You will forgive us for the wrongs we have done others and we ask You too to forgive those who may have slaughtered our reputation and said unkind things about us. We thank You Father that You are a loving and forgiving God and that You want us to become more like You. Enable us Dear Lord to love all those with whom we come in contact in the name of Jesus, Your Son. Amen.

# November

# The Benefits of Righteousness

*Day 15*

*The fruit of righteousness will be peace; the effect of righteousness will be quietness and confidence forever.*
Isaiah 32:17

God's people should seek after righteousness as there are rewards to be gained. The Bible tells us in Proverbs 14:34 that righteousness exalts a nation but sin is a reproach to any people. In this contrasting verse, the Prophet Isaiah tells us the benefits of righteousness are peace, quietness and confidence forever. There are two paths we can travel in this life, either the path of the righteous or the path of the ungodly or foolish. We have to decide as Christians whether or not we will follow the path of the righteous by standing up for what is right, just, honest, truthful, and morally correct or we choose to follow the things of this world that lead us to a dead end in our lives with no hope for us or for our nations.

*Lord, You have declared in Your word that by our fruits others will know whose we are. Help us Father to remain steadfast in our belief and to live lives that are acceptable unto You. Lord we know that Your word has said that righteousness exalts a nation but sin condemns us and yet Lord we keep on sinning. We pray Father that You will enable us to seek after righteousness so that we might be able to come into Your holy presence to thank You and to praise Your name for ever and ever.*

*Father in heaven, we thank You that You are a God of righteousness, compassion and peace and that as Your children You require of us to live holy and righteous lives. Lord help us to examine our lives to see if there is anything in our lives that is displeasing to You so that we can seek Your forgiveness. Father God help us to choose to follow the path of righteousness and not the foolishness of this world. We thank You Lord that there are benefits to be gained when we follow after righteousness and we ask You to help us to do so in the name of Jesus, Your Son. Amen.*

# November

# Forever Trusting God

## Day 16

*As it is written: See, I lay in Zion a stone that causes men to stumble and a rock that makes them fall, and the one who trusts in him will never be put to shame."*

Romans 9:33

Jesus Christ is the main corner stone of our lives and we should put our trust in Him at all times. We all know that in building a house, the foundation is very important as it holds up the entire structure of the building and corner stones are very important to the strength of the building. For us to have a strong foundation and become well grounded in our faith, Jesus Christ must be the corner stone of our lives. He is the one who can deliver us and keep us from falling prey to the temptations of the world. Once we put our faith and trust in Him, He will never put us to shame.

*Lord Jesus Christ, thank You that You are our rock, our sword and our shield and if we put our faith and trust in You, we shall never stumble or fall. Lord Jesus we thank You for being the bedrock of our lives and the foundation on which we stand is firm and solid and we do not have to be afraid of the storms of life that may come our way. Jesus our Lord, we thank You for the reassurance You have given to us to keep us safe from life's tempestuous seas.*

*We thank You Lord Jesus that You are our sure foundation and when we put our faith and trust in You, we shall not be moved no matter what storms might be blowing. Lord Jesus, we acknowledge that our lives without You would be on shaky ground and so we thank You for being the corner stone of our lives and for giving to us stability in our faith so that we can stand firm and well-rooted in You. Lord Jesus, we pray that You will hear our prayer and make our cry come unto You. Amen.*

# November

# God's Purpose For Us

## Day 17

*The LORD will fulfill his purpose for me; your love O LORD endures forever—do not abandon the works of your hands.*                                          Psalm 138:8

God has demonstrated His love for us time after time and He will certainly not abandon us for that is not His purpose for our lives. When we remain faithful and true to the Lord, He will fulfill His purpose for our lives in ways we would not expect Him to. God's love for us is immense and intense and it is from generation to generation. No matter how much we sin or try to run away from God, He still loves us and He never gives up on us. One thing we cannot do is to hide from God even as Jonah tried to do because just as how His eye is on the sparrow, even so much more His eye is on us His children. We must always show our love and appreciation to God every day by giving Him all the praise and glory for His goodness towards us.

*Almighty and most merciful father, we thank You that Your power and love work together to protect us from the evil one. We pray Father that You will grant us Your grace today to put our trust and faith in You. Lord Jesus, we thank You that You will fulfill Your purpose for our lives and we thank You for Your love which endures forever. Father help us this day to come to You in prayer and thanksgiving and to live our lives according to Your will and purpose.*

*Heavenly Father, we thank You that Your love for us will endure forever as You have promised. We know Father that as long as we remain in You and You remain in us, we will be able to live with You forever and ever. Grant us dear Father the ability to make our lives shine for You in this dark world of ours. You are the only one Father who can enable us to be what You want us to be and to do what You want us to do and for this we give You thanks. Lord we thank You for all Your countless blessings on us in the name of Jesus we pray. Amen.*

## November

# God Guarantees Our Victory

*Day 18*

*For the LORD your God is the one who goes with you to fight for you against your enemies to give you victory.*

Deuteronomy 20:4

Sometimes we feel that we are fighting a losing battle with certain issues over which we have no control. Remember, we cannot do it alone but with God being there for us, we do not have to worry. He has reminded us in His Word many times that the battles we fight are not ours but His and so we must trust Him to give us the victory. Many times we have tried to fight our own battles and we fail because we did not include our Father God in our plans. When we try to do things on our own without involving God, it becomes more difficult for us to overcome the issues we are fighting. However, when we take our challenges and difficulties to God and seek His guidance, He helps us to be victorious. Let us remember that it is the Lord who goes before us and with us to fight against those who would bring harm to us and cause us to stumble and gives us the victory over them.

*Gracious and ever-blessed Father, we thank You that as holy and transcendent as You are, You have throughout the ages shown Yourself to be accessible to the prayers and cries of feeble people such as we are. Thank You Father for Your understanding and the way in which You so graciously and lovingly supply our every need. Father we thank You that we do not have to fight our battles alone because You have promised to be always there to defend and shield us from those who would harm us.*

*Dear Father God, we thank You that we can always turn to You especially when we are faced with the difficulties of life because Your Word tells us that You always go before us to ensure that the way ahead of us is safe. We thank You Lord that You are our refuge and strength and a very present help in times of trouble and because of this You will not only defend us but lead us to victory. We praise You and magnify You Father for always looking out for us and we give You thanks in the precious name of Jesus. Amen.*

## November

# Respecting Those Who Are Weak

## Day 19

*Blessed is he who has regard for the weak; the LORD delivers him in times of trouble. The LORD will protect him and preserve his life; he will bless him in the land and not surrender him to the desire of his foes.*

Psalm 42:1-2

Let us thank God our Father for guiding, protecting and guarding us from difficult, treacherous and troublesome times. We are thankful to God that He is in control of every facet of our lives. When we are feeling weak He delivers us in times of trouble; He protects and preserves our lives and His blessings are always upon us. Like the Psalmist, we need to bless the name of the Lord for all the wonderful blessings He keeps on pouring down on us. We are so undeserving of God's love and mercy and yet out of the abundance of His heart, He keeps on showering His manifold blessings on us. We should make every day of our lives a time of giving thanks to Almighty God for all that He has done for us and will continue to do.

*Lord our thanks go to You for delivering us in times of troubles and hardships and for keeping us safe from our enemies. We are weak Father but You are strong and we thank You that we can lean on You when we feel weary and depressed. Lord You know life is not always kind to us but we praise and thank You for the way in which You reach down to us and put Your loving hands around us and give us Your peaceful reassurance that all will be well.*

*Heavenly Father, we thank You that You will keep us in perfect peace if our minds are fixed on You. Help us Father to trust in You forever, for You are our Rock eternal. With You Father in charge of our lives, we know that You will deliver us in times of trouble and that You will preserve and protect us from all those who would do us harm. We give You thanks Father for being such a good and wonderful God to us and for Your protection and guidance always. Help us Lord to defend those who are weak and are often times disadvantaged in the wonderful name of Jesus, we pray. Amen*

## November

# Love Begets Love

### Day 20

*Whoever has my commands and obeys them, he is the one who loves me. He who loves me will be loved by my Father, and I too shall love him and show myself to him.*
John 14:21

As Christians we cannot say we love the Lord and yet behave contrary to what He expects of us which is plain hypocrisy. We as Christians are called to a higher standard to be in the world but not of the world and to always be obedient to God's Word. The Lord expects us not only to talk the talk but to walk the walk so that others will truly know that we belong to Him. God is love and because He is love, those who follow Him must not only love Him but must also obey what His Word tells us to do. Jesus has given us His assurance that those who follow His commands and do the things He has commanded us to do, are the ones who love Him and by so doing we will also be loved by God our heavenly Father.

Father in heaven, we thank You that we have no other choice but to love You since You first loved us and gave to us Your only Son to be our Savior and our Lord. No one else Father has ever done or will do what You have done not only for us but for the whole world in giving the greatest gift of all to humanity-Your one and only Son to die in order that we might have new life. Thank You Father that one day we will come face to face with Your Son, Jesus who has gone to prepare a place in heaven for us.

Lord, we thank You that there is no other love like the love of Jesus which He demonstrated by dying on a cross to save us from our sins. We thank You Father for first loving us and for putting Your love into action through the gift of Your only Son, Jesus to the world. Help us Dear Father to learn how to love You and to be obedient to Your Word. May we love You Father with our whole being and help us to love others even as You love us. It is in Your name we pray. Amen.

## November

# The Sinless Becoming Sin

### Day 21

*God made him who had no sin to be sin for us, so that in him we might become the righteousness of God.*
2 Corinthians 5:21

Let us thank God for Jesus who took on our sin and paid the price at Calvary with His life. God in His love for lost humanity, clothed Himself in mortal flesh so that through the surrender of His Son Jesus who became the sacrificial Lamb of God, we could be fully identified with Him. God in His mercy, grace and love, adopted us as His children and made us joint heirs with Jesus. God loved the world so much that He made Jesus who knew no sin to be sin for us that in Him we would become the righteousness of God. This is just so awesome to know the extent to which God went in order to redeem us from our sins.

*Today O Father, we thank You for Jesus who gave His life to redeem us, Himself for our example, His word for our guide, His grace to save us and His body on the cross to wash away our sin and that of the whole world. How can we thank You enough Lord for all that You have done for us even though so undeserving of it all. Lord Jesus we love You and we want to thank You for all that You have done for us.*

*Father God, we can scarcely take in the depth of Your love for us sinners who deserved nothing but condemnation. We praise You Father for Your grace, love and wisdom towards us and we thank You Father that You made Jesus who knew no sin to be made sin for us so that we might become the righteousness of God in Him. We thank You Lord that through Christ there is no condemnation for those who believe in Him as their Savior and Lord. We give You thanks Father for all that You have done for us in the name of Jesus, we pray. Amen.*

# November

# Restoring Health

## Day 22

*But I will restore you to health and heal your wounds, declares the LORD.*

Jeremiah 30:17

Our God is the greatest of all physicians and He is in the healing business. During times of health challenges and when everything we have tried to get relief fails, we look to our great Healer, Almighty God who alone is able to help us through the difficult moments of our lives. We all tend to suffer from some physical or spiritual wounds and our only hope for being healed in one way or another is to seek God's healing touch and power on our lives. When we put our total faith and trust in the Lord, He has promised to be with us through the most difficult and challenging periods that we will experience in this life. We must recognize that our healing is not only physical but it is also spiritual and He does both to relieve us from any form of suffering.

O God our Father, we thank You for making us as we are. We thank You Father for blessing us with healthy bodies and healthy minds. Lord we thank You for all the interests of life and for the opportunity to learn new things and to know new places. We thank You precious Father for all the people who mean so much to us-our families, friends, teachers, spiritual leaders and all those with whom we come in contact from day to day.

Heavenly Father, thou who art our Healer and Great Physician, we thank You for restoring our health and healing our wounds as only You can do. Father our sins have left us sick and truly wounded and only You Lord can restore us in a right relationship with You by forgiving us of our sins and cleansing us from all unrighteousness. Lord Jesus help us to always put our faith and trust in You so that when we are going through the trials and tribulations of life, we will lean on Your everlasting arm. This we pray Father in Your name and for Your sake. Amen.

# November

# God's Saving Grace

## Day 23

*In him we have redemption through his blood, the forgiveness of sins, in accordance with the riches of God's grace that he lavished on us with all wisdom and understanding.*

Ephesians 1:7-8

It is through God's grace that we are saved and not through any good work that we may have done. Our Lord sent His only Son, Jesus into the world so that He could bear the weight of our sins on a cross. His shed blood made atonement for our sins and now we have been redeemed through His blood and forgiven of our sins. When we consider how undeserving we are of God's love, grace and mercy due to our sinful nature, yet He saw the need to sacrifice His very Son in order that we might have new and abundant life in Christ Jesus. Let us give to God our lives in return for all that He has done for us and live according to His will and purpose.

*Accept, O Lord God our Father, the sacrifices of praise and thanksgiving that we offer unto You this day. Thank You Lord Jesus that through Your shed blood on the cross, You have redeemed us from all our sins and made us new creatures. You have taught us many things Father and this one thing we know is to respect and honor Your most precious and holy name and give to You our continuous praise and thanksgiving.*

*Loving Lord Jesus, we thank You for the ultimate sacrifice You made for us all by giving Your life in order that we might be saved. Lord Jesus, we know that You did not have to do what You did by dying on a cross because You committed no sin, yet You willingly surrendered Your life for lost humanity. We thank You Lord Jesus that through Your shed blood, our sins have been washed away and we are now redeemed and forgiven. To You Lord Jesus, we give all the praise and glory. Amen.*

## November

# Do Not Allow Sin To Be Your Master

### Day 24

*For sin shall not be your master, because you are not under law, but under grace.*

Romans 6:14

    Thank God that we are no longer under the heavy weight of the law, but under His grace through which we are saved. When Christ died for our sins it was a once and for all payment and there is nothing more to do but to simply believe God's Word that Christ died for our sins and the result of it is that we are no longer under the bondage of Satan but we are now all part of the family of God. We thank God that Christ died to break the power of sin in our everyday life which means that sin no longer has the power to dominate our lives as believers in Christ as it does with those who do not believe.

    *Lord there is so much for which we have to give You thanks. We thank You Father that we are no longer under the law but under Your grace and therefore sin is no longer our master. We thank You Lord for this beautiful and interesting world that You have made and the way in which everything works in unison. We can just imagine Lord how much worst living in this world would be had You not been in control. We are amazed at this great wonder and we thank You for every detail of Your creation.*

    *Lord Jesus, we thank You for dying on a cross to break the power of sin in our lives and because of this, sin no longer has the power to dominate our lives as believers. Help us Dear Lord Jesus to surrender our lives to You so that You can have full control of all our being. We confess Lord Jesus that many times we have messed up by turning away from You and seeking the pleasures of this world. Forgive us Dear Jesus of all our sins and we ask You to draw us closer and closer to You each and every day. It is in Your name we pray. Amen.*

## November

# The Humble Reaps Rewards

*Day 25*

*Humility and the fear of the LORD bring wealth and honor and life.*

*Proverbs 22:4*

When we humble ourselves before the Lord, we will reap untold benefits. Humility is a virtue we should all strive to possess. Jesus Himself is the greatest example of what it means to live a life of humility. He was the Son of God, but He gave up all the privileges and comforts of this world of living in a kingly state to become poor and homeless for the sake of the lost. He humbled Himself on a cross and bore the pain and agony for the sins of lost mankind. He loved as no one ever loved, He healed as no one ever healed, He gave as no one ever gave and He suffered as no one else ever suffered. We too are called upon to be humble in everything we do even as Christ has taught us.

*Lord Jesus, we thank You for this day You have made. Help us Father to use at least some part of it to think about You and to thank You for Your wonderful creation. We thank You Lord that this is not the only world so help us to live well in this world that we are prepared for the world to come. Father we thank You that if we humble ourselves and fear You, we will be honored by You. Lord we thank You that You will always bless and prosper us.*

*Lord Jesus, we thank You that if we humble ourselves before You, our rewards will be great. Help us Lord Jesus to pattern our lives after Yours as Your life on earth was the greatest example of what it means to be truly humble. May we never be afraid Lord Jesus to do whatever we are asked to do no matter how menial the tasks might be. We know Lord Jesus if we want to be great in this life we need to humble ourselves by becoming true servants who are willing to serve. This we pray and ask in Your mighty and powerful name. Amen.*

# November

# God's Immovable and Unshakable Love

## Day 26

*Though the mountains be shaken and the hills be removed, yet my unfailing love for you will not be shaken nor my covenant of peace be removed, says the LORD who has compassion on you.*

Isaiah 54:10

God's love for His people is unshakable and immovable and no one can pluck us from His hand. The love of God for those who trust and believe in Him never fails and no one can take it away from us. His compassion for us is always available and so we must trust Him at all times to take care of our needs. As Christians we should never be afraid to seek God's favor because He sees us as the apple of His eyes and therefore He cares more for us than we can even think or imagine. Whatever might be happening around us and out of our control, we must remember that God is always in control of our lives and He will continue to bless and protect us.

Thank You Lord God that You are great and mighty and powerful and that You are always in control. Father we thank You that Your love for us will never be shaken and that You will never let go of us. In the midst of danger and threats, we thank You that through Your unfailing love for us, You will protect and guide us from anything that could harm or destroy our lives.

Loving Lord, we thank You that Your love for us is unshakable and immovable and it is from everlasting to everlasting. Thank You Father for Your covenant of peace and for Your compassion on us Your erring children. Father God, thank You for the assurances You have given us through Your Word that You will never leave us nor forsake us and that we can depend on You to deliver on Your promises. All these and other mercies we ask in the name of the Father, Son and Holy Spirit. Amen.

# November
# Not Afraid of Sharing The Gospel

## Day 27

*I am not ashamed of the gospel, because it is the power of God for the salvation of everyone who believes: first for the Jew, then for the Gentile.*

Romans 1:16

As God's elect, we must be prepared at all times to defend our faith and the teaching of God's holy word as contained in the Bible. The Apostle Paul declared that he was not ashamed of the gospel that he preached because it is the power of God for the salvation for every believer. Unfortunately today many of us are afraid and maybe ashamed to share the gospel with others for fear that we will be rejected or challenged and we are not too certain how to respond. We must remember that God never sends us out alone but His Holy Spirit is always with us to intervene on our behalf when we do not know what to do or to say. God's Word is powerful and sharper than any two-edged sword and which is able to penetrate the hardest of hearts and so our task is simply to tell others about what the Lord has done for us and how through belief in Jesus Christ, their lives can also be transformed.

*Lord we thank You that You have made us strong and bold enough to stand up and defend the good news about Your Son, Jesus Christ. Help us Father to never be afraid of testifying to the world that Jesus saves and He is the only one who can make a difference in our lives. Father we thank You that through the gospel our salvation is secured and all we need to do is to keep on serving You faithfully.*

*Lord Jesus help us never to be afraid or ashamed to carry out the mandate of the Bible and that is to go into all the world and tell the good news to everyone. We thank You Father that Your Word changes and transforms lives and all those who seek after You will experience everlasting life. Thank You Father for preparing us to spread the gospel to all those with whom we come in contact and help us to continue to be consistent in all that we do to enlarge Your kingdom here on earth. Loving Lord, it is in Your name and for Your sake we pray. Amen.*

## November

# Give And Be Blessed

### Day 28

*In everything I did, I showed you that by this kind of hard work we must help the weak, remembering the words the LORD Jesus himself said: "It is more blessed to give than to receive."*

*Acts 20:35*

We receive our blessings when we give until it hurts especially to those who are less fortunate than we are. The Lord has blessed us with so much and in return He wants all of us to be a blessing to others. It should be our duty as Christians to pour out bowels of kindness, mercy and compassion on those who are less fortunate than we are. Jesus Himself declares that it is more blessed for us to give than to receive because it is in giving that we too truly receive. Remember that God gave to us His very own Son because of His love for us and so the least He expects us to do is to give back some of what He has blessed us with to the less fortunate and needy.

Wonderful Father, we thank You that You have said in Your word that there is more blessing in giving than in receiving. We realize Father that it is only when we empty ourselves and truly share with others that we in return receive in abundance. Thank You Lord that You have set us the example to give without counting the cost even as You gave Your only Son to be our Savior and Lord.

Heavenly Father, please help us to see others through Your eyes of love and to share the blessings with which You have blessed us with the poor and needy. We thank You Father for the gift of Your Son, Jesus Christ to the world, the greatest of gifts anyone could offer. Give us hearts we pray Father filled with love and compassion for others and the willingness to be ready to give of our best to those who might be desperately in need. Lord we pray that You will hear our prayer and let our cry come unto You. Amen.

# November

# Always Seek Humility

## Day 29

*For whoever exalts himself will be humbled, and whoever humbles himself will be exalted.*
Matthew 23:12

It is a good thing for us to be humble in everything we do so that we might be exalted by our Father in heaven. Simply put this verse is saying to us Christians that it is better for all of us to be humble and consider ourselves a part of those who are lowly, rather than assuming or acting like we are better than others. Too often we see many persons including Christians who have tried to exalt themselves to the extent of forgetting where they are coming from until they are brought low they realize that the only person worthy of being exalted is God. Let us take heed of God's Word and humble ourselves at all times so that if He sees fit to exalt us, He will do so.

*Lord help us today to come to You with a humble and contrite heart so that we might be able to praise and thank You with our whole being. Father, we pray that You will enable us to humble ourselves before You and worship You in spirit and in truth. We thank You Father that Your word is truth and if we know the truth then it will indeed set us free. Thank You today Father for the example Jesus has left us to be humble in all things.*

*Loving Lord, give us the wisdom and strength to remain humble in all that we do. We know Father how it is so easy for us to fail and to fall by being haughty and puffed up and forgetting that it is You who controls our lives. Father God, give us we pray the right attitude to show humility at all times and to wait on You to elevate us if You so desire. Help us Father never to take anything for granted but to keep trusting You and to leave our destiny into Your hands. It is in Your name we pray Father. Amen.*

# November
# Everything on Earth Belongs To God

## Day 30

*Moreover when God gives any man wealth and possessions and enables him to enjoy them, to accept his lot and be happy in his work—this is a gift of God.*
Ecclesiastes 5:19

We should acknowledge that all that we possess is a gift from God to be used to glorify Him and to help others. Before any of us can enjoy our possessions, we must first receive them from God's hands. Once we have received the gifts from God, it is left to us to be either good or bad stewards of what we have received from Him. Some of us will invest those gifts and do well with the returns on our investments while others will waste what has been entrusted to their care by God. The gifts we receive from our Father God are to be used to expand His kingdom here on earth and to be of help to others. None of us should boast about the wealth we have acquired because it is truly not ours but a trust from God who is the Provider of all things.

*Gracious and loving Father, we thank You that nothing that we have belongs to us but it is a gift from You to be used wisely and unselfishly. Help us Lord never to put material things before You since these are temporary, but rather to invest in the things of heaven which are eternal. We thank You Father that we can always depend on You to give to us all that we need to live and enjoy a happy and peaceful life.*

*Providing and Providential Father, we acknowledge that the gifts we receive from You are to be used in the expansion of Your kingdom here on earth. Kindly help us Father to become good stewards of the resources You have entrusted to our care and to use them wisely in helping others. We know Father many times we have taken credit for the success and fame we achieved instead of giving to You all the praise and glory because had it not been for You we would never have attained anything worthy of recognition. We give You thanks merciful Father for all Your blessings in the name of Jesus we pray. Amen.*

# December

# Yielding To Temptation

## Day 1

*When tempted, no one should say, "God is tempting me." For God cannot be tempted by evil, nor does he tempt anyone.*

*James 1:13*

Too often when we are tempted and fall prey to temptation we place the blame on God. The Bible makes it abundantly clear that God does not tempt anyone. Satan we know is the devil of lies and the one who uses every strategy he knows to lead us astray and so we need to be very careful and watchful of the subtle ways he tries to tempt us and gets us to commit actions that are contrary to God's Word. All of us are subjected to being tempted even as our Lord Jesus was, but what is wrong about the temptation is when we yield to it and that is where we sin. If we stand firm in our faith and put our trust in God, He will certainly deliver us and protect us from the snares of the devil and He will find a way for us to overcome the temptations.

*Heavenly Father there is no source of greater joy for us than worshipping You. Thank You Lord that we can come into Your holy presence with praise and thanksgiving and worship You this day. Lord we thank You that when we are tempted we do not have to yield to the temptation but all we need to do is to look to You for the strength to overcome. Father we thank You for helping us to resist the temptations of the devil time and time again and for strengthening our faith in You.*

*Gracious and Loving Father, we thank You for the constant watch You keep over us Your children. Father, without Your guidance and protection we could be trapped constantly by Satan, and fall into many temptations that we would find very difficult to resist. Help us Dear Lord not to yield to temptations when tempted because yielding is sin, but give us the capacity to resist the devil even as You were able to do for those forty days and forty nights in the wilderness. All these and other petitions we ask in the name of Jesus. Amen.*

# December

# Good and Wise Discipline

## Day 2

*My son, do not despise the LORD'S discipline and do not resent his rebuke, because the LORD disciplines those he loves, as a father the son he delights in.*
                                              Proverbs 3:11-12

Without discipline in our walk with God, we would be easily swayed by every wind of doctrine that blows by us. Discipline is a good thing for us to establish in our walk with the Savior. The more disciplined we become in the study of His Word and in prayer and fasting, the more we will be drawn closer to God. Our Father God disciplines us when we need to even as our earthly fathers correct us when we do wrong. This discipline is done out of an abundance of love for our own good and so we must accept with humility when God says no to us when our requests are not answered the way we want them to.

*Eternal and everlasting Father, we thank You for the discipline and the good counsel You make available to us so that we stay on the straight and narrow path. Father it is so easy for us to become rebellious in our attitude towards You and we thank You for Your rod of correction which You use to draw us back to Yourself. We are very grateful and thankful to You Lord for being such a loving, caring and forgiving Father.*

*Loving Lord Jesus, help us not to follow the voices of strangers especially those who would want us to travel down the wrong road that leads to destruction. So many peoples' lives Father have been marred because they have chosen not to listen to You but instead they have chosen to listen to the ill advices of others. We thank You for the wise counsel we receive through Your Word and for disciplining us when we step out of line. In Your mercy Father, we ask You always to protect and keep us safe from all that is evil and may learn to stick to the straight and narrow path. It is in Your mighty and powerful name we pray. Amen..*

# December

# Qualities To Obtain

## Day 3

*For if you possess these qualities in increasing measure, they will keep you from being ineffective and unproductive in the knowledge of our LORD Jesus Christ.*
2 Peter 1:8

The child of God must make every effort to exhibit goodness, self-control, perseverance, kindness, love and godliness so that he or she may have a deeper knowledge and understanding of the God whom we worship. There is the tendency for us as Christians to dabble into the things of the world and acting and behaving like those who are not of God. Every action we take and every word we speak, will determine whose we are and we will be ultimately judged by others who are watching every move we make. The qualities Paul speaks about in the preceding verses will enable us to be effective and productive in all that we do for the Lord.

*Thank You Lord for Your love, peace, joy, faithfulness, grace, mercy, kindness, truth and healing. Lord we thank You that we can depend on You for Your Word is unfailing and that You are the same yesterday, today and forever. Father we praise and lift up Your name today for You are good and Your mercies endure forever and ever. Today loving Father, we worship You in the splendor of Your holiness and give to You all the praise and glory due to Your precious name.*

*Father we thank You for making us new creatures in Your Son, Jesus Christ, our Lord. We thank You Lord Jesus for having transformed our lives from the old ways of life into an entirely new creation. Give us Lord Jesus we pray those qualities we need to make a difference in the lives of others and be consistent in living out our Christian beliefs. We ask You Father to cause Your face to shine upon us and to grant us Your peace in the name of Jesus we ask. Amen.*

# December

# Avoiding God's Condemnation

## Day 4

*Whoever believes in me is not condemned, but whoever does not believe stands condemned already because he has not believed in the name of God's one and only Son.*

John 3:18

It is vitally important that as Christians we demonstrate our belief in the God who created us in His very own image. God's love was demonstrated for us by sending His Son, Jesus to us. Jesus came to save whosoever would believe in Him. According to the Bible we are all guilty of sin and deserve to be separated from God but God sent Jesus to deliver us from our sins and to give us a chance to be reconciled to Him. The Bible tells us that we are saved through God's marvelous in Christ and so those who do not believe in Him cannot and will not find eternal life. Jesus says that those who believe in Him will not be condemned but those who do not believe in Him will be condemned. Let us all embrace this wonderful opportunity of believing in the one and only true living God who makes all things possible.

*Gracious and loving heavenly Father, we thank You that You have called us out of darkness into Your marvelous light. Lord, help us to always trust and believe Your Son Jesus Christ and to thank Him for the hold He has on our lives. Father we thank You that all things work together for good to those who love You and are called according to Your purpose for their lives. We thank You Father for ensuring that nothing draws us away from the plan You have for our lives.*

*Providing and Providential Father God, we give You thanks for not condemning us if we trust and believe in Your Son, Jesus Christ, our Lord and Savior. In Your wisdom Father, You have seen the need to give us the opportunity to seek You and to accept You as our Father. We praise You Lord that through faith in Jesus Christ, we are saved and we become Your children. We thank You Father for never giving up on us no matter how much we sin against You. Father, we give You thanks always in the precious name of Jesus we pray. Amen.*

# December

# Never Forsaken or Forgotten

## Day 5

*Those who know your name will trust in you, for you, LORD, have never forsaken those who seek you.*

Psalm 9:10

When we seek God, we will find Him and He will never forsake us. The Bible tells us that we are to seek the Lord while He may be found and to call upon His name while He is near to us. Failure to seek after God will result in us seeking after the things of this world that are temporary. To seek after God means that we have to read and study His Word and put His Word into action. God reveals Himself to us through His Word and that's why we must devote much time in studying it. He shows Himself to us in the evidence of grace in others so we can seek Him through the lives of believers. The seeking after God is the conscious effort we make to get through the natural means to God Himself and to constantly set our minds and hearts toward Him in all our experiences.

*O Holy and Righteous Father, we thank You that if we trust in You, You will never forsake us but You will be there for us at all times. Father thank You that when those closest to us turn away from us and shun us, that You will stand by us and uphold us with Your righteous right hand. Father we thank You for Your promise that You will never forsake those who put their faith and trust in You.*

*Merciful and Gracious Father, forgive us for the times when we have sought the things of this world instead of seeking after You. Your Word tells us Father that those who seek You will find You but too often we seek after the wrong things and in the process we miss finding You. Forgive us we pray Father for not spending enough time reading and studying Your Word so that we can become more grounded in our faith. We praise You Father for not forsaking or forgetting us once we put our faith and trust in You. Hear our prayer we pray Lord in the name of Jesus. Amen.*

# December

# The Truth Sets Us Free

### Day 6

*Do not lie to each other, since you have taken off your old self with its practices and have put on the new self, which is being renewed in knowledge in the image of its Creator.*

Colossians 3:9-10

    A Christian's life is characterized by being truthful and honest at all times. It is our duty to mortify our bodies that are inclined to the things of this world. We must continually be opposed to any form of corruption and do not become involved in anything that is carnal minded. God wants us to avoid as much as possible any lust of the flesh, the love of the world, covetousness, greed and the worldly pleasures which are not of God. We are encouraged not to lie to others since we are new creatures in Christ Jesus and our lives must be renewed in the knowledge of God our Creator.

    *Father in heaven, we thank You that ever since we accepted Your Son, Jesus Christ into our lives, we have become new persons in Christ. Sometimes we find it very challenging Lord to stay on the straight and narrow path, but thank You for ordering our steps when we go off track. Lord thank You that every day we are being renewed in knowledge in Your own image.*

    *Loving Father help us to keep our tongues from speaking lies and from saying anything that would cause hurt and injury to others. Thank You Lord Jesus that You have made us new creatures because we have forsaken the things of this world and have accepted You as our Lord and Savior. Fill our hearts we pray Jesus with the desire always to seek after You and to do the things You have called us to do. Lord help us always to speak the truth in the name of Jesus. Amen.*

## December

# Always Doing Good

### Day 7

*Command them to do good, to be rich in good deeds, and to be generous and willing to share. In this way they will lay up treasure for themselves as a firm foundation for the coming age, so that they may take hold of the life that is truly life.*

1 Timothy 6:18-19

God through His Son Jesus has taught us to be generous in our giving even as He gave to us His only Son to be our Savior and Lord. Paul exhorts us as believers in Christ to be rich in good deeds and to be generous and willing to share with others. Our goal must be to store up riches in heaven where it will be safe and not on earth where we are vulnerable to lose what we have. God has blessed us all with time, talents and treasures and He wants us all to use what He has given to us wisely to glorify Him and for the benefits of others.

Generous and loving Father God, we thank You for the opportunity You have given to us to be kind and generous to others. Lord we thank You for having blessed us with so much and we ask You to help us always to seek out ways and means of being a blessing to others even as You have been to us. We thank You Father that it is indeed much better to give than to receive and this we need to do more of.

Lord Jesus we thank You for laying down Your life for us and for making such a great sacrifice in order for us to be saved. We acknowledge Father how much You have blessed and prospered us in so many different ways and we want to thank You for all Your blessings bestowed upon us. Help us Father to give back to You by way of our tithes and offerings which can be used in the extension of Your kingdom here on earth and to help those who are less fortunate than we are. We give You thanks Father for all these and other blessings in the name of Your Son, Jesus. Amen.

# December
## Making The Right Decision
### Day 8

*Therefore everyone who hears these words of mine and puts them into practice is like a wise man who built his house on the rock. The rain came down, the streams rose, and the winds blew and beat against that house; yet it did not fall, because it had its foundation on the rock.*
Matthew 7:24-25

God is our Rock and sure foundation and on Him we should build our lives. Jesus Christ is not only our sure corner stone but He is the foundation on which we build our faith in Him. Whatever decisions we make in this life we must choose wisely. Some decisions we make could either be profitable or unprofitable and that is why it is so important to put our trust in the Lord who can guide us into following the right path. Let us seek to build our lives on the Lord Jesus Christ who is our solid foundation and not on the shaky grounds of this world. We can build up our faith and trust in Him by reading, studying and applying His Word in everything we do. In this way when the storms of life keep blowing, we will remain solid in His Word.

*O Lord our God, we thank You for being our Rock, our Shield and our sure Foundation. Thank You Father that we do not have to be afraid of falling or failing because we know in whom we believe and that You are able to keep us safe from the storms of life. Father today we want to thank You for Your Word which is the rock on which we build our faith and trust in You. Lord, if we adhere to Your teachings and remain faithful, then no matter what storms might be brewing, we will be able to overcome.*

*Lord Jesus we thank You that if we build our lives on Your Word and not on the things of this world, that when the storms of life come blowing from every direction, we will be able to withstand the force of the wind, because we know that we are protected by You. We thank You Lord Jesus for all the wonderful things You have done for us and what You will continue to do in the future. Thank You Jesus for being our Protector and our Fortress in times of trouble and great tribulations. We know Lord Jesus, with You in the midst of us, everything will be alright and we do not have to fear. We give You thanks and praises in the wonderful and precious name of Jesus. Amen.*

## December

# The Lord Is Our Tower of Strength

### Day 9

*The name of the LORD is a strong tower; the righteous run to it and are safe.*

Proverbs 18:10

God is certainly our strong tower and in Him we can take refuge and be safe. The only safe refuge we can truly rely on in times of trouble is that of the God whom we worship. When we are feeling fearful and terrified about life's challenges, we need a strong tower we can run into and be safe whenever we need it. Nothing can breach this safety, for our strong tower is the Lord and there is no other place for such protection from danger. We have the freedom to call upon the name of the Lord at any time and we should not be afraid to call upon Him and be saved.

*O God, our Refuge in pain, our Strength in weakness, our Help in trouble and our Strong Tower in danger, we thank You merciful and loving Father that we can come to You anytime in our hour of need. Father we thank You for hearing our cry and listening to our prayers from the ends of the earth and for leading us to the rock that is higher than us. Mighty God we thank You for allowing us to live in Your shadow and to know that we are protected by You forever.*

*In these difficult and troublesome days Father, where doubts and uncertainties abound, we crave Your continued protection from all the dangers that are always present. We thank You Father for forming a hedge around us to protect and keep us safe from anything that would cause harm and injury to Your loved ones. Father, we acknowledge that there is no other name under heaven whereby we can be saved but by the name of Your Son, Jesus Christ our Lord. It is in Your name we pray Father. Amen.*

# December

# No One Excluded

## Day 10

*This is good, and pleases God our Savior, who wants all men to be saved and to come to a knowledge of the truth.*
1 Timothy 2:3-4

Our Father God does not want His children to suffer or perish and that's why He has made His Son Jesus available so that all those who believe in Him, can be saved from their sin. Jesus said that He is the Way, the Truth and the Life and all who follow Him will know the truth because He is the Truth. The psalmist describes truth as the sum of God's word and he reminds us of how God draws near only to those who call upon Him in truth. (Psalm 119:160). We as Christians will falsely claim to know the truth if we do not live it out in our daily lives as truth is something that we do and we would not be faithful to the Lord if we are not concerned to walk in His true way.

*O loving and tender Father in heaven, we thank You that through belief in Your Son Jesus Christ we do not have to perish but we can experience eternal life with Him forever. Father we thank You that if we remain faithful to Your word, You will remain faithful to us and bless us. Lord we thank You that although we cannot see the future You have planned for us and though the way is sometimes dark and hard to understand, we thank You for the faith You have given to us to carry on.*

*Righteous and Holy Father, we thank You that Jesus is our Way, our Truth and our Life and that without Him we are lost. We pray Lord Jesus that You will help us to live for You and to follow in Your footsteps. We thank You Lord Jesus for not wanting any of us to perish, but to have eternal life by believing Your Word. Grant us Lord Jesus the capacity to read and study Your Word so that we may not depart from Your teachings. This we ask in Your wonderful name. Amen.*

## December

# Growing In Our Faith

## Day 11

*And how from infancy you have known the holy Scriptures, which are able to make you wise for salvation through faith in Christ Jesus. All Scripture is God-breathed and is useful for teaching, rebuking, correcting and training in righteousness.*

2 Timothy 3:15-16

We as followers of Christ, need to immerse ourselves more in studying His holy word so that we can share the good news of the gospel confidently with others. For many of us Christians, our first encounter with the Word of God could have come from our parents, grandparents or from others. Whoever it was that influenced our lives in our early days, we owe them a debt of great gratitude for had they not inculcated in us the importance of God's Word, we may not have been what we are today. We need to immerse ourselves in the Word of God because we will find it useful for teaching, rebuking, correcting and for training in living right with God and our fellow men.

*Thank You heavenly Father that Your word is useful for teaching, rebuking, correcting and for training in righteousness. Help us Father to apply ourselves in the study, interpretation and application of Your word so that we might be better able to impart it to others. Lord we thank You that because of the teaching of the Holy Scriptures, our faith has been made stronger in Jesus Christ.*

*Father God, we depend on You to help us overcome the obstacles and hurdles in our lives. Lord Jesus help us to hold on to the sound teachings we received from our parents, grandparents and others about You and thank You for guiding and protecting us through all the days of our lives. Lord God, we cannot do without You and so we ask You to keep us ever so close to You in everything we do. We thank You Father that the more we dig deep into Your word, our faith grows and we are not afraid to share Your word with others. Lord we ask You to grant us Your grace everyday in the name of Jesus we ask. Amen.*

# December

# Obeying And Serving Are Rewarding

## Day 12

*If they obey and serve him, they will spend the rest of their days in prosperity and their years in contentment.*
Job 36:11

God has called us into His service to be obedient servants of His and if we obey His commands, we will be blessed by Him abundantly. As servants of the Lord, we are expected to show our allegiance to God by putting His Word into practice and to demonstrate that He is indeed Lord of our lives by being truly obedient to Him. Being obedient to God means that we are prepared to do what He calls us to do no matter what it may cost us. Jesus said that if we are going to follow Him we must take up our cross and to do so we cannot count the cost of following Him.

Lord we thank You that You are our Shepherd and nothing shall we lack. Thank You for leading us beside the still waters and for restoring our souls. Father we pray that You will enable us to obey Your word and to serve You all the days of our lives so that we may spend the rest of our days in prosperity and contentment. We thank You Father that with You all things are possible and there is no need for us to worry or to be afraid of the future.

Father God we thank You that it is never too late for us to become obedient to Your Word and once we obey You, we will become successful in all that we do. We thank You Father that You have called us to serve You and by so doing we will receive abundant blessings from You. Help us Father to seek You while You may be found and to call upon You while You are near. It is in Your name we pray. Amen.

## December

# Bearing Insults For Christ

### Day 13

*If you are insulted because of the name of Christ, you are blessed, for the Spirit of glory and of God rests on you.*
1 Peter 4:14

As Christians living in a somewhat hostile world, we have to be prepared to suffer insult and persecution for the sake of Jesus Christ. Once we name the name of Jesus, there are those who will become annoyed and oppositional to hearing His name, but we must continue to speak in the name of Jesus, When we speak the name of Jesus even the very demons have to disappear because they know how powerful and mighty the name of Jesus is. We are indeed blessed when we suffer insult and humiliation for standing up and proclaiming the wonderful and awesome name of Jesus to the world.

We thank You most gracious heavenly Father that if we are going to truly follow You to the end, we must be prepared to suffer hardship, persecution and even death. Father we thank You that Jesus suffered and died for our sins when He did not have to, so we too must bear our cross with His help. Today we want to thank You Lord that nothing can separate us from Your unconditional love for Your children.

Dear Father in heaven, we do not want anything or anyone to separate us from You and all that You have in store for us. Father God, help us to remain faithful to You even if we are persecuted for Your name's sake because we know that Your Holy Spirit will always be there for us. Make us bold Father to declare the name of Jesus to a world that is hurting and longing for someone to make a difference in their lives and You are that special person. We pray loving Lord that You will continue to strengthen our faith in the name of Jesus we ask. Amen.

# December

# Reward in Worship

## Day 14

*Worship the Lord your God and his blessings will be on your food and water. I will take away sickness from among you.*

Exodus 23:25

Our obligation to God as Christians is to worship Him and none other as He says we should have no other god beside Him. The Lord has made it abundantly clear that those who fervently worship Him and keep His commandments will receive His blessings and favor. The Lord will undoubtedly bless everything that we need for survival and protect us from anything that would cause us harm. Just as God promised the Israelites to bless them and to take away from them sickness, in the same way He will bless us and ensure that we remain healthy and protect us from all diseases such as the coronavirus that is plaguing the world.

Lord Jesus we thank You for our hearts, our souls and our voices, all of which we can use to worship You and to praise and magnify Your holy and magnificent name. Father we thank You that when we worship You in spirit and in truth, Your blessings will continually be upon us and our loved ones. Today we want to thank You Lord Jesus for dying on Calvary's cross so that we can have new lives knowing You as our personal Savior and Lord.

Lord God we pray that You would keep us from having a divided heart and divided loyalty. Help us Lord that our loyalty will be to You and to no other gods and that we will always seek to bow down and worship You in Spirit and in Truth. Father as we seek to worship You, help us to stay in close touch with You through our constant and fervent prayer, and may we learn to separate ourselves from anyone or anything that would separate us from You. Father it is in Your name and for Your sake we pray. Amen.

# December

# Watch and Pray

## Day 15

*Do not love sleep or you will grow poor; stay awake and you will have food to spare.*

Proverbs 20:13

In this life we are encouraged to watch and pray or else we fall into diverse temptations. We must have a balance in life and by so doing we can make wise use of the time God has given to us. We should not spend all of our time focusing on our basic necessities such as food, shelter and sleep as important as these are. We must also give to God some of our time to spend reading and meditating on His Word and in prayer and fasting. It is so easy for us to spend our days being busy with everything else except being busy doing the work of the Lord. When we fail to do what He has called us to do and to invest in His Word, that is when we can become spiritually poor.

*Thanks be to You O God our Father in heaven for giving us the victory through Jesus Christ over sin and death. Lord, we thank You that through the death and resurrection of Jesus, we can have everlasting life. Help us dear Father to be consistent in our watching and praying because we know not when You will return. Thank You Lord for preparing a way for us to live with You in eternity soon and very soon.*

*Loving Father, we ask You to help us to live a more balanced life and to put everything into perspective. We know Lord that there is the tendency for us to spend so much time on doing other things instead of focusing more on You and Your Word. Lord we thank You that You are always there for us and no matter what we do You will still love and care for us. Forgive us Lord for disappointing You many times and for not giving to You more of our time. All these and other mercies Lord we ask in Your most precious and awesome name. Amen.*

# December

# Wise Counsel

## Day 16

*Yet I am always with you; you hold me by my right hand. You guide me with your counsel, and afterward you will take me into glory.*

Psalm 73:23-24

The one person who is always with us providing good counsel and guiding us in the path we should take is the God of heaven whom we worship. God is our Provider and Sustainer and He will always make a way for us. He provides us with wise counsel and we have His Word to point us in the right way. Our journey on this earth is so that we can prepare ourselves to be with the Lord when He comes again to take us to that place which He has prepared for us. It should be our desire each and everyday to draw closer and closer to God so that we can get to know Him better and to appreciate Him more.

O Heavenly Father, give us a heart like that of Jesus, a heart more ready to minister than to be ministered to, a heart full of love and compassion especially for the weak and oppressed. Thank You Father for Your loving-kindness and tender mercies shown to us each and every day. We thank You for the guidance and good counsel that You provide us Father, so that one day if we remain obedient to Your word, You will take us with You to paradise.

Lord God, You have declared in Your Word that You are always with us and that You hold us by Your righteous right hand. Father, we are well protected by You and You provide good counsel for us through Your Word. You have promised Father that there is nothing that can separate us from Your deep and affectionate love for us. We give You all the praise and glory Father for all the wonderful things You have done for us and will continue to do for us. It is in Your name we pray. Amen.

# December

# Faith is Believing

## Day 17

*And without faith it is impossible to please God, because anyone who comes to him must believe that he exists and that he rewards those who earnestly seek him.*

Hebrews 11:6

Without faith we can do nothing and we cannot please God who created us since faith helps us to believe that our God truly exists. Christianity is a faith based religion since we believe in a God we cannot see because He exists as a spirit and those of us who worship Him must worship Him in Spirit and in Truth. Many people doubt the existence of God because they cannot see him but do not doubt the reality of electricity which they cannot see but can feel the effects of it. We as Christians know that we cannot see God but we can feel His presence near us and we can see His handiwork all around us. Our faith and trust in God will one day bring us great rewards since He's coming back to earth to claim those whom have remained faithful to Him.

Father we thank You that we are not ashamed to own and confess You as our Lord or to defend Your cause. We thank You Lord for increasing our faith and for having helped us to acknowledge that You are indeed the Creator of heaven and earth and that there is no other god besides You. Lord we thank You that one day You will reward us for trusting and believing in You.

Lord Jesus, our faith looks up to You the crucified One who gave Your life so that those who believe might be saved. We know Lord Jesus that without faith it is impossible to please You and Your Father in heaven. We ask You dear Lord to strengthen our faith each and every day so that we will never drift far away from Your presence. May our faith Lord become deeply rooted and grounded in You so that we will have the boldness to share Your Word with those who are seeking. We ask Father that You will grant us our requests in the wonderful and precious name of Your Son, Jesus. Amen.

# December

# God's Cleansing Power

*Day 18*

*I will sprinkle clean water on you, and you will be clean; I will cleanse you from all your impurities and from all your idols. I will give you a new heart and put a new spirit in you; I will remove from you your heart of stone and give you a heart of flesh.*

Ezekiel 36:25-26

Only God can truly cleanse and purify our hearts by the outpouring of His Holy Spirit upon us. When we as God's people have sinned and wandered far away from Him, He makes allowances for us to be cleansed of our sins and be restored in a right relationship with Him. The children of Israel who were God's chosen people did abominable things in the sight of God even though He had provided them with so many blessings and protected them from their enemies. They transgressed the commandments He had given them as a guide on how to live and for worshipping Him by turning away from Him and worshipping idols instead. God is merciful to us too because we have sought to have our own way as well and have put the things of this world before those pertaining to God.

*Father in heaven, we thank You that we are precious, beautiful and spotless in Your eyes and in Your sight. We thank You that only You alone can wash us and make us clean. Thank You for putting a new heart and a new spirit in us and for softening our hearts. Lord , we thank You for sending Your Son Jesus into the world to heal our broken hearts and to heal us from all our infirmities.*

*Lord God we repent of all the wrongs we have done and for having caused Your Son to suffer and die for our sins. We know Father that we can never repay You for this great sacrifice You made for us especially that Christ did no wrong and He lived a perfect life while He tabernacled amongst us. We offer up ourselves to You Lord and ask that You will accept us as we are and use us as You would have us be used to do Your work here on earth. It is in Your name we pray Father. Amen.*

## December

# Be Not Afraid

### Day 19

*"Do not be afraid, little flock, for your Father has been pleased to give you the kingdom.*

Luke 12:32

The hope of every believer is to one day become residents with our Lord and Savior in His kingdom. In order to do so, we must be obedient to His Word in reading and meditating on it and applying it to our lives. When we immerse ourselves in the Word of God and stay in tune with Him through our prayers, the Lord will be pleased with us. We are grateful and thankful to Him that He is preparing a place for us so that where He is there we may be also. Like a good shepherd, He constantly keeps watch over His flock and makes sure that there is a safe place for all His sheep to stay. We bless the name of the Lord for never leaving us or forsaking us but for always keeping a watch on us.

*Patient and Merciful Father, we thank You that Your kingdom is not of this world and that You are preparing a heavenly kingdom for us where we will live with You forever and ever. Lord we thank You that we do not have to be afraid of living or dying because in which ever state we may be, You are there with us. We thank You Lord Jesus for being our Good Shepherd and for assuring us of Your constant care, protection and provision.*

*Lord Jesus, we come before You with high hopes and anticipation that one day when we leave this earthly realm, we will be ushered into that place which You have prepared for us. Grant us loving Jesus the desire to seek You always and to dedicate our lives in serving You. We thank You for all that You do for us and for having died for us in order that we will be able to be with You in Paradise one day. Father, we give to You all the praise and glory in the name of Jesus. Amen.*

# December

# Good Counseling

## Day 20

*I will instruct you and teach you in the way you should go; I will counsel you and watch over you.*

Psalm 32:8

God does not slumber nor sleep and so His eyes are always on us to guide us in the path we should follow. God's holy Word as contained in the Bible, is our guide to living the way God wants us to live. If we follow His instructions we shall remain on the right track but if we fail to follow it, then we will find ourselves drifting further and further away from God. It is in our best interest to be obedient to God's Word and to walk on the straight and narrow path so that we will never stray far away from Him. Like the psalmist, the Lord will instruct and teach us in the way we should go and He will provide us with good counsel and keep His eye on us.

Lord God, we thank You that because Your eyes are always on the sparrow, You are also watching over us at all times. Father we thank You for the plans You have for us to bless and prosper us and we thank You for the sound instruction You give to us to achieve our utmost. Lord we thank You for etching out the direction You want us to follow and for providing us with the instruction that we need to guide us as we embark on our journey.

Forgive us O Lord Jesus for being reticent and reluctant at times in heeding Your wise counsel. Lord we have often times paid more attention to what others are saying instead of what Your Word says we are to do. We ask You Father to forgive us for not following Your instructions and for having sinned against You. Help us Dear Father to listen to Your wise counsel for our lives so that we may receive Your blessings. This we ask Father in the mighty name of Jesus. Amen.

## December

# Watch Your Speech

### Day 21

*You will be protected from the lash of the tongue, and need not fear when destruction comes.*

Job 5:21

The tongue is used to say good things as well as to say unkind and hurtful things about others. As Christians we need to be mindful of our speech because we must remember that we are not only judged on what we do but also on what we say. When we experience the lash of the tongue from someone, it means that whatever awful and degrading that could be said by that person was said about us. The Bible tells us that by our fruits the world will know who we are and so if we are to avoid being spoken about in a bad way, we need to take heed to God's Word and do what is right and acceptable in His sight.

*Heavenly Father we thank You that we have hidden Your word in our hearts so that we are able to control what comes out of our mouths. Lord, You know how easy it is for us to say the wrong things which can cause hurt and ill-feelings and that's why we are so thankful to You for bridling our tongues so that we can refrain from uttering unhealthy, unwholesome and unkind thoughts.*

*Father we ask You to forgive us for the times when we have uttered unclean thoughts and have been disrespectful to Your name. Lord Jesus, we are sorry that we have not always lived up to our expectations as Your children and for behaving in a manner which has not been different from those who do not know You. Father God we humble ourselves before You and truly repent of all our sins and ask You to forgive us. All these mercies we seek in the name of Your Son, Jesus, our Lord and Savior. Amen.*

# December

# Marvelous and Amazing Grace

## Day 22

*For we do not have a high priest who is unable to sympathize with our weaknesses, but we have one who has been tempted in every way, just as we are-yet was without sin. Let us then approach the throne of grace with confidence, so that we may receive and find grace to help us in our time of need.*

Hebrews 4:15-16

God has made His grace through Jesus Christ available to all who trust Him so that when we are faced with diverse trials and temptations, His grace will help us to overcome. We thank God for Jesus who became flesh and lived on earth so that He could sympathize with our human weaknesses and when we fall into diverse temptations. Jesus who knew no sin became sin for us so that through His death on the cross we would be able to receive eternal life by believing in Him. God has made His free gift of grace available to us so that it will help us in our time of need. Let us all hold on to what God has given to us through Jesus Christ and look to Him always who is the Author and Finisher of our faith.

*Father in heaven, we thank You that Jesus Christ is our High Priest who is able to sympathize with all our weaknesses and temptations as He too was tempted to the extreme and yet did not yield to the temptation. Thank You Lord that if we approach Your throne of grace with confidence, we will receive and find grace that will help us in our time of need.*

*Almighty and Merciful Father, we thank You for the grace You have given to us so freely and which is sufficient to meet all our needs. We thank You for Your Son, Jesus Christ, our Lord, whom You sent into the world to live among us so that He could become acquainted with all the challenges of life that we go through. Father help us to hold on to Jesus who alone understands our human frailties and weaknesses. This we pray Father, in the name of Your Son, Jesus. Amen.*

# December

# God With Us

## Day 23

*The LORD your God is with you, he is mighty to save. He will take great delight in you, he will quiet you with his love, he will rejoice over you with singing.*
Zephaniah 3:17

God is always on our side and He delights in doing good for us at all times. Those who put their faith and trust in the Lord will never be disappointed because He always fulfills His promises no matter how long the timing may seem. The Lord delights in those who call upon His name and He rejoices and is pleased when we come seeking Him. The Lord our God desires all His children to seek after Him, to come to Him, to draw near to Him even as He draws near to us and to rest and abide in His truth, because He is God.

*Gracious Lord, we thank You for Your faithfulness in providing our daily needs and for taking great delight in all that we do. Father we thank You that as Your children, we can glory in Your righteousness. Lord help us to seek always to lift You up and may our words tell of Your goodness and not our own. Father we thank You that when we do that which is right and pleasing in Your sight, You are pleased with us and You grant us Your favor.*

*Our Father we pray that You would create in us clean and right hearts before You at all times. We thank You Father for all the promises that You have made and for keeping all Your promises. Heavenly Father we thank You for delighting in us Your wayward children and for constantly loving us the way You do and for Your provisions and protection which are new each and every day. Loving Lord, we ask that You will see fit to bless us in the name of the Father, Son and Holy Spirit. Amen.*

# December

## Love is Costly

### Day 24

*But he was pierced for our transgressions, he was crushed for our iniquities; the punishment that brought us peace was upon him, and by his wounds we are healed.*
Isaiah 53:5

Our Father God loved us so much that long before His Son was born, He had in His plan to send Him into the world to redeem lost humanity from their sins and make it possible to be reconciled to Him. Yes, Jesus was pierced for our transgressions, He was crushed for our iniquities and He bore the punishment on the cross so that we could be healed from our sins. We can only imagine the pain and agony Jesus suffered on the cross for our sins. Without this sacrifice God made for us His lost and wayward children, we would never have the chance to be saved and spend eternity with Him in heaven.

*Lord Jesus, we thank You that You died so that we might live. We thank You Jesus that You were pierced for our transgressions and was crushed for our sins considering we did absolutely nothing to deserve such a sacrifice. Father God, we truly thank You for what You did for us by giving Your only Son, Jesus to die on a cruel cross to redeem us from our sins. No one would ever do what You did for us and we will ever be thankful to You for this great gift of love.*

*Dear Lord Jesus, how grateful we are that You came to earth as our Savior and Lord to save and redeem us from our sins. We thank You Lord Jesus that You paid the price that You did not owe so that we would have a second chance of being forgiven and to be with You in heaven. Lord Jesus we are truly sorry for having put You through all the agony and pain You endured because of us and we ask You to forgive us. All these mercies Father we ask You to grant us in Your name and for Your sake. Amen.*

## December

# New Birth

## Day 25

*While they were still there, the time came for the baby to be born. And she gave birth to her first born, a son. She wrapped him in cloths and placed him in a manger, because there was no room for them in the inn.*

*Luke 2:6-7*

Jesus the Son of God was born in the most unlikely of all places-a stable and yet look at His contributions to the whole world. As we celebrate this most memorable occasion in the history of the world, where God chose to send His only Son, born of a woman, into the world to become our Savior and Lord, let us do so with a deep sense of joy and gratitude to Almighty God. The world in which we live has never been the same again since the birth of Jesus over two thousand years ago. The lives of millions of people have been transformed and God continues to transform the lives of people every day. We are indeed grateful to our God for this priceless gift to humanity and for the love and peace Jesus brings to all those who follow Him.

*O God our Father on this Christmas day we thank You for Jesus. We thank You Father that He took our ordinary lives upon Himself and made them extraordinary. We thank You that He was born not in a palace but in a stable and yet He became the greatest human being who ever walked this earth. We thank You Father that it was not earthly wealth or ease that He knew, but that He was born into a humble home, where He had to work for a living.*

*Heavenly Father we appreciate Jesus for being our Savior and Lord and for His love for the world. We thank You for the sinless life He lived while He walked this earth and the lives that were transformed through His teachings. Lord there is no other time so precious to us than this event, when You sent Jesus into the world to be a part of lost humanity. His coming into the world has made a significant difference in the lives of millions of people and we just praise You for the difference He has also made in our lives. This we pray Father, in the wonderful name of Jesus, our new born King. Amen.*

# December

# Reward in Giving

## Day 26

*I tell you the truth, anyone who gives you a cup of water in my name because you belong to Christ will certainly not lose his reward.*

Mark 9:41

    Jesus wants us to consider the needs of others and provide whatever help we can so that we will be rewarded accordingly. We give God thanks for not holding back on the greatest gift He gave to us-the gift of His only Son, Jesus. We are called upon to make sacrifices for others too without counting the cost. The Bible tells us that it is more blessed to give than to receive because it is in giving that we are truly blessed. There is no condition attached in giving to others. As long as people are in need no matter their color, class, creed or gender, we should respond to their cry for help and much more so being children of God. There is a blessing awaiting all those who have been kind, generous and loving and who remained faithful in carrying out the will of God.

    Father in heaven, help us to thank You over and over again for the blessings You have blessed us with especially when we consider the many who are so desperately in need. Lord we thank You for the blessings that have little to do with wealth such as Your love, peace, joy, good health and the work of the Holy Spirit in our lives. Remind us Father of the great cost of our salvation and let us praise You forever and ever.

    Loving Father God, we thank You for all of the wonderful blessings You have poured down upon us in the past, that You are doing for us today and for all the blessings You will give to us in the future. We thank You that You are always giving to us and we ask Father that You would give us generous hearts so that we too can be a blessing to others. Lord, Your Word tells us that it is more blessed to give than to receive and so this is what we want to do, to give to others especially to those who are so desperately in need. Continue to bless us Father so that we can be a blessing to others and it is in the name of Jesus we pray. Amen.

## December

# Being Strong and Hopeful

### Day 27

*Be strong and take heart, all you who hope in the LORD.*
*Psalm 31:24*

All God's people who put their hope in Him will receive from Him strength for the journey of life. Those of us who put our faith and trust in God who is the Creator of all things, He will give us the courage and the strength to remain in Him despite all the crazy things that are happening around us to challenge our faith in Him. We are encouraged by the psalmist to be strong and take heart because of our hope in the Lord. When we put our God first in everything we do, then He will deliver and protect us from all harm and danger. Our God is a good God and is faithful in every way. He keeps His promises and we do not have to worry whether or not He will fulfill them. Let us all take heed of His Word and apply it to our lives so that we will find favor in His sight.

*Loving Father in heaven, we thank You for all Your promises and provisions. We thank You Lord for touching our lives in so many ways, never denying us that which we need to flourish and grow in Your grace. Lord we thank You for making us strong as we put our trust and hope in You. Thank You dear Father for opening the portals of heaven and showering on us Your bountiful blessings from on high.*

*Father God, we thank You that if we put our faith and trust in You, we will get to know You better because we will learn to depend on You more and more and be drawn closer and closer to You. Lord make us strong and bold to resist every attempt made by the devil to woo us away from You. Awesome Father, all our hope is vested in You and You alone so keep us very close to You always. This we pray Father in Your loving and tender name. Amen.*

# December

# Peace That Heals

## Day 28

*Peace, peace to those far and near," says the LORD. "And I will heal them."*

Isaiah 57:19

True and lasting peace can only come from our heavenly Father who has given to us His Prince of Peace, Jesus Christ our Lord. The world is longing for the kind of peace Jesus gives, but it is elusive as Jesus is not at the center of how people are seeking for what they consider to be peace. The peace that Jesus offers us is everlasting but what the world offers is only temporary until there's the outbreak of war. When we seek God's peace that passes all wisdom and understanding, only then will the people of the world experience true and lasting peace. Jesus Himself said that His peace He not only leaves with us but He also gives it to us and that it is a different kind of peace than what the world has to offer.

*Merciful and Gracious God, we thank You for giving to us the peace that passes all understanding that the world cannot give to us. We thank You Father that Jesus, Your only Son is indeed the Prince of Peace and that we have full access to Him. Father we thank You that when our lives are full of turmoil and tribulation, we have Jesus as our Savior to look to for that peace and quiet that only He can provide.*

*Father in heaven, we acknowledge that true and lasting peace in this world can only come from You. Lord, even though leaders try to broker peace when there are disputes, this is only temporary and nothing we can rely on. We thank You Father for reassuring us that Your peace is available to all those who ask and it is from everlasting to everlasting. Thank You Father for the peace that Jesus gives to all who seek Him and may His perpetual peace reign in our hearts for ever and ever. It is in Your name we pray Father. Amen.*

## December

# Proud Parents

### Day 29

*Children's children are a crown to the aged, and parents are the pride of their children.*
Proverbs 17:6

We being God's children are no doubt a pride to Him when we obey and love Him. In the same way our earthly parents are proud of their children and grandchildren so is the Lord proud of all those who call Him Abba Father. God has demonstrated His love for His children again and again and like any good Father, He is always present when we need Him. Let us follow the wise counsel we receive from our earthly parents but even more so let us follow the wise counsel we receive from Almighty God because all good things come from Him.

*Most loving and ever merciful Father, we thank You that our faithfulness to You does not depend on our abilities or our social status in life. So often Father we try to be faithful and yet we still mess up miserably. Lord we thank You for Your faithfulness which is part of Your perfect nature. It never changes or leaves us helpless. Father we thank You for that faithfulness and we pray that it may seep into our hearts and souls even as we follow You today and always.*

Father God we worship You and thank You for being proud of us Your children when we follow in Your footsteps. Your love, guidance and protection throughout the years Lord have enabled to become the best of what You want us to be. Help us Dear Father to continue to follow the wise counsel of all those who have guided us along the way, but more importantly to give You all the praise and glory for having transformed our lives the way You have done. Lord we ask You to hear our prayer and let our cry come unto You. Amen.

# December

# Godly Fear

## Day 30

*Through love and faithfulness sin is atoned for; through the fear of the LORD a man avoids evil.*
Proverbs 16:6

    If we love and fear God and remain faithful to Him, He will keep us safe from the evil one. God is a God of love, mercy, grace and justice and He expects us to respect this truth. He does not separate the work of His grace from His truth. It is by His mercy and truth that our iniquities are atoned for when God is working in us and through us. God brings His truth to us through the Holy Spirit when His Word convicts us. Without God's work of truth showing us our sin, we are not fit for His mercy because mercy presumes that we realize that we are not deserving of God's grace but His judgment. So we are encouraged by this Proverb to fear God so that we will not sin against Him.

    Lord we are grateful and thankful to You that if we love and fear You and remain steadfast in our faith, You will guide and protect us from all that is evil. Father we thank You that when we are stepping out of line and wandering far from You, You pull us back unto Yourself and place us on the right path. We are ever thankful to You Lord for making us who we are and for blessing us so abundantly.

    Most gracious and ever loving Father, we thank You that it is through Your mercy and truth that our sins are atoned for when You are working in us through Your Holy Spirit. Father we realize that without Your work of truth in our lives showing us our sins, we are not fit to receive Your mercy because mercy tells us that we are not deserving of Your grace but Your judgment. We thank You for being a God of love, mercy and grace and for extending these to us. It is in Your name we pray Father. Amen.

# December

# Pleasant Words

## Day 31

*Pleasant words are a honeycomb, sweet to the soul and healing to the bones.* — Proverbs 16:24

    The words we utter as Christians should be encouraging and pleasing to our Maker. So often we resort to saying unkind things to and about others without thinking about the hurt and injury we can inflict on them. Jesus wants us as His followers to take the high road of love and kindness even as He demonstrated to us. This should be a time of reflection and introspection on the year that is now behind us and to assess all the things we said or done that were not pleasing to our Creator. It is a time when we should seek to correct the hurts and divisions we might have caused to others and to seek God's forgiveness even as we leave this year behind. May we heed the words of this Proverbs that pleasant words are a honeycomb, sweet to the soul and healing to the bones.

    *Father as we come to this the last day of another year, let us vow to make the new year one in which we show more love and compassion to all those with whom we come in contact. Lord we want to thank You for having brought us safely through another year and to especially this the last day of the year. Thank You for all Your blessings, love, guidance, protection and faithfulness to us throughout this year, and thank You Father for the way in which You have helped us to minister to others through the written word. We pray Lord that You will continue to use our gifts and talents as You see fit. Thank You again for all that You have done for us and for what You will continue to do in the year ahead.*

    *Lord Jesus we ask You to help us to be more kinder and gentler towards others and the words we speak. Guide our lips and our tongues Lord Jesus from uttering unpleasant things that can only cause much pain, hurt and injury to others. Father, it is our desire to be more encouraging and thoughtful in the things we say and what we do in the coming year. May we learn Lord to lean not to our own understanding but rather to acknowledge You in all our ways and give to You all the praise and glory. Father God, we ask You to continue to bless us in and through the name of Your Son, Jesus our Lord and soon coming King. Amen.*

Made in United States
Orlando, FL
09 October 2023